The "Old is New" NPM Guidebook

Splendors of the New National Palace Museum

Editor-in-Chief / Lin Mun-lee

國立故宮博物院
NATIONAL PALACE MUSEUM

July 2007

The Sky's the Limit for the NPM
Director's Preface

The National Palace Museum (also referred to in this guidebook as the Museum or the NPM) was established in 1925, turning a treasure house of the imperial family into a public institution for the people. Now standing at more than eighty years old, these eight decades can be divided roughly into two forty-year periods that also reflect different period backgrounds and historical fates.

In the first forty-year period, the National Palace Museum went through an initial stage of feeling its way through China's early modern period. Its birth also happened to bear witness to several entirely different historical processes. It went from a period originally as a centralized authoritarian institution in the hands of the emperor into an initial society with democratic ideals, and then into chaotic periods marked by imperialistic colonial invaders and civil war that waged with Communists. All along, the National Palace Museum has been a part of this turbulent period of Chinese history, which the hundreds of thousands of objects in the collection have stood by and watched with cool indifference. For the people entrusted with their care, however, the first few years of its existence were followed by a period of over twenty years, in which the National Palace Museum went through one of the most difficult and arduous journeys in the history of world museums. The ups and downs are known to many people, as masterpieces of the collection were transported over thousands of kilometers across many parts of China. Some people say that ancient objects have a spirit of their own, and it must have been the case with these treasures in order for them all to survive their journeys across China and finally make it by boat safely to Taiwan. There are two good things that have come about as a result of this. The first is that these hundreds of thousands of objects were not scattered all over the land, instead finding a place in Taiwan to set down roots as a whole. The other is that we in Taiwan are the envy of the world in having these cultural treasures, many of which represent the greatest legacies of Chinese culture that have become a part of our home here.

In the second forty-year period of the National Palace Museum's history, the collection has been able to enjoy a period of rest and recuperation. Several generations of personnel and caretakers devoted to the collection have given the best of their years to build a home for the storage and display of these treasures, to edit and record professional inventories for them, to research and publish their rightful place in the course of history and aesthetics, and also to care for, restore, and plan conservation principles for their future over the coming centuries. In short, the people at the National Palace Museum have given in return to these treasures their due respect after a tumultuous start, providing these treasures the public honor that they have rarely, if ever, had seen in the past. And the National Palace Museum during these forty years has worked diligently to establish a system and organization to improve its operational capabilities, taking one step after another in the steady progress of heading in the direction of a modern museum.

At this very moment, we are now in the third phase of the history of the National Palace Museum, and our mission and responsibilities have become ever greater. This is, after all, part of the challenge of living in a new millennium, and what we face in the museum field today are completely new fields waiting to be developed. We must shoulder the responsibility of this new outlook and mission, which requires new vision, organization, and people of talent in order to develop innovations and value for the role of the museum as a whole in society and for its collection. After the new organizational statutes are passed, we look forward to the National Palace Museum possessing even more efficient and professional administrative work teams and an overall system, so that we may be able to develop operational strategies to respond more flexibly and quickly to trends in society. In this process of rapid change and transformation, the NPM must play the role of an all-around, comprehensive member of the new century and society. Now, with the completion of the renovation project of the Museum's main building, the National Palace Museum now has a solid infrastructure to step into the new century and create an ideal museum-park to present to the world, the first steps of which have now been taken. And in the future, with the successful completion and operation of the National Palace Museum Southern Branch in Taibao, Chiayi, we will be able to open our eyes even further to all of Asia, thereby firmly establishing the status of the National Palace Museum as a central hub among museums of the world.

With the publication of this guidebook, I envisioned it as not only one of the fine publications of the National Palace Museum. In addition, with the beginning of the third phase of the Museum's history, I hope that this guidebook can do justice and honor the continuous efforts and hard work of several generations of Museum personnel dedicated to the preservation and study of the collection, thereby allowing the importance and beauty of these treasures to be appreciated by all of us today. This guidebook is also dedicated to everyone in the previous two forty-year phases who have protected and preserved these cultural objects in their journey to the present, to each and every member part of and associated with the Palace Museum who valued these objects and treasured every one of them. This guidebook, however, is by no means a commemorative tribute, but it is also another milestone in the journey of the collection, symbolizing a whole new series of hopes and aspirations to which we strive to make the National Palace Museum a part of in the new century. After all, when it comes to the future, the sky's the limit, and that's where we must all strive to reach in our endeavors, including the National Palace Museum.

Lin Mun-lee
Director of the National Palace Museum

CONTENTS

Accounting for the Art: The Registration Department

The Original Collection and New Acquisitions

The cultural objects in the collection of the National Palace Museum are currently divided into the three major categories of antiquities, painting and calligraphy, and books and documents, which originally belonged to the Palace Museum in Peking and the Preparatory Office of the Central Museum in Nanking. After arriving in Taiwan, the collections were temporarily stored at Pei-kou in Wu-feng, Taichung. In 1965, the two collections were joined together in Wai-shuang-hsi, Taipei, to form that of the current National Palace Museum. The holdings from the Palace Museum included 46,100 antiquities, 5,526 paintings and calligraphic works, and 545,797 rare books and archival documents. The collection from the National Central Museum included 11,047 antiquities, 477 works of painting and calligraphy, and 38 rare books. In sum, the combined holdings consisted of 608,985 cultural relics, making already for a huge repository for the legacy of Chinese culture.

The current collection of the National Palace Museum features not only the objects brought to Taiwan from the two institutions mentioned above, but also acquisitions made after the Museum's official inauguration in Taiwan. These new additions have come from transfers from other institutions, donations made to the Museum, and Museum purchases, of which the latter two are the most significant.

The Palace Museum in Peking and the Preparatory Office of the National Central Museum had begun expanding their collections long before their collections were moved to Taiwan. Since opening in Taipei, the National Palace Museum has never ceased in expanding the scope of its collection. Towards this end, a set of measures was drawn in 1969 to facilitate making acquisitions with budgetary funds and to encourage private donations and entrustments with a system of official channels and guidelines. In the current stage, the National Palace Museum is actively expanding the collection through the three methods of purchases, donations, and entrustments.

As of September 2006, a variety of works of painting and calligraphy, antiquities, and books and documents has been added to the collection. The total of 46,294 works of cultural and historical significance added since January 1967 include 1,651 transferred from other institutions, 32,001 donations, and 12,642 purchases. These have enriched the collection and preparation of exhibitions at the National Palace Museum considerably.

Among these treasures in their own right, some more notable examples include the Tzu-fan set of bells from the Spring and Autumn period, gilt bronze Buddhist sculptures from the Northern Wei and later periods, jade tablets used by the T'ang emperor Hsüan-tsung in homage to the God of the Earth, the "Spring Thunder" zither of the T'ang dynasty, the calligraphic work by Ch'en Po of the Northern Sung, the scroll "Cold Food Observance" by Su Shih of the Northern Sung, "A Calligraphic Rendition of the Hsi-tz'u Chapter of the I-ching" by Chu Hsi of the Southern Sung, a set of hanging scrolls of bamboo in monochrome ink by Shih-t'ao of the Ming-Ch'ing dynasty transition, sandalwood furniture from

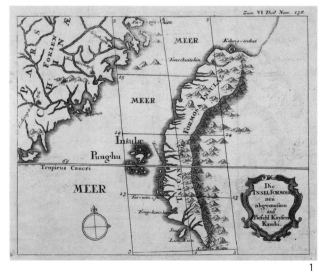

1

2

the residence of the Ch'ing dynasty prince Kung-wang, and the painting "Mount Lu" by the modern master Chang Dai-chien. The National Palace Museum has also acquired a large number of prehistoric jades and ceramics, Shang and Chou bronzes, ceramics, as well as famous paintings and calligraphic pieces from the reign of the Chia-ch'ing Emperor of the Ch'ing dynasty down to the modern era. These acquisitions have all served to fill some of the few gaps in the original collection of the Ch'ing emperors. In response to pluralistic developments in art world in recent years, as well as changes in society, the Museum has also been enriched by more than three hundred examples of Buddhist and religious sculpture from throughout Asia donated by Mr. Peng Kai-dong. Purchases have also been made of other Asian artworks, thereby expanding the depth and range of the collection even further as we branch out from the original model of the NPM based primary on the collection of Chinese artworks and objects from the Ch'ing court.

Tabulation of the Types and Numbers of Artworks in the Collection

The objects in the National Palace Museum collection are great in both number and variety. They can be divided as follows:

Bronzes	5994	Ceramics	25310	Jades	12103
Studio objects	2379	Lacquerware	707	Enamelware	2510
Carvings	651	Miscellanea	12293	Coins	6952
Silk tapestries, etc	279	Fans	1641	Paintings	5257
Calligraphy	2959	Stele works	450	Rubbings	756
Seal impressions	7	Textiles	88	Rare books	176713
Ch'ing archival documents	386729	Books and documents in Manchu, Mongolian, and Tibetan		11501	

Total: 655279 objects

The above represents the total number of objects in the collection of the National Palace Museum as of the end of September 2006. According to a statute in the presidential and vice-presidential management of cultural objects, the National Palace Museum transferred the care of 27 objects for preservation at Academia Historica.

The National Palace Museum, in order to establish a meticulous and all-around digital registration system, has reinforced object documentation common to the archival management, registration, and collection departments. This includes such procedures as data organization, classification, measurements, and photography. In addition, a complete registration and inventory system for the objects has been created, establishing a unique and permanent registration number system for each object. At the same time, in order to control the state of preservation of the collection objects, the National Palace Museum has already established a system of annual unannounced random selections every season. The director personally checks the record of each selected work against the actual objects in all of the collection departments, and registration personnel accompany those from the collection department, conservation department, and civil ethics office in checking the condition of the objects randomly selected for inspection, making a record of their inspection. Only by putting collection management into practice and establishing rules and regulations to be strictly enforced can the task of the registration of objects be done properly and completely. (Jen Li-li, Fang Chan-li)

3

4

1. Map of Formosa, dated 1715 (Donation 031976). Gift of Mr. Johannes Hajime Iizuka in July 2004.
2. Sculpture of Shiva and consort, India, 11th-12th century (Donation 031620). Gift of Mr. Peng Kai-dong in August 2004.
3. *Yüeh* beast-mask battle-axe with turquoise inlay, late Shang dynasty (Purchase 009058). Bought in March 1995.
4. Stone axe, late Neolithic period (Donation 031448). Gift of Mr. Lin Chen-yao in March 2002.

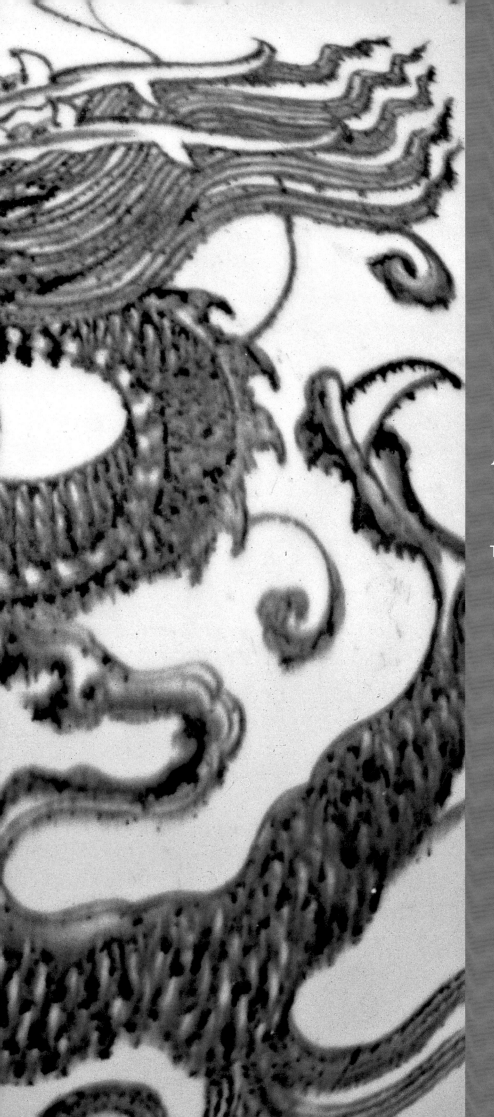

All Kinds of Treasures:

The Antiquities Department

1

All Kinds of Treasures:
The Antiquities Department

The National Palace Museum's Department of Antiquities is divided into four sections: bronzes, ceramics, jades, and treasured objects (previously known as curios). For years, professional curators working in these sections have directed their research to both general and specific aspects pertaining to these art forms, exploring topics in related areas even further to advance their own studies.

Bronzes

Research on bronzes is conducted to integrate recent archaeological discoveries with findings from more traditional studies on bronze and stone inscriptions, making important inroads into understanding the historical and cultural significance of bronze vessels during the Shang and Chou dynasties. In particular, progress in the studies of *tz'u*-grain containers, wine vessels, and weaponry has been significant in the interpretation of the connection between the making of bronze vessels and civilization of the Shang and Chou dynasties. Scholarship on Chinese bronzes has traditionally emphasized the inscriptions on Shang and Chou vessels, because they are crucial in the study of Chinese written forms and are primary source materials for the study of early Chinese history. Several pieces in the Museum's collection of bronzes feature inscriptions, sometimes with hundreds of characters. Collectively, they constitute an invaluable aid to understanding the history of the Western Chou as well as Spring and Autumn periods. These pieces include the Fu *chung* (also known as Tsung-chou *chung*) bell, Mao-kung *ting* food vessel, San-shih *p'an* plate, and the Tzu-fan *pien-chung* bells.

Porcelains

The collection of ceramics in the National Palace Museum is internationally renowned and boasts some of the finest pieces of imperial porcelains from the Sung, Yüan, Ming, and Ch'ing dynasties. The Museum's collection of Ming and Ch'ing official porcelains is particularly impressive for its comprehensive range of vessel types. Imperial wares of the Sung are equally prominent, and specimens of Ju ware are unrivaled anywhere else in the world. The studies by the Department's professional curators on Sung official wares, including those commissioned and made by the Palace Maintenance Office (Hsiu-nei-ssu) and those made in the kilns at Chiao-t'an-hsia, Ju ware, Chün ware, Ting ware, and associated topics have been comprehensive, and a large number of treatises and monographs have been published. Their research on Ming and Ch'ing official wares are also highly regarded by the academic community. The recent excavation of an early kiln site at Ching-te-chen in Kiangsi has yielded a wealth of information crucial to the study of Ming ceramics, with which researchers in the Department have been able to more precisely identify and authenticate the Hung-wu and Yung-lo reign pieces in the collection and to probe into the rich collection of Hsüan-te wares in a more systematic manner. In addition to examining stylistic changes in official wares and the development of decorative patterns and firing techniques through the dynasties, the Department's professionals have also combined the study of historical materials and the scientific analysis of artifacts to determine the origins and background of the production of imperial ware, presenting a systematically formulated hypothesis on the making of official wares in 12th-century China.

Jades

The Museum's renowned collection of jades features many of cultural and historical significance. Notable examples include the Neolithic *kuei* tablets with falcon or mask motifs, Shang dynasty *p'ei* ornaments with bird design, Han dynasty pieces rendered in the form of a *pi-hsieh* creature, ritual tablets used by the T'ang emperor Hsüan-tsung and the Sung emperor Chen-tsung, exotic Hindustan pieces with intricate openwork carving that stand apart from their Chinese counterparts, and the perennial favorite, a carved piece of jadeite in the form of cabbage and insects from the Ch'ing dynasty. While Chinese jade has been studied for well over a thousand years, it was originally under the realm of ancient stone inscriptions with an emphasis on the identification of the names and functions of objects. Entering the 20th century, archaeological discoveries have contributed a great deal of materials that have been essential to the advancement of scholarship on jades. Coupling the examination of these findings with cross-disciplinary studies in mineralogy, the humanities, and astronomy as well as a return to historical literature, researchers in the Department have been able to develop many fresh perspectives in deciphering China's jade cultures and to gain new insight into the dating of objects, distinctive regional characteristics, clan organization, and artistic styles.

1. Flower *tsun* pot with grape-violet glaze.
2. Exhibit gallery of the Antiquities Department.
3. New storage facilities.
4. Arrangement of metal cases in the cave storage facilities.

Treasured Objects

The treasured objects (curios) section of the Antiquities Department features the widest array of pieces in the collection, naturally encompassing an even broader range of research. Groundwork has already been laid in the study of carved lacquer from the Yüan, Ming and Ch'ing dynasties. However, the scope of research on pre-Sung lacquer works is rather limited due to constraints in the field itself. Even so, preliminary steps towards outlining and summarizing the development of lacquer production in China over 7,000 years have already been undertaken with materials garnered from archaeological excavations. Enamelware entered the realm of Chinese handicrafts in late Ming and was much favored by the Ch'ing court over Hsüan-te incense burners, Ch'eng-hua porcelains, and Yung-lo lacquer wares. Department researchers in the field have attained a comprehensive understanding of the development of this foreign-borne craft in China and are able to discern stylistic period characteristics based on designs, changes in enameling materials, and cloisonné techniques.

The majority of costumes and accessories in the Museum collection date to the Ch'ing dynasty, except for some jade ornaments that had been passed down from earlier periods. Many ornaments were produced by court artisans, some were gifts from provincial governors, and others were presented to the court by minority groups in border regions. Ornaments in the latter two groups were produced by regional craftsmen and submitted as tribute to the court. Research in this field has yielded important evidence in connection between official ranking and the types of precious stones and pearls used in court regalia. Through textual studies and actual comparisons, Department curators have explored regulations concerning court headwear, cap insignia, belts, court beads, gold diadems, and torque necklaces.

Buddhist Objects

The vast array of Buddhist ritual implements in the National Palace Museum is mainly composed of Tibetan Buddhist objects, and they are divided based on the origin of their production into Tibetan and Ch'ing palace items. The latter, greater in number, was mainly presented as gifts to Mongol and Tibetan leaders or temples, given as birthday gifts, or used in the Buddhist halls within the Ch'ing court. These Tibetan Buddhist ritual implements illustrate the influence of religion in Tibet on the Manchu Ch'ing emperors, who ordered the production of such beautiful ritual objects not only out of devotional piety, but also to have political sway over the Mongols and Tibetans.

Studio Implements

It became a tradition since the Sung dynasty for literati to collect and treasure implements of the scholar's studio. With major political, social, and economic changes after the mid-Ming in the Cheng-te and Chia-ching eras (16th century), literati placed even more emphasis on the pursuit of refinement in daily life through collecting and appreciating studio objects. Even emperors came under the sway of this trend. The three Ch'ing emperors K'ang-hsi, Yung-cheng, and Ch'ien-lung were especially fond of these implements, and nearly all of the brushes, ink, and inkstones in the Museum collection were from the Ch'ing court. In 1778, the Ch'ien-lung Emperor ordered the compilation of the *Imperial Catalogue of Hsi-ch'ing Inkstones*. Ninety-five of the inkstones registered in the catalogue are still today in the Museum collection. Green Sung-hua ink stones, with purplish-green and yellowish-green veins, were particularly admired in scholarly circles. Apart from their imperial pedigree, they were also given as state gifts to improve relations with foreign countries and bestowed upon government officials who had made important contributions to the court. Vital research work on other objects under the realm of the Department, such as bamboo carvings, *ju-i* scepters, and snuff bottles, has also been established through archaeological studies and historical literature.

As for exhibition planning, the Department will continue to organize and launch displays that present specific themes. The feasibility of having different objects from the Department's four sections integrated into a coherent whole for more comprehensive exhibitions in the future will also be further reinforced. (Chi Jo-hsin)

Crystallization of Nature: Jades

Chinese culture features several unique phenomena, one of which is an almost indescribable love of minerals known by the term "jade". Some people have compared the Chinese love of jade to the Western passion for gold, but actually the latter has more to do with the sparkling luster and preciousness of this metal, whereas the former has even deeper cultural implications and roots that go far beyond its monetary value.

In the Chinese language, there are many terms that use the character for "jade (yü 玉)" to describe various virtues, from a beautiful woman to incomparable looks, fine music, virtuous conduct, good fortune, riches beyond compare, and great purity. These are all associated with things or qualities that are happy, precious, noble, admirable, solid, and eternal. In everyday life, the purchase, wearing, and giving of jades marks a life of abundance that signifies behavior when one is joyous in both body and mind. Many Chinese people believe that wearing or handling jade has the effect of protecting one from evil spirits and influences, therefore beneficial to cultivating one's health and well-being. So, for example, at the bustling "Jade Weekend Market" in Taipei and in communities in Europe and America where Chinese people live, the best-selling items in gem shops is not the diamond so highly admired in the West, but jades made of jadeite and nephrite. People from around the world travel to Taiwan, Hong Kong, and mainland China and purchase jades as souvenirs of their visits. Such phenomena reinforce the age-old traditions of "admiring jade" and "respecting jade" found in Chinese culture, thus adding further to the "love of jade" so common among people of all classes in Chinese-influenced societies.

Jade, whether the soft and glossy nephrite variety or the shining and glassy jadeite form, is beautiful and remarkably tough. Over thousands of years, the art of jade carving has developed along with the changes in culture. Consequently, over the past few decades, the display of jades at the National Palace Museum includes some of the oldest objects of Chinese culture and traces the continuous and unbroken culture of jades in its later and more innovative incarnations. Mysterious ancient jades act like strong magnets that attract throngs of visitors, and the Museum's jade displays are often filled with viewers all day long. The objects in the permanent display are rotated to present the full spectrum of this art form, with beautiful jades covering eight thousand years of history. Divided by period into different display halls, the jades are also often displayed along with other antiquities of the same period, leading viewers to gain a fuller understanding of the cultural changes that took place as a whole.

Some jade lovers may be a little upset with this arrangement, but if you are able to make a lateral leap into other types of antiquities with the guide of beautiful jades from the ages in

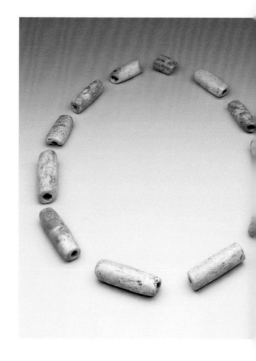

▲ **Fig. 1. Set of jade tubes**
Hsing-lung-wa Culture, Neolithic age
Length: 2.8-6.9 cm, tube diameter: 1.5-2.25 cm

▶ **Fig. 2. Animal-head jade figure**
Hung-shan Culture, Neolithic age
Height: 6.6 cm, width: 1.41 cm, width: 1.65 cm

these new displays, perhaps you will come away with a greater appreciation of the formation, developments, changes, and fusion that took place in Chinese culture over the centuries. Since many of the most famous Museum pieces have already been published in various books and catalogues, we here have tried to select a wide range of works from the collection that are both aesthetically pleasing and culturally significant so as to explain the developments that took place in the culture of jade. Many of them are already on display, so can go to the displays and search for them?

The permanent displays are on the second and third floors of the east wing of the Main Building. If viewers start from the section on the "The Neolithic Age: The Beginning of Civilization" on the third floor and pass through the displays entitled "Classical Civilization: The Bronze Age" and "From Classic to Tradition: Ch'in and Han Dynasties", you will find that you have traveled from the Neolithic Age all the way through the Hsia, Shang, Chou, and Han dynasties, taking a trip through time with jades from eight thousand to eighteen hundred years ago, covering more than six millennia.

In East Asia, the three main rivers known as the Liao, Yellow, and Yangtze Rivers gave birth to cultures in ancient times, and over the years they ebbed and flowed both independently and reciprocally. They absorbed wave after wave of outside cultural influence from western regions and to the north, and in the Han dynasty this cultural fusion reached a peak. Afterwards, a political and cultural entity took form that also took part in exchange with surrounding areas. This is why, even up to the present day, the main trends of Chinese cultural circles is known as "Han culture", the people of this main group known as "Han Chinese", and the language they use as "Han Chinese".

In the ancient past, people in their experiences of using tools to grind and polish stone materials learned that certain minerals were not only extremely tough and durable, but also quite beautiful. After grinding and polishing, these minerals would give off a radiance and luster that earned them the term "*yü*", which means "beautiful stone" in Chinese. The sun is the source of almost all life on our planet, and in the simpler belief systems of Chinese ancestors, they felt that such objects as beautiful stones and fine silks radiating with luster and sheen from the light of the sun both contained this source of energy--the "quintessential force". As a result, "jades and silks" became used as ceremonial objects in rituals for the gods and spirits. Silk disintegrates quickly over the millennia, but jade is enduring and can thus be displayed here before your eyes to show how ancestors of the Chinese communicated with the gods, which was done primarily through the use of jade.

In addition to the notion of a "quintessential force", the ancients in simpler times also developed the idea of "receptivity" in terms of "objects of like quality". They believed that the shape and decoration of objects had a supernatural power of producing a similar response in communication. Therefore, according to

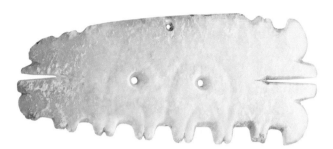

their model of the workings of the universe, the forms of clan ancestors and spirit animals were carved in jades and then used to conduct rituals in ceremonies in the hopes that the spirits and ancestors would be able to read their hopes and what was in their minds. In other words, since antiquity, jades played the role of a "spirit medium", and the "culture of reverence for jade" was born at this time.

There are a total of two displays in the section on "The Neolithic Age: The Beginning of Civilization", one presenting the works of coastal cultures in Eastern China and the other showing inland objects from more westerly regions. Although expressions of stone and ceramic objects in the lives of people at the time are somewhat lacking here, one can gain a great understanding from the wealth of these jade objects, some of which are extremely rare.

The prehistoric inhabitants of China's northeast mostly subsisted on fishing and hunting, and they apparently often wore chains of bone objects to show off their prowess in hunting. Figure 1 is a jade tube from seven to eight thousand years ago that imitates a bone tube. Close examination of this object shows that the jade was first carved into a rectangular piece. Then its edges were gradually rounded, with the hole in the center still revealing obvious traces of the circular grinding process.

The inhabitants of the northeast who depended on fishing and hunting for their existence practiced a primitive form of shamanism (in which religious figures communicated with an unseen world of gods and spirits). In their worship of animistic beliefs, they believed that many animals possessed the supernatural ability to assist humans in communicating with the gods and spirit world. They often used beautiful pieces of jade

▲ **Fig. 3. Toothed animal-mask jade ornament**
Hung-shan Culture, Neolithic age
Height: 5.9 cm, width: 13.3 cm, width: 0.6 cm

▼ **Fig. 4. Jade bird of prey staff**
Hung-shan Culture, Neolithic age
Top length: 10.2 cm, width: 3.25 cm, width: 1.1 cm
Bottom length: 6.9 cm, width: 1.8 cm, width: 1.0 cm
The two pieces were inserted into both ends of a wooden pole and used as a staff of authority by someone of prominence.

▲ **Fig. 5. Two jade finials of birds on stands**
Liang-chu Culture, Neolithic age
Height: 2.7 cm, bird length: 1.47 cm,
pole width: 0.68 cm; thickness: 0.4 cm
Height: 3.0 cm, birth length: 1.6 cm,
pole width: 0.65 cm; thickness: 0.5 cm

▼ **Fig. 6. Jade *pi* disc**
Liang-chu Culture, Neolithic age
Outer diameter: 13.17-13.44 cm,
hole diameter: 2.16 cm, thickness: 1.5 cm
The outer diameter of the disc had been cut
at some time, thereby damaging the original
symbol of the bird on the back. See the detail
for the engraving in special light and the line
drawing based on it.

carved in the form of larval insects and mammalian fetuses to emphasize the life force of change and immortality. The display here includes two "pig-dragons" in such fetus shapes. These ancient peoples also often combined different parts of animals and humans into a single form, such as the beast-head human jade figure in Figure 2. Its head not only looks like a wild bear, even the two hands in front of its chest appear to have curved claws.

The jade pendant in Figure 3 was apparently worn for a long period of time. The small hole at the top, used to loop through a piece of string in order to suspend the object, still bears traces around its edges of wear and tear caused by the movement of string. Originally the area around the pair of eyes and that above the row of teeth below were once ground into arcing grooves. However, due to the grinding, the grooves have become much less obvious and can only be seen clearly when light is shown at a certain angle. This toothed animal-mask jade pendant and another famous piece clearly carved with vortex eyes is different in style, revealing the mysterious beauty and religious contents of the ancient past.

Birds possess an ability that humans and most other animals naturally lack--that of flight. It is therefore of little wonder that many ancient peoples worshipped birds. In the belief system of the peoples who lived in eastern China, the divine dark bird was originally considered as a messenger of the mysterious life forces of nature and therefore felt to be an ancestor of clans who descended from the gods. In different ecological habitats appeared various so-called "dark bird" forms. In the expansive regions of the northeast, the bird often took the shape of a fierce falcon or bird of prey, thereby accounting for the carving of the jade bird-of-prey finial from the Hung-shan Culture seen in Figure 4. In the beautiful scenery of the Kiangnan area, one often finds swallows darting about or birds like turtledoves among the trees, hence

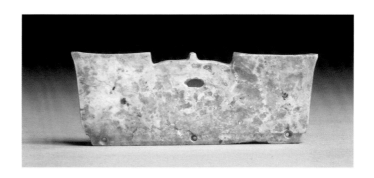

◀ **Fig. 7. Jade** *ts'ung* **tube**
Lung-shan-Ch'i-chia System,
Neolithic age
Height: 32 cm, width: 10 cm,
hole diameter: 8 cm

▲ **Fig. 8. Jade crown ornament**
Liang-chu Culture, Neolithic age
Height: 2.3 cm, width: 6.3 cm,
thickness: 0.4 cm
The drawing to the left is a line drawing
reconstruction of its original purpose
based on archaeological evidence.

▼ **Fig. 9. Jade knife**
Liang-chu Culture, Neolithic age
Height: 8.1 cm, width: 15.5 cm,
thickness: 0.55 cm,
hole diameter: ca. 1.03 cm

the appearance of the mysterious symbol of the "bird standing on a ritual platform" seen engraved on round discs or square tubes by the peoples of the Liang-chu Culture, which they used as a "password" to communicate with the gods. The edge of the jade disc in Figure 5 has been partially cut away, resulting in the engraving of the dark bird only retaining its beak and frontal area as well as the pole stand on which it is perched. The ritual stand itself is decorated with another bird-like symbol apparently wearing a crown and with its wings spread out. The peoples of the Kiangnan area seem to have been immersed in a fascinating and mysterious world of beauty and illusion, which accounts perhaps for the attraction we find in the two adorable jade sculptures of birds standing on poles seen in Figure 6.

Ancient peoples also noted that the sun rose in the east and set in the west, forming part of the notion of the trajectory and roundness of certain forms in the universe. In the exhibition hall is an explanation that the round shape of the jade disc corresponds to the trajectory of the sun (the so-called "Yellow Path") in the known universe at the time, as explained in a section of an ancient Chinese mathematical treatise. The shape of the *ts'ung* tube, with its unique square external form and circular hole, appears to have had no practical function. It was nonetheless quite common in the Liang-chu Culture in the lower reaches of the Yangtze River valley during the late Neolithic period as well as the Miao-er, Lung-shan, and Ch'i-chia Cultures of the middle reaches of the

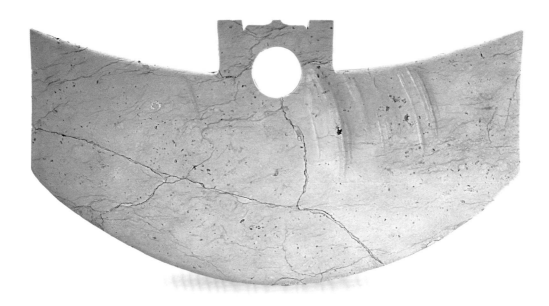

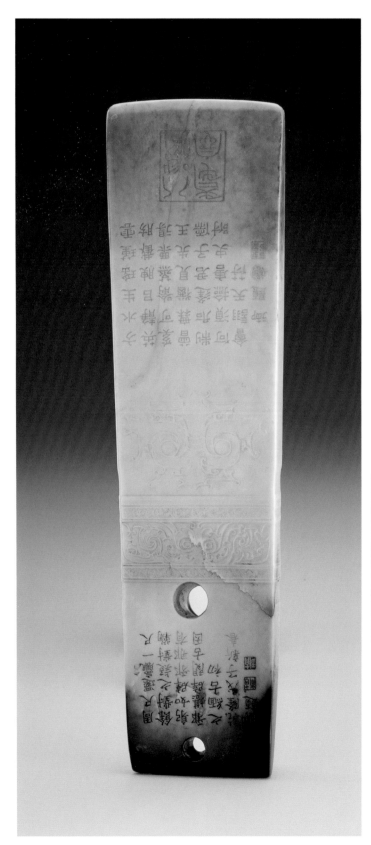

Line drawings

Details

Fig. 10. Jade *kuei* tablet
Shantung Lung-shan Culture, Neolithic age
Height: 24.6 cm, width: 7 cm, thickness: 1.2 cm
Both sides of this jade tablet are carved with
abstract and concrete images of spirit figures.
During ceremonies, the wider part of the tablet
would have been held upwards. However, back
in the Ch'ing dynasty, the Ch'ien-lung Emperor
did not understand this function and ordered jade
craftsmen to engrave his poetry and seals on the
tablet with its narrow side facing upward, hence
the characters appearing upside down here.

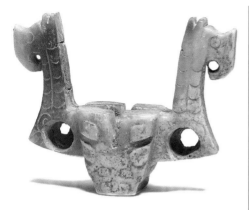

▲ **Fig. 11. Twin-bird jade stand**
Shang dynasty
Height: 5.6 cm, width: 7.4 cm
The groove along the necks of
the birds and along the top of the
animal's head is originally where a
now-lost insert would have been.

▼ **Fig. 12. Handle-shaped jade**
with phoenix pattern
Western Chou period
Height: 8.7 cm, width: 3.1 cm

Rubbing

Yellow River valley. The round disc and square tube perhaps represent the simple, ancient belief of the duality of nature as "the heavens are round and empty (all encompassing) and the earth is square (solid)". For example, the square *ts'ung* tube in Figure 7 reveals the plain and simple geometricized style that the peoples of the northwest admired.

The jade piece in Figure 8 has a small notch in the upper edge that reflects the idea of "exaltation" or "communicating with the heavens" that is found in the Liang-chu Culture. The bottom edge would probably have been attached to an ivory or wooden comb and inserted into the hair of a shaman, appearing somewhat like a crown when worn. Due to the fact that it looks a little like the modern Chinese character for "*chieh* 介", it is also known as a "*chieh*" crown.

The Liang-chu people believed that the "*chieh*"-character crown allowed the wearer to communicate with the heavens. Not only was it worn on the head of religious figures, it also decorated the images of the gods along with such weapons and tools as the jade battle-axe, jade knife, and jade sickle. Figure 9 shows a jade knife with a "*chieh*"-character crown. Judging from the penetrating coloring and other features, this probably was a ritual object of the highest order in the middle period of the Liang-chu Culture.

The lower reaches of the Yellow River lie precisely in between the northeast and the lower reaches of the Yangtze River. There, the peoples of the Lung-shan Culture in Shantung absorbed the "*chieh*"-character crown from the south as well as the large vortex eye shape from the north, creating an abstracted ancestral spirit mask of their own. Although they possessed a high level of carving skill, they intentionally carved the spirit-ancestor mask form very shallow in order to make it difficult to distinguish. Here in the display galleries, we need to use special reflective lighting in order to allow visitors to be able to somewhat make out the details of this decoration.

In the late Neolithic Age, when the area of the middle reaches of the Yellow River valley had entered the Hsia dynasty of Chinese history, the surrounding archaeological cultures of Shih-chia-ho, Lung-shan, and Ch'i-chia continued to develop. The jades of this age belong to the historical period corresponding approximately to the Hsia dynasty at the time.

In the Neolithic Age, cultures revering jade emerged and developed. The most important ritual objects made of jade were discs, which symbolized the sun and the heavens and continued to be produced in later dynasties. The prehistoric "animistic beliefs" and "reverence of the dark bird" yielded the development of two auspicious and mystical animals of the historical age in China-- the dragon and the phoenix. Starting from the "The Neolithic Age: The Beginning of Civilization" gallery, the forms associated with the dragon and the phoenix appear and come to stay throughout the history of Chinese culture.

Rubbing

Figure 12 is a jade paired-bird object stand. The lower part of the stand bears a groove, indicating that it was fastened to the top of some other object. The top part of the stand is comprised of two bird-head forms facing out to the left and right, also forming what appear to be the horns of the animal head in the middle. There is also a groove that runs down the necks of the birds and along the top of the animal's head. Some now-lost decorative insert was probably placed into this groove. A similar jade object is in the collection of Harvard University, in which a human head appears between the two birds.

Although the jade in Figure 11 is not on display in the permanent galleries, but it and a famous phoenix-décor pendant with dragon crown from the Shang dynasty as well as a phoenix-décor handle-shaped object from the Western Chou (Figure 12) all reveal a similar notion. The lower part of the latter has a plain area that would have been inserted into a tall pole. The ancient Chinese believed that inserting a bird-head or bird-decorated jade carving into the top of a tall pole would allow it to invite the spirit of the dark bird in during rituals and thereby listen to the prayers of people.

▲ **Fig. 13. Jade *huang* pendant with dragon pattern**
Middle Eastern Chou period
Length: 12.2 cm, inner width: 3.7 cm, thickness: 0.4 cm

▼ **Fig. 14. Phoenix-shaped pendant and grain-pattern jade *pi* disc**
Late Eastern Chou period
Phoenix: height: 4.8 cm, length: 7.94 cm, thickness: 0.39 cm
Disc: diameter: 7 cm, hole diameter: 3.1 cm, thickness: 0.43 cm

▶ **Fig. 15. Jade *pi* disc**
Western Han period
Outer diameter: 20.6 cm, hole diameter: 5.9 cm, thickness: 0.4 cm

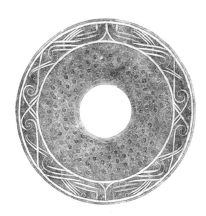

Rubbing

The dragon-décor *huang* pendant in Figure 13 is a typical jade object of the Spring and Autumn period, offering proof that the cloud pattern derived from the disintegration of the dragon pattern. Both ends of the jade *huang* are carved with a large dragon head sticking out its tongue. The lower jaws of the large dragon heads are also engraved with small dragon heads facing in the opposite direction. The upper area of the arcing form of the jade *huang* is also decorated with a carving of four small dragon heads. Except for the head areas still preserving the features of their eyes, the rest of the areas have disintegrated into a cloud pattern similar to "S" and "C" shapes.

By the Warring States period, the cloud pattern again developed into a grain-like pattern that looks like a series of commas. Figure 14 shows that jade craftsmen at the time were fully able to work with jade, taking side materials in the production of the grain-pattern disc and designing them into a

Rubbing

phoenix bird looking back. The elegant shape perfectly matches the refinement of the carving.

The round disc symbolizing the sun and sky was produced in large numbers in the Han dynasty, for people at the time believed that the whole in the middle was the passageway connecting to the realm of the heavens. Therefore, when many members of the nobility passed away, small pieces of jade were sewn together to form jade suit (commonly called a "gown of jade sewn with gold") to cover the entire body. In order to allow the deceased to "breath in" the essence of the jade, a jade disc was sewn onto the top of the jade suit, allowing the deceased's soul to pass through the opening of the jade disc and to the heavens and the afterworld. Perhaps as a result of this, the top of a person's head in Chinese is known as the "cover to the gate of the heavens".

The jade disc in Figure 15 is divided into inner and outer rings. The inner one is carved with a grain pattern, while the outer one is engraved with a "dragon and phoenix" pattern. The center of this part is a patternized dragon face seen frontally, with eyebrows, eyes, and nose. Emerging from both eyebrows appears a floating phoenix bird. Other archaeological evidence indicates that this type of jade disc may have been used in ritual ceremonies or perhaps in burials. However, the surface of this particular jade has already changed to a dark brownish color and fitted with a sandalwood stand from the Ch'ing dynasty. Only by viewing the ink rubbing hanging on the wall can one see the decoration clearly.

Figure 16 is a jade disc engraved with the characters for "everlasting happiness" in openwork, revealing the interest in decorative flourish from the late Eastern Han period. The inner ring is engraved with a raised dot pattern, while the outer ring is carved in openwork with the "Four Spirit Animals" that represent the lucky animals associated with the four directions:

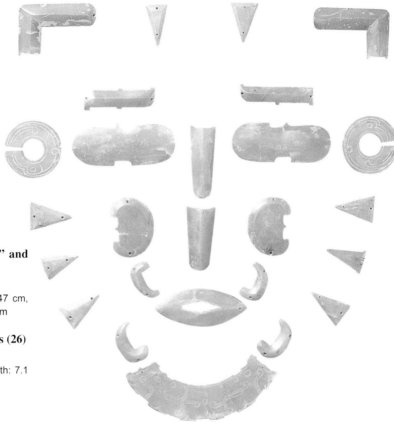

◀ **Fig. 16. Jade *pi* disc of "eternity" and "happiness"**
Eastern Han period
Height: 16.55 cm, outer diameter: 13.47 cm, hole diameter: 2.9 cm, thickness: 0.47 cm

▶ **Fig. 17. Jade and stone mask pieces (26)**
Western Chou period
Huang length: 10.6 cm, eye piece length: 7.1 cm, ear piece diameter: 4 cm

◀ **Fig. 18. Jade cicada**
Han dynasty
Height: 6.1 cm, width: 2.9 cm, thickness: 0.85 cm

▼ **Fig. 19. Two jade pigs wrapped in gold foil**
Han dynasty
Height: 2.8 cm, length: 10.9 cm, thickness: 2.85 cm

green dragon (east), white tiger (west), crimson bird (south), and dark tortoise (north). The dark tortoise in the lower right corner, however, is rendered in the form of a small dragon. The upper parts of the bodies of the dragon and tiger extend beyond the rim of the disc, while the center of the upper part of the arcing portion is an open place for slipping a string to hang the piece, perhaps once in some ancient palace wall or part of a lavish canopy.

In sum, the initial stage of the reverence for jade in prehistoric cultures continued to develop in the Shang and Chou dynasties and down into the Western and Eastern Han period. In addition to popular animals used for decoration in jade pendants, it was also common to make jades solely for the purpose of funerals. The jade pieces in Figure 17, for example, symbolize the features of the face and were once sewn together and laid on the face of the deceased. Figure 18 represents a jade cicada that was once placed in the mouth of the deceased, while the two gold-wrapped jade pigs in Figure 19 were put in the hands. Together, they symbolize the ideas of "rebirth" and "wealth".

In the period from the Six Dynasties to the Sui and T'ang dynasties, Buddhist thought emerged and came to grip the consciousness of many Chinese. The culture of jade and their association with the quest for immortality gradually went into decline. At the same time, China was subject to waves of foreign cultural influence that had an increasing impact on society, eventually yielding the refinement and classicism of Sung dynasty culture. At this time, many jades began to appear in the form of lively plants and animals, such as lotus-leaf brush washers, geese, cats, and even children. However, in the second floor galleries devoted to the Sung and Yüan dynasties, you will find that among the most valued historical objects are the jade tablets used by the Sung dynasty emperor Chen-tsung in his sacrifices to the gods of the earth. At the time, the jade tablets were not only placed in a

Rubbing

◄ **Fig. 20. Jade tablets and inlay for Emperor Chen-tsung's Sacrifices to Gods of the Earth**
Sung dynasty
Tablet length: ca. 29.8 cm, overall width: 48 cm
Inlay length: ca. 17.3 cm, width: ca. 12.8 cm, thickness: ca. 0.4 cm

▲ **Fig. 21. Pieces of a jade belt (20)**
Ming dynasty
Longest piece: length: 16.18 cm, width: 6.5 cm
Narrowest piece: length: 5.7 cm, width: 2.42 cm

▼ **Fig. 22. Three concentric jade rings**
Ming dynasty
Outer diameter: 11.6 cm, hole diameter: 6.0 cm, thickness: 0.8 cm

box inlaid with many pieces of jade, but the central jade pieces of both sets were engraved with a dragon pattern and the surrounding pieces adorned with phoenix décor and hooked-cloud decoration (Figure 20).

The custom of inlaying a piece of jade into a belt for decoration originally derived from Central Asian sources. After it was introduced in the T'ang dynasty, it became part of the requisite clothing of the Chinese official. According to records, only the highest officials were allowed to wear a jade belt, followed by that of the silver belt. In the display for the Ming dynasty is a set of twenty jade pieces decorated with dragon patterns. Because it was never buried, the quality of the jade remains pristine white and lustrous. In the collection of the National Palace Museum is another jade belt that had been buried, and the dragon pattern is just as robust and the coloring elegantly archaic from burial in the ground (Figure 21).

Figure 22 shows a very interesting jade composed of three concentric rings that form a round disc. The central ring is engraved with the sun, clouds, and stars to represent the sky. The outer ring is engraved with mountain peaks and ocean waves to represent the earth, while the central ring is decorated with a dragon pattern to represent the ruler (emperor) in the human world. The three rings act as an armillary sphere that also

Rubbing

symbolizes the harmonious workings and interaction of the universe in three-dimensional form. The noble and mysterious dragon in the pattern represents the role of the emperor as an important link in the object and functioning of the Chinese cosmology. Jade seals decorated with the dragon were also an indispensable accessory of the emperor, Figure 23 showing a grand and imposing jade seal once used by the Ch'ien-lung Emperor of the Ch'ing dynasty.

The Ch'ien-lung Emperor greatly appreciated ancient objects. Not only did he collect antiquities with great passion, he also encouraged current artistic production to emulate them. Figure 24 shows a miniature jade mountain that uses the natural reddish-brown coloring of the jade boulder to create the illusion of mountains with trees in autumn. On the back, the jade craftsmen also engraved the poem personally written by the Ch'ien-lung Emperor onto the piece, filling in the characters with gold pigment. This is the largest miniature jade mountain in the collection of the National Palace Museum.

In the late Ch'ien-lung reign (corresponding to approximately the end of the 18th century), many quarries for jadeite were gradually discovered in the mountains along the border between Yunnan and Myanmar (Burma). The court often referred to this new jade material as "Yunnan green jade" and it quickly became the fashion among women in the palaces, the jadeite cabbage in Figure 25 being an example from the 19th century. Here, the craftsmen used the natural coloring of the jade to design the intended subject and form. A larger locust and smaller katydid appear at the top of the vegetable, and both of these insects represent the desire for numerous offspring due to their large numbers in nature. The design of the entire piece conveys the notion of "pure as white and many children", which suited exactly the hopes and desires of many a parent in traditional China when presenting a gift to their daughter upon her marriage. Since this piece was originally part of the display in the Yung-ho Palace, it is generally regarded by many to have been part of the dowry of its occupant, Concubine Chin.

(Teng Shu-p'ing)

▼ **Fig. 23. Pair of jade seals**
Ch'ing dynasty
Left: height: 10.5 cm, seal face width: 13 cm
Right: height: 10.4 cm, seal face width: 13 cm
These two seals were produced on the occasion of the Ch'ien-lung Emperor's seventieth (left) and eightieth (right) birthdays.

◄ **Fig. 24. Miniature jade mountain depicting red trees in autumn mountains**
Ch'ing dynasty
Height: 16.6 cm, width: 39.5 cm, thickness: 8.2 cm

► **Fig. 25. Jadeite cabbage**
Ch'ing dynasty
Height: 18.7 cm, width: 9.1 cm, width: ca. 5.07 cm

Vessels of State Importance: Bronzes

Bronzes in the Museum Collection

The Museum's collection of bronze vessels illustrates the development of this art in the valleys of the Yellow and Yangtze Rivers over a period of nearly 2,000 years from the Shang to Han dynasties.

The types of bronze vessels and methods of casting differed from one ancient bronze civilization to another. In Egypt, Mesopotamia, Greece, and Rome, wrought bronze was made with lost-wax casting techniques into weapons and statues; bronze vessels, however, were relatively rare. Inhabitants of the Central Plains in ancient China also took advantage of the hardness and sharpness of bronze, turning it into weapons of various sorts. Of greater significance, though, was that they applied the piece-mold approach to casting wine, food, and water vessels to pay homage to their ancestors and to serve as ritual implements for betrothal and marriage. Moreover, they realized the melodious tonal quality of the metal and the reflective nature of polished bronze, casting a number of full-scale musical instruments (such as the Tzu-fan *pien-chung* bells from the Spring and Autumn period) and mirrors (such as one with sea animal and grapevine décor from the T'ang dynasty). Hence, the Museum's collection of bronzes is rich in ritual vessels, musical instruments, weapons, and mirrors.

The animal-mask *ku* wine goblet serves to prove that the casting of bronze into a range of vessels, including wine, food and water containers, was already being practiced in the Yellow River valley during the early Shang dynasty. The deep banding of the animal-mask pattern on the surface of the vessel was an

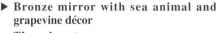

▶ **Bronze mirror with sea animal and grapevine décor**
T'ang dynasty
Diameter: 17.7 cm
Popular at the height of the T'ang dynasty, the décor here is typical of designs on bronze mirrors at the time. The back is ornamented with patterns of butterflies, flowers, birds, winding grapevines and a sea animal (known as suan-ni, which is actually probably a lion) in a prominent relief, fully illustrating the pluralistic splendors of T'ang culture.

▼ **Bronze Tzu-fan *pien-chung* bells (set of eight pieces)**
Middle Spring and Autumn period
Height: 28.1-71.6 cm

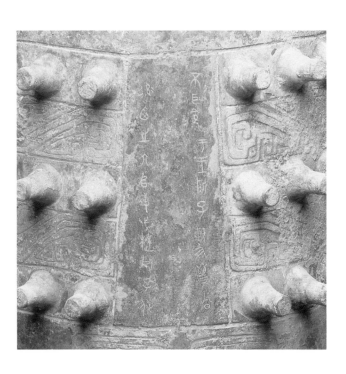

ornamental motif with significant meaning to the Shang people. The circular base and carved holes in the body show the technical achievement of arriving at fixed inner and outer edges. On the other hand, the animal-mask *ting*, with its shallow hook-shaped angled ridges, reveals a southern style. It can be inferred that a certain degree of interaction from the 16th to the 14th centuries BCE occurred between the bronze cultures of the Yellow and Yangtze River valleys.

The coiled-dragon *p'an* plate features a dragon head in the center with its body coiled around and encircled along the rim with fish, *k'uei* dragons, and bird patterns covering the interior surface. This reveals a new trend in bronze casting after the capital of the Shang dynasty was moved to Anyang. With its unusual square shape and handles of animal heads holding birds, the Ya-ch'ou square *kuei* vessel provides evidence of the creativity of the Ya-ch'ou clan in the Shantung area in the late Shang and early Chou. Another example is the twin-dragon *kuei* container. While maintaining the traditional round body, the different angles of the two coiled dragons and the unified design on the lid and body illustrate a rather novel style of the late Shang and early Chou.

Towards the end of the 11th century BCE, the ruler of the Chou became the overlord of the entire realm, and the content of bronze vessels that feudal states competed in casting was mainly used as symbols of socio-political status. Originality within inherited traditions was still witnessed from time to time. The Chao *yu* kettle, cast in separate pieces and with linear animal mask designs, marks a departure from the unified style of the Shang, and the hook-shaped angled ridge reveals a new development in the art of bronze. The ox-head *kuei* vessel with phoenix motif, on the other hand, has large and small ox heads carved in relief on its handles, body, and square base, revealing a wealth of local characteristics of the northwestern region, possibly of Pao-chi in modern Shensi.

▲ **Bronze *ku* wine vessel with animal-mask décor**
Early Shang dynasty
Height: 15.3 cm; depth: 11.3 cm

▼ **Bronze *p'an* plate with coiled-dragon décor**
Late Shang dynasty
Height: 16.7 cm; depth: 7.2 cm

▲ **Square bronze *kuei* container of the Ya-ch'ou clan**
Late Shang or early Chou dynasty
Height: 20.7 cm; depth: 11.9 cm

▶ ***Kuei* bronze container with twin-dragon décor**
Late Shang or Early Chou dynasty
Height: 21.3 cm; depth: 13 cm

◄ **Bronze Chao *yu* kettle**
Early Western Chou dynasty
Height: 29.8 cm; depth: 22.9 cm

▶ **Bronze Sung *hu* pot**
Middle to Late Western Chou dynasty
Height: 63 cm; depth: 44.4 cm
The flat form of this *hu* vessel with its geometrically curved pattern and coiled-dragon décor marks the birth of a new style in mid-Chou bronze casting. The inscription is an account of how a person by the name of Sung was appointed by the Chou ruler to an official post and how he commissioned the casting of the vessel to eulogize the ruler's virtue.

▼ **Bronze *tsun* wine jar in the shape of a bird-headed animal**
Warring States period
Height: 11.4 cm; depth: 10.5 cm

The Hsing-chi *tsun* wine jar of the Hsing state during the mid-Chou (between the 10th to 9th centuries BCE) features a body covered with ornamental phoenixes, and the new design is considered by many as announcing the end of the animal-mask motif of the Shang. The Sung *hu* pot is covered with a geometric curved pattern, fish-scale décor, and ornamental coiled dragons. Along with the Mao-kung *ting* tripod from Ch'i-shan in Shensi and the pair of *pu* containers of the Duke of Chin from Ch'u-ts'un in Shansi, they illustrate the popularity of unique designs during the middle and late Western Chou--ornamental animal pattern and geometric décor. This kind of large square *hu* was used along with *ting* and *kuei* in ritual ceremonies and usually carried inscriptions relating to the conferring of honors and favor. Representing the status of the nobility, the vessel type was popular among feudal lords of the Central Plains. After the middle of the Western Chou, the system regulating the use of bronze vessels in ritual practices gradually became fixed.

◄ **Bronze *fang* wine vessel with décor
of hunting scenes**
Warring States period
Height: 45.3 cm; depth: 39.9 cm

► **Bronze I-ch'u *tuan* wine vessel**
Late Spring and Autumn period
Height: 20.3 cm; depth: 18.1 cm

► **Bronze standard measure**
Wang Mang Interregnum period
Height 25.5 cm; depth: 23 cm

▼ **Tseng-chi Wu-hsü bronze *hu* pot**
Late Spring and Autumn period
Height: 78.1 cm; depth: 57.5 cm

At the beginning of the Spring and Autumn period from the 8th to 7th centuries BCE, the bronze casting traditions in the Central Plains from the late Shang and early Chou was still preserved in such southern kingdoms as Hsü, as evidenced in the style of the *tuan* wine vessel of I-ch'u. However, in response to the new political milieu, various kingdoms competed against each other with new techniques and styles, ushering in a trend in bronze casting towards a higher level of ornamentation in the middle of the period.

The Tseng-chi Wu-hsü *hu* pot from the late Spring and Autumn state of Tseng in the Ch'u cultural sphere, for example, features handles of relief-carved *k'uei* dragons with heads turned and a lid with tall, hook-shaped feet. The vivid and lively form is considered a masterpiece of cast welding. The hunting décor on the *fang* wine vessel, with its transformed ornamental style, is illustrative of scenes of nobility at leisure and war. The pattern may have originally been inlaid with metals, exhibiting a new style close to what was popular in the Central Plains (of present-day Honan). The *tsun* wine vessel in the shape of a bird-headed animal represents a tradition of exchange in the northern pastoral region. Decorated with vividly molded animals, it may be a rendition of the style popular in the Shansi area. The unique stylistic development of each region eventually grew into a plurality of artistic patterns in the Warring States period.

With the Ch'in and Han dynasties, feudal political structure began to disintegrate, and the use of bronze ritual vessels declined. Along with the standard measure used to unify the system of the realm in the Wang Mang Interregnum at the beginning of the 1st century CE, the development of seals and mirrors clearly mark a change in the practical and socio-political functions of casting bronze. (Ch'en Fang-mei)

The Evidence of History: Engraved Writing on Bronzes

While the inscriptions on Shang and Chou dynasty bronzes (known as *chin-wen*) had been meticulously collated and documented since the Sung dynasty, serious in-depth study of the writing system did not take place until the Ch'ing dynasty when the practice of scholarly textual verification arose. Bronze inscriptions, along with newly discovered inscriptions on oracle bones, were recognized by paleographers as ancient writings of the Shang and Chou. Moreover, they were valued by calligraphers as authentic examples of ancient writing and looked upon by scholars of ancient history as first-hand historical material.

The National Palace Museum is home to nearly a thousand bronze vessels (not including mirrors and seals), of which almost half carry inscriptions. This collection may be small compared to the more than 13,000 inscribed Shang and Chou bronze vessels extant today, but it does boast the longest example of text on a bronze in the world--the Mao-kung *ting* food vessel with its 500-character inscription, and the most unrestrained example of ancient calligraphy--the inscription of 357 characters on the San-shih *p'an* plate. Furthermore, many pieces in the collection, such as the bell-shaped Fu *chung* musical instrument (cast by King Li-wang of the Western Chou and formerly known as the Tsung-chou *chung*), the paired Hsiao-ch'en-lai *kuei* containers, the Sung *ting* tripod, the Sung *hu* kettle, the Shih-sung *kuei* vessel, and the Warring States standard measures of Ch'en-hou-wu *kuei* and Ch'en-hou-wu *tun*, can be used to confirm historical facts. In other words, the Museum's collection of inscribed bronze vessels is rich enough to well illustrate the evolution of *chin-wen* in ancient China.

Late Shang bronze inscriptions are usually less than ten characters; they typically serve to indicate the maker's name, family emblem, and name of the person being sacrificed to, as seen in the Chu-fu-i *ting* tripod or the Chu-ko-fu-ting *ho* wine vessel. The contrast between the thicknesses of the lines in these inscriptions is considerable. The start and finish of a character show more of a point (or, in some, a rounded dot), and the pictographic quality of the forms is strong. The thick lines (*fei-pi*) and dots (*mo-ting*) are quite evident in the tops of the characters "*tzu* 子," "*fu* 父," "*ting* 丁" and "*ko* 戈."

▲ **Ink rubbing of the inscription on the Fu-i *ting* tripod**
This inscription found on the inner face of the *ting* identifies it as a vessel used by the Chu (🜩) clan to commemorate the ancestor Fu-i.

▼ **Fu-i *ting* tripod**
Late Shang dynasty
Height: 23.1 cm; depth: 7.5 cm

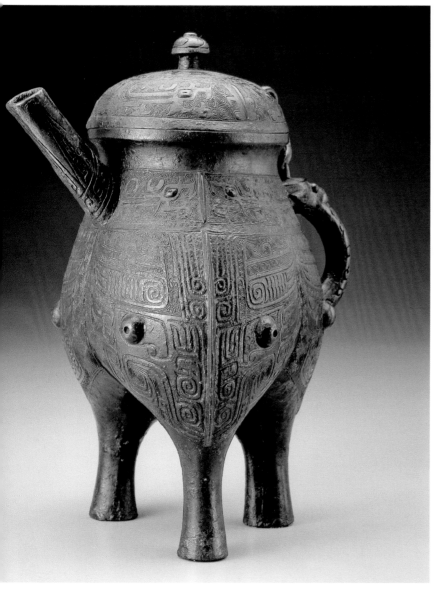

▲ **Bronze Fu-ting *ho* ewer**
Late Shang dynasty
Height: 28 cm; depth 15.3 cm
The vessel was used by the Chu-ko clan to
venerate their ancestor Fu-ting.

▶ **Ink rubbing of the inscription on the lid**
of the Fu-ting *ho* ewer.
The inscription on the lid is found in the center.

▶ **Ink rubbing of the inscription on the body**
of the Fu-ting *ho* ewer.
The inscription on the vessel body was engraved
on the exterior surface of the lower part.

Bronze inscriptions were produced by first using a brush to write on a clay template, and, after being corrected and engraved with a knife, were then cast. The character "i 乙" is done with space, showing that the knife was first employed to cut an outer frame and something left out when the bottom of the middle was carved out.

Bronze inscriptions of the early Western Chou are relatively longer, and the form of characters appears to change with the number of strokes. In general, character size is irregular and columns unaligned, the K'ang-hou *fang-ting* and Hsien-hou *li-ting* being examples of such. Recording the conquering of eastern barbarians, the Hsiao-ch'en-lai *kuei* containers feature four inscriptions. Not only are they first-hand documents of military affairs of the time, they are also ideal for comparing differences in calligraphic renditions, as the same inscription was done on different templates.

Clear examples of early Western Chou clan insignias are 「冗」 on the Huan *tsun* wine vessel and 「㸚」 on the Che-ling *fang-tsun* (pronunciation of both characters unknown). The clan insignia of 「㸚」 is also seen on the Tso-tse ta *fang-ting* tripod, proving that these two vessels were part of the same clan collection.

▼ **Bronze Hsiao-ch'en-lai *kuei* container**
Early Western Chou dynasty
(reign of King K'ang)
Height: 24.5 cm, depth 10.9 cm; height 24.5 cm, depth 11 cm
This *kuei* features a set each with two pieces; each lid carries a pair of inscriptions, and there are four sections in all. They document how Hsiao-ch'en-lai and Earl Mao-fu had led eight divisions of Shang soldiers to fight the Tung-i tribe. After the victory, their respective service to the Chou was evaluated, and Hsiao-ch'en-lai received cowries and royal commendation. The *kuei* was cast to commemorate this event.

"Conquering the Tung-i"

Rubbing of the vessel inscription

Bronze Hsiao-ch'en-lai *kuei* container
Comparison of details of the inscriptions on the four parts.

▲ **Bronze Che-ling *fang-tsun* wine vessel**
Early Western Chou dynasty
(reign of King Chao)
Height: 28.6 cm; depth; 21.6 cm

▶ **The vessel carries the insignia of the 龗 clan.**

▶ **The vessel carries the insignia of the 龗 clan.**
The inscription reads, "The Duke came to cast handled ritual *fang-ting* for King Wu and King Ch'eng. On the *chi-ch'ou* day in the first half of the fourth month, the Duke of Shang, Tso-tse Ta Pai-ma, made this treasured *i* vessel in gratitude to Yin, Ta-pao. (Insignia 龗)."

After the middle Western Chou, the number of inscriptions conferring titles gradually increased, and long inscriptions of more than fifty characters were not uncommon. In addition to clan insignias, sacrifices, military conquests, and records of ritual ceremonies of royal households, records of ceremonies conferring titles (such as the Sung *hu* and Sung *ting* from the time of King Hsüan), royal decrees, expressions of the riches of conferrals and rewards (such as the Mao-kung *ting* from the time of King Hsüan), the filial piety for ancestors (such as the Chuei *kuei* and Tsung-chou *chung* from the time of King Li), and agreements on surveys of land disputed by states (such as the San-shih *p'an* from the time of King Li) can be found. They all serve to illustrate the historical character of Western Chou bronze inscriptions and are highly valued as original documents. (Yu Kuo-ch'ing)

▲ Bronze Huan *tsun* wine vessel
**Early Western Chou dynasty
(reign of King Chao)**
Height: 20.3 cm; depth: 14.9 cm
The 27-character inscription is a record of how
Tso-tse-huan received the charge of King Chiang
in the 19th year of King Chao's reign to send
greetings to I-po, and how he was rewarded
for his work. It was cast at the same time as
the Tso-tse-huan *yu* kettle to bring glory to his
descendants, and the inscriptions on these two
vessels are thus quite similar in content.

◄ Bronze Tso-tse ta *fang-ting*
**Early Western Chou dynasty
(reign of King Chao or Mu)**
Height: 26.4 cm; depth: 10.8 cm

▶ **Bronze Mao-kung *ting* tripod**
Late Western Chou dynasty
(reign of King Hsüan)
Height: 53.8 cm, depth: 27.2 cm; rim diameter: 47 cm

The duke Mao-kung, in commemoration of the charge and ritual implements conferred upon him by the Chou ruler, had cast this vessel with 32 columns of 500 characters. The first half eloquently narrates how Mao-kung received this conferral. Finely composed and rendered, the value of the inscription was thought to be as important as a chapter from the *Book of Documents*.

▼ Ink rubbing of the right half of the inscription on the Mao-kung *ting* tripod.

The style of writing is classic and simple, with movement within the order and elegance in its strength.

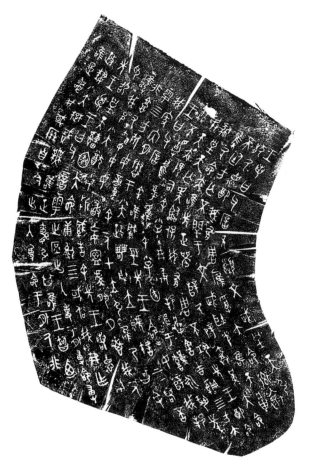

**Bronze Fu *chung* bell
(formerly known as the Tsung-chou *chung*)**
**Late Western Chou dynasty
(reign of King Li)**
Height: 65.6 cm, width: 30 cm
The 122-character inscription on this bell
commemorates a successful military expedition
against the Nan-i and Tung-i tribes undertaken
by King Li to the south of his territory. The
bell was cast to be placed in a shrine to be used
in sacrificial ceremonies and rituals entreating
the gods for good fortune, long life, and the
protection of his realm.

Bronze San *p'an* plate
Late Western Chou dynasty
(reign of King Li)
Height: 20.6 cm; depth: 9.8 cm;
rim diameter: 54.6 cm

The 350-character inscription on this vessel records how the state of Che invaded and occupied the territory of the state of San. The San people thereupon asked the powerful states around them to unite and bring the offending invaders to justice. The first half of the inscription is a commentary of the situation, followed by the names of individuals involved in the dispute and the oaths taken by the Che people. The inscription displays grand and powerful lines with bold, unconstrained, and varied composition. The treatment of identical characters (such as *yü* 于, *feng* 封, *chih* 至, *san* 散, and *i* 以) are different from one to the next. This is considered an exquisite example of large seal script.

Classical Beauty: Porcelains

The collection of ceramics and porcelains in the National Palace Museum exceeds 25,000 pieces, of which about 24,000 came from the former holdings of the Ch'ing dynasty court. The NPM collection of ceramics originated with the court and includes works from famous kilns of the Sung to Ming and Ch'ing dynasties. Nearly all are of superior grade, making this collection of ceramics and porcelains one of the greatest in the world in both quantity and quality.

The economy flourished in the Sung dynasty and the production of ceramics rose to unprecedented levels as kilns spread throughout the north and south and ceramics became requisite objects for both daily utilitarian use as well as display at home. The most famous monochrome colors of Sung dynasty porcelains are white, celadon green, black and bluish-white. Not only are the glaze colors exceptionally beautiful, their forms are also quite elegant. With the exception of bluish-white glaze wares, Sung porcelains mostly inherited from the developments of the T'ang dynasty known as "White (wares) in the north and green (wares) in the south". The green celadons of Yüeh kilns and white porcelains of Hsing kilns were highly prized by scholars of the T'ang dynasty, while poets also sang the praises of the glaze colors of Yüeh wares, likening them to the purity and luster of jade and ice. The production of Yüeh wares took place in the area of Shang-yü and Yü-yao in Chekiang, which in ancient times was known as Yüeh-chou and in the late T'ang and Five Dynasties period had produced ultra-refined celadons of mysterious glaze color as annual tribute for use at the court. The collection of the National Palace Museum includes such a Yüeh "secret color (mi-se)" porcelain washer from the late T'ang and Five Dynasties period. Covered completely in a beautifully light

▲ **White porcelain long-necked vase with incised floral and lotus décor**
Ting ware, Northern Sung period
Height: 25.2 cm, rim diameter: 6.6 cm, base diameter: 6.7 cm

▼ **"Secret color" celadon porcelain washer**
Yüeh ware, Five Dynasties period
Height: 10.3 cm, rim diameter: 30.7 cm

▲ **Reclining child-shaped white porcelain pillow**

Ting ware, Northern Sung period

Height: 18.8 cm, length: 31 cm, width: 31.2 cm

▼ **Sky-blue lotus-blossom porcelain warming bowl**

Ting ware, Northern Sung period

Height: 10.4 cm, rim diameter: 16.2 cm, base diameter: 8.1 cm

and creamy glaze with a hint of green, the glaze is very thin and evenly distributed, making this a masterpiece among surviving "secret color" celadons. In the T'ang dynasty, the silver-white glazed wares of the Hsing kilns had an enormous influence on those of the Ting kilns, leading to the saying that "the whites of Ting kilns are the best in the land". In fact, each of the kiln areas in the Sung dynasty had their own unique features and received orders to fire products for tribute to the court and its use. The simple and elegant features of the forms and decoration of Sung porcelains reveal the introverted and tranquil beauty appreciated in the Sung dynasty, reverberating with the spirit of the times and not unrelated to the rise of Neo-Confucianism and Ch'an (Zen) Buddhism at the time.

The center of production for Ting wares in the Sung dynasty was located in Ch'ü-yang, Hopeh. The ancient name for this site was Ting-chou, hence the name of the ceramics produced there. The glaze colors of Ting wares are characterized as ivory white, and porcelains are often molded, engraved, or impressed with subtle designs below the glazes to add a touch of liveliness to the plain appearance. In the early Northern Sung period, this was included as a porcelain type for use at the court. Ting wares with engraved and impressed designs more commonly appear starting from the middle Northern Sung. The method of production at the Ting kilns mostly included being stacked upside down, which would leave the rim unglazed. As

Plain sky-blue oval narcissus porcelain planter
Ju ware, Northern Sung period
Height: 6.9 cm, length: 23 cm, width: 16.4 cm

Examples of undecorated Ju ware are exceptionally
rare, the term for undecorated here referring to the
fact that the glaze is not crackled. At the present,
this is the only surviving example in the world. It
is perfect in terms of both shape and glaze, being
regarded as the supreme example of Chinese
porcelain.

Ash-green hollyhock-rim porcelain bowl
Ko ware, Southern Sung period
Height: 5.5 cm, rim diameter: 14.7 cm,
rim diameter: 3.9 cm

Celadon *kuei* vessel with raised-line décor
Kuan (Official) ware, Southern Sung period
Height: 12.7 cm, rim diameter: 17.5-19.7 cm

a result, a band of gold or silver was often added to the rim, a technique that has popular for quite some time and became a unique feature of Ting wares. The collection of white Ting wares in the National Palace Museum collection is considerable, including mostly objects of daily use, such as bowls, plates, teacup saucers, and display objects.

The most famous green celadons of the Sung dynasty are those of the Ju kilns and Kuan (Official) kilns of the Southern Sung. Records of Sung authors reveal that Ju wares were considered the best of the Sung porcelains, the kiln site for which has now been identified as the Ch'ing-liang Temple in Pao-feng County, Honan. Ju wares were submitted to the court and produced only during a very brief period of time for a few decades in the late Northern Sung, which is why extremely few Ju wares are found in collections around the world. The National Palace Museum leads all collections with 21 pieces. The production of Ju wares was quite refined. In general, they were completely covered in glaze, with only the bottom revealing very fine spur marks the size of sesame seeds indicating where separators were used for stacking pieces in the firing process. The number of spur marks generally was related to the weight of the object, heavier pieces requiring more spurs. This attention to detail reveals the Sung pursuit of perfection in the art of porcelains. Ju wares also feature delicate clay bodies and sky-blue glaze colors that appear with a hint of green where thicker. The rim and raised edges often have thinner glaze, revealing a reddish-brown tint from the clay body underneath. This is perhaps the reason behind the saying in the Sung dynasty that "Ju wares were fired solely for the court, their contents include

◀ **Porcelain bowl in sky-blue glaze with violet splotches**
Chün ware, Chin to Yüan period
Height: 16.4 cm, rim diameter: 16.2 cm, base diameter: 8.1 cm

▼ **Celadon vase with phoenix handles**
Lung-ch'üan ware, Southern Sung period
Height: 25.5 cm, rim diameter: 9.4 cm, base diameter: 9.6 cm

agate for the glaze". The development of this glaze has also been praised since Emperor Shih-tsung of the Latter Chou in the Five Dynasties period commented, "The blue of sky breaking through clouds after a rain, it is the sort of color associated with the hereafter". As a result, sky-blue glaze became an ideal and standard hardly matched afterwards. The glaze surfaces of Ju wares are often covered with a fine pattern of crackle similar to the shape of crab claws, hence the saying that "those with crab-claw patterning are divine, but those without (crackle) are exceptionally rare." Indeed, Ju wares without crackle are almost unknown, the National Palace Museum having in its collection two pieces without crackle that are unmatched and without rival in the world--an oval narcissus planter and a lotus-blossom shaped warming bowl.

The Southern Sung Kuan (Official) kilns were established by the court to supervise the production of porcelains in the capital city of Lin-an (Hangchow) after the Sung had moved south. There were two sites, one at the Palace Maintenance Office (Hsiu-nei-ssu) and the other at Chiao-t'an-hsia (the Suburban Altar) at Wu-kuei (Turtle) Hill. The excavation of the Kuan kilns at Chiao-t'an-hsia took place in the early 20th century. Archaeologists in recent years have also discovered a kiln at Lao-hu-tung (Tiger Cave) at Feng-huang (Phoenix) Hill in the Hangchow area, which may have been the site of the Hsiu-nei-ssu kilns. The masterpieces of Southern Sung Kuan court wares in the National Palace Museum collection include examples of pieces from both of these two kiln sites. The forms and glaze colors of Southern Sung Official wares mostly imitate those of Ju wares, the forms being equally classical and often

▲ **Porcelain tea bowl in black glaze with tree-leaf décor**
Chi-chou ware, Southern Sung period
Height: 5.2 cm, rim diameter: 15.2 cm,
base diameter: 3.4 cm

▼ **Porcelain tea bowl with hare's-fur black glaze**
Chien ware, Sung dynasty
Height: 6.5 cm, rim diameter: 11.5 cm,
base diameter: 4.2 cm

covered with glaze crackle. The patterns of crackle both deep and superficial in the glaze are akin to that of cracked ice, being a major distinguishing feature of Kuan wares. The glaze colors of these Kuan wares often have a tinge of pink and bear thicker glazes on thin bodies that appear to have congealed like grease. The places where the glaze is thinner on the foot and rim of the pieces shows the dark color of the clay body, hence the term "purple mouth and iron foot" applied to them. The National Palace Museum collection of Southern Sung Kuan wares is quite refined in quality and elegant in color. Display objects tend to be patterned after the shapes of bronzes and jade *ts'ung* tubes, also being classical and upright in manner.

There is also another type of Sung porcelain known as Ko ware, but its period and place of firing remain today a matter of speculation. Most information comes from a later Yüan dynasty record on the "Kiln at Ko-ko Cave", which indicated that production had already occurred in the Southern Sung. Many of the Ko wares in the National Palace Museum collection are small objects of daily use in the scholar's studio. The glaze color tends to be grayish-green with a tinge of white or grayish-yellow, while the glaze surface is generally covered with a blackish or yellowish pattern of large and small crackle. This is what connoisseurs in the Ming and Ch'ing dynasties appreciated as "silk of gold and threads of iron".

In 1184, under the Chin dynasty to the north, the name of the place known as Yü-hsien in Honan was changed to Chün-chou, hence the name given to Chün wares. These porcelains break with the tradition of monochrome celadon colors and feature the addition or fusion of violet and reddish spots and splotches, indicating that craftsmen at the time had already fully grasped the control of the element of copper that leads to these colors. The milky glaze of Chün wares tends to be relatively thick with a rose-colored tinge, while the violet tends to be in grape-like splotches, forming a radiant contrast with the colors of sky-blue and moon-white for a beautiful effect. The Chün wares in the collection of the National Palace Museum include mostly objects of daily use, such as bowls and plates as well as flower holders. The inverted-cup flower holder in sky blue glaze with violet splotches was used at the court as a planter for arrangements of calamus and narcissi that complemented each other perfectly.

Chekiang was the main area for the production of celadons in the Sung dynasty. In addition to official Kuan wares, one of the most famous types was known as Lung-ch'üan ware. Starting from the 11th century, Lung-ch'üan wares were also made for export, and examples have been found in shipwrecks along the

"Silk Route of the Seas". The finest of Lung-ch'üan wares were submitted to the court as tribute items. One of the examples in the National Palace Museum collection is a phoenix-handled vase that continues in the mallet-vase type that was produced at the Ju and Kuan kilns, except for the addition of the handles. Upright and elegant in form, the glaze is a pastel green that has a luster like that of jade, this being considered a typical example of the finest of Lung-ch'üan porcelains.

Black-glazed porcelains were also used extensively in the Sung dynasty and produced at all the major kiln sites in the north and south. People in the Sung dynasty paid particular attention to the refinement and aesthetics of life, using black-glazed tea cups and saucers to highlight the color of powdered tea when brewed therein. The Chien kilns in Fukien became famous for their production of tea cups. Black-glazed tea cups were not only fired to meet market demand, the finest of impressed design and hare's-fur tea cups were also presented to the court for "imperial use" and as "gift chalices". Although the kilns at Chi-chou in Kiangsi produced common wares, they also developed a unique technique in which paper-cut floral designs were added to their products. In the National Palace Museum collection, a leaf-pattern tea bowl differs from those commonly used by the people, because the interior of the bowl is decorated with a branch of plum blossoms and the moon done in gold pigment. The subtle fragrance wafting from the cup when sipping tea would enhance the visual and tea experience considerably. The Ching-te-chen kilns of Kiangsi were the main center for the firing of bluish-white porcelains in the Sung dynasty, with its products marketed both domestically and abroad. Bluish-white is also known as "shadow blue" and features a thin and delicate body mainly decorated with incised and impressed floral designs. Unfortunately, this ware is not well represented in the National Palace Museum collection, perhaps being related to the tastes of the imperial family in the past. Nevertheless, the representation of Sung porcelains is remarkably consistent in its simple and elegant presentation, the straightforward forms and tranquil colors setting an eternal standard for all later successors to compare.

In the Ming and Ch'ing dynasties, the official kilns at Ching-te-chen entered a phase of producing painted and colorful wares. In all facets of ceramic production, whether it be technique, glaze coloring, or shapes, major and discernible differences compared to the emphasis on simple and elegant monochrome porcelains of the T'ang and Sung dynasties appeared. The National Palace Museum has a very rich collection of Ming and Ch'ing dynasty official porcelains with a complete representation from each reign period of these

▶ **Underglaze-blue porcelain globular vase with lotus-and-dragon décor**
Yung-lo reign, Ming dynasty
Height: 42.6 cm, rim diameter: 9.7 cm, base diameter: 15.8 cm

The globular vase is one of the innovations of the official kilns of the Yung-lo reign. The body is covered with bright blue underglaze coloring that depicts a three-clawed dragon prancing among scrolling lotus plants. With its mouth agape and its hair and whiskers flowing in an animated pose, the dragon appears quite majestic and imposing as it runs across the surface of the vase. A dragon that has not yet ascended the heavens is known as a p'an dragon, which is why this type of vase is also known as a ***p'an*-dragon globular vase.**

▼ **Porcelain flat vessel with figures in underglaze blue**
Yung-lo reign, Ming dynasty
Height: 29.7 cm, rim diameter: 3.6 cm, base diameter: 12 x 8 cm

dynasties. Starting from the Yüan dynasty, Ching-te-chen came to serve as the main center for the production of porcelains for the country. The court established a kiln factory at Chu-shan in Ching-te-chen to make porcelains specifically for the court, the imperial pieces that were fired being submitted as tribute to the emperor. The wares produced at the imperial kilns were exquisite and came in a variety of forms, each with the reign mark of the emperor. Ming dynasty official wares used *ma-ts'ang* and kaolin clay near Ching-te-chen for production, resulting in the refined and pure white body that was fired. Generally speaking, Ming porcelains can be divided into early, middle, and late phases. Underglaze blue painting and colors with underglaze blue were the main types of porcelains fired at the official kilns. From the underglaze blue porcelains of the Yung-lo and Hsüan-te reigns and the underglaze blue porcelains with color to the "competing colors" of the Ch'eng-hua and "five color" wares of the Wan-li reigns, the colorful and rich evolution of official wares of the Ming dynasty can be found in the National Palace Museum collection.

The most famous of early Ming dynasty official wares are underglaze blue porcelains of the Yung-lo and Hsüan-te reigns. These underglaze blue wares are upright and beautiful in manner, representing the use of Su-ma-li cobalt blue pigment imported from Western Asia. This gives the color its bright and gorgeous appearance. The "rust spots permeating the blue" have a dripping wet and unbridled manner like the natural staining and washing of a monochrome ink painting. This became its trademark feature that was continually emulated and imitated by official kilns later in the Ming and into the Ch'ing dynasty. The extremely thin "sweet white half bodiless" porcelains of the Yung-lo reign and ruby-red, clear-blue, and underglaze-blue colors of Hsüan-te wares, as well as the underglaze blue and overglaze yellow, red, and five-color underglaze blue porcelains, all served as a fountainhead for the production of later ceramics. The early Ming dynasty also witnessed closer interaction between Chinese and Western Asia and Islamic cultures, resulting in its influence on the decorative styles and porcelain forms produced in China.

The official porcelains of the Ch'eng-hua, Hung-chih, and Cheng-te reigns of the middle Ming dynasty enter into a world of colors. The gorgeous hues of "competing color" glazes of Ch'eng-hua porcelains are extraordinarily refined, being best represented by the cups decorated with either chickens or human figures. *P'ing-teng* blue pigment was used for the production of underglaze blue porcelains, resulting in the light and elegant coloring. The bright yellow wares of the Hung-chih reign involved the application of low-temperature yellow glaze over white glaze, thereby softening the hue. Green-colored yellow-glaze wares are most distinctive of the wares made in this period. Accompanying the popularity of Islam at the court during the

▲ **Porcelain saucepot in sacrificial red glaze with incised floral petal décor**
Hsüan-te reign, Ming dynasty
Overall height: 10.6, rim diameter: 2.8 cm, base diameter: 7.1 cm

▼ **Underglaze-blue porcelain dish with dragon-and-phoenix décor**
Hsüan-te reign, Ming dynasty
Height: 4.4 cm, rim diameter: 20 cm, base diameter: 12.5 cm

▲ **"Competing colors" porcelain wine cup with figures**
Ch'eng-hua reign, Ming dynasty
Height: 3.7 cm, rim diameter: 6.2 cm,
base diameter: 2.4 cm

▼ **Blue-ground tricolor porcelain planter with scrolling lotus décor**
Cheng-te reign, Ming dynasty
Height: 12.5 cm, rim diameter: 25 x 24 cm,
base diameter: 15 x 14.1 cm

▶ **Hundred-deer five-color porcelain *tsun* vessel**
Wan-li reign, Ming dynasty
Height: 24.6 cm, rim diameter: 20 cm,
base diameter: 16.3 cm

Cheng-te reign, Arabic script became increasingly popular as a form of underglaze blue decoration. Quarried blue pigment from Jui-chou in Kiangsi was the source of cobalt used in the production of underglaze blue, yielding the grayish-blue hue of these wares. Tricolor wares on a blue background and overglaze five-color wares became the distinguishing features of porcelains from this era.

During the Chia-ching, Lung-ch'ing, and Wan-li reigns of the late Ming dynasty, official wares were produced in enormous numbers, unfortunately with a corresponding decrease in the level of quality compared to the past. Objects often depict patterns with auspicious objects or immortals. The gorgeous hues of five-color wares of the Wan-li era involve patterns covering the surface, featuring little blank background left behind. All kinds of studio objects and utilitarian objects were also made.

Ch'ing dynasty official wares continued in the precedents set by those in the Ming dynasty, in which Chu-shan in Ching-te-chen further served as the bastion for production. However, the Ch'ing court changed the Ming dynasty practice of having a eunuch oversee production, choosing instead to have a Supervising Ceramics Official knowledgeable in the art and technique to be in charge of the entire process. The court sent such officials as Lang T'ing-chi, Nien Hsi-yao, and T'ang Ying to the imperial kilns to take charge of the design and production of ceramics, leading to numerous innovations in official wares. At the height of the Ch'ing during the K'ang-hsi reign, plain tricolor, five-color, red-glazed, and underglaze blue porcelains all achieved renown. During the reign of the following Yung-cheng Emperor, official wares were elegant and beautiful. Enamels painted on white porcelain bodies as fine as jade represented various subjects and included such details

as inscriptions and seal impressions, making these enamelware porcelains the most famous in the Ch'ing dynasty for their fusion of the fine arts of poetry, calligraphy, painting, and seals along with that of ceramics. Innovations continued to roll out in official wares in the reign of the Ch'ien-lung Emperor. A bewildering array of styles and decorations were produced-- everything from innovations in painted enamels on porcelain bodies to the rendering of Western-style subjects and faithful imitations of various forms and décor from the past. However, in the late Ch'ing, dynastic power declined, and the official kilns at Ching-te-chen could no longer continue the strides it had made in its heyday, leading to a reduction in the number of innovations made after the reign of the Chia-ch'ing Emperor. In the Hsien-feng and Kuang-hsü reigns, Empress Dowager Tz'u-hsi used porcelains distinguished by the mark known as "Ta-ya chai (Studio of Great Elegance)". Nonetheless, they do not quite compare with the porcelains made at the height of production under the K'ang-hsi, Yung-cheng, and Ch'ien-lung Emperors, as official wares gradually slid into a decline that saw its demise with that of the dynasty and the establishment of the Republic of China in the early 20th century.

Among the most noteworthy official wares of the Ch'ing dynasty in the collection of the National Palace Museum are the "porcelain-body painted enamelware" and "porcelain-body Western enamels" so described in the court archives of the period. Both of these types were forms of porcelain with painted enamels. The technique of "painted enamels" had begun in the late K'ang-hsi reign and its production had been personally ordered by the K'ang-hsi Emperor to take place at court. The white porcelain and dark clay bodies that it required were supplied by the Ching-te-chen and I-hsing kilns, respectively. Transported over long distances all the way to the capital, they were painted and fired at the Imperial Workshops at court. In the early period of development, bronze body enamelwares were used as models, and the materials used for enamel pigments were imported from the West. Afterwards, however, the Imperial Workshops made continual efforts at research and development. By 1728, under the Yung-cheng Emperor, painted enamels were given additional splendor with the development of Western painting styles. With the creation of "porcelain-body Western colors" (*fen-ts'ai*, or so-called "pale colors", "famille rose") by the Supervising Ceramics Official T'ang Ying, the art had reached a level of exceptional molding and beautiful decoration. The production of the porcelain body to the firing of porcelain-body Western-color painted enamels were all completed at the official kilns at Ching-te-chen. A variety of highly advanced and difficult skills in the art of ceramics was developed and combined at one site, including openwork, revolving, and

▲ **"Kuan-yin" porcelain *tsun* vessel with ruby-red glaze**
K'ang-hsi reign, Ch'ing dynasty
Height: 25.6 cm, rim diameter: 7.3 cm, base diameter: 11.1 cm

◀ **Five-color *k'uei*-dragon openwork porcelain incense burner**
K'ang-hsi reign, Ch'ing dynasty
Height: 24.6 cm, rim diameter: 23.4 cm,
base diameter: 19.4 cm

Porcelain-body tea cup in painted enamels of spirit fungi blessings for immortality on a yellow ground
Yung-cheng reign, Ch'ing dynasty
Height: 6.1 cm, rim diameter: 10.5 cm, base diameter: 4.4 cm

The most precious of porcelains in the Ch'ing dynasty were painted enamelwares combining the arts of painting, poetry, and calligraphy, the Ch'ing court referring to them in records as "porcelain-body painted enamelware". Painted on a yellow ground of this tea cup are spirit fungi, orchids, and a longevity stone on one side, hence the name for this auspicious assemblage as "blessings for long life". On the other side is an inscribed poem on the spirit fungi and fragrance of orchids in the land of immortals.

interlocking forms. Gathering together some of the greatest talents in the country, they gave even greater beauty, majesty, and innovation to these materials from the earth. Painted enamelware porcelains were treasures of the Ch'ing court and their production from start to finish (including forms, colors, and decoration) was personally directed by the emperor. With such strict quality control, almost none were presented as gifts to underlings. In fact, starting from the Ch'ien-lung reign, they were gathered and managed as a collection. Not until the establishment of the Palace Museum as a public institution in the early Republican period did this secret court collection of the Ch'ing become known to the outside world.

The collection of porcelains in the National Palace Museum collection extends from the Sung down to the Ch'ing dynasty. Preserved and treasured at the court, they were assembled and unified as a whole under the Ch'ien-lung Emperor, representing the finest gathering in the world in terms of range, quantity, and quality. The porcelains of daily use in the Ch'ing dynasty were not graded and counted among these, being kept mostly in storage at the Ning-shou Palace. Amounting to tens of thousands of pieces, these were not transported with the Palace Museum collection to Taiwan when the government moved. Here, however, we have been able to assemble some of the finest examples of porcelains from the National Palace Museum holdings to present the most distinguished and greatest developments in the development of the collection as well as Chinese ceramics as a whole. (Liao Pao-hsiu)

▼ **Porcelain-body teapot in painted enamels of a blue landscape on a white ground**
Yung-cheng reign, Ch'ing dynasty
Overall height: 9.2 cm, rim diameter: 7.5 cm, base diameter: 8.1 cm

▶ **Four-inch porcelain-body plate of figures in painted enamels**
Ch'ien-lung reign, Ch'ing dynasty, dated 1742
Height: 1.8 cm, rim diameter: 13.5 cm

▼ **Auspicious conjoined flat round porcelain vases with floral patterning of red and blue in Western colors**
Ch'ien-lung reign, Ch'ing dynasty, dated 1741
Height: 19.7 cm, rim diameter: 4.1 cm,
base diameter: 5.9 x 2.7 cm

Working with Nature: Treasured Objects

In the collection of the National Palace Museum is a category of antiquities often called by the name "miscellaneous", or "curio objects", but which we now refer to as "Treasured Objects". The term "miscellaneous" was a reflection of earlier art historical concepts of such three-dimensional antiquities as bronzes, porcelains, and jades as crafts, rather than the traditional two-dimensional fine arts of Chinese painting and calligraphy. However, nowadays, this enormous field of objects is felt to be otherwise, for these art forms combine the highest of technical achievements with the finest of aesthetic consideration in the lives of the ancient Chinese.

The NPM collection of treasured objects is comprised of more than 25,000 pieces, including the colorful forms of lacquerware and enamelware, crafts that would have adorned and signified majesty in the palaces of the court. This category also includes intricate carvings, engravings, and openwork sculptures in ivory and wood, their often small size comprising a whole world of appreciation unto themselves. Objects of the traditional scholar's studio include all the implements required by the refined Confucian of learning. The beautiful and intricate accessories and items worn on the body were meant for both ritual and decorative purposes. As for the gifts that the emperor would bestow upon favored court officials and family members, there are also scepters, snuff bottles, and flint lighters. The collection of Tibetan Buddhist implements is an expression of the exchange with the religious authority of Tibet on the part of the Ch'ing dynasty court. Curio boxes are small cases of the Ch'ing emperors that often include a wide range of ancient and contemporary as well as domestic and foreign objects; these could be taken out at any time for appreciation and reflected the Ch'ing court fascination with the art of packaging, spatial arrangement, and design.

These works reveal not only the taste of the Ch'ing court in collecting antiquities, but they also serve as an overview of the attitude towards arts and crafts by the Ming and Ch'ing dynasty courts. Throughout the dynasties in China, there had always been official agencies in charge of managing the objects required by the emperor and the court. These institutions oversaw and supervised craftsmen in the production of these objects, including the Directorate of Imperial Manufactories, Supervisory of Imperial Manufacturing, Institute of Crafts, and Palace Provisions Commission. More specifically, in the Ch'ing dynasty, the Palace Workshops in the Imperial Household Department were directly established under the auspices of the Yang-hsin Hall of the emperor and the Tz'u-ning Palace of

▶ **Jade-inlaid coral planter sculpture with pearls and jadeite of the God of Examinations and constellation**
Ch'ing dynasty
Height: ca. 30 cm

The God of Examinations is the Chinese celestial deity in charge of the civil service examinations, the path to success in traditional China. Here, he holds a representation of a constellation in his right hand and a branch of plum blossoms, indicating that he is head and shoulders above all the rest. He stands on one foot on the head of a carp-turned-dragon, symbol of coming in first place in the transformation of a commoner into a member of the elite in society. Five bats are show encircling the pattern of longevity on the jade planter, representing the notion of "five fortunes" (a synonym for bat) upholding longevity. Thus, this colorful and gorgeous decorative planter inlaid with many semi-precious materials conveys a complete sense of auspiciousness and blessings.

▼ **Hair crystal horseback monkey ("fast track to nobility")**
Ch'ing dynasty
Length: 8.95 cm

Carved red lacquerware paper-mallet floral vase
Yung-lo reign, Ming dynasty
Height: 16.4 cm

The walls of this vase are filled with carvings of flowers ~~of~~
the four seasons, their stems and leaves sprawling abou~~t~~
in an elegant and natural composition. The layers of r~~ed~~
lacquer are thick and lustrous, while the carving is refin~~ed~~
and polished. Engraved on the underside along the edge ~~is~~
an inscription that reads, "Produced in the Yung-lo Reig~~n~~
of the Great Ming", indicating that this is a masterpiece ~~of~~
the official workshops of the early Ming dynasty.

▲ **Carved color lacquerware plate of nine dragons**
Chia-ching reign, Ming dynasty
Diameter: 19.7 cm

▼ **Carved red lacquerware treasure box with a scene of floating cups**
Ch'ien-lung reign, Ch'ing dynasty
Diameter: 18.5 cm

the empress. Within the Palace Workshops were specialized workshops for producing various handicrafts, including those for gold and jade, clocks, glasswares, and cases and mountings. There, the finest craftsmen from all over the country were assembled, including those with specialized talents from Tibet, Nepal, Mongolia, and even Europe. Together, they worked with materials of nature to create the dazzling and skillful objects used by and adorning the court.

1. Lacquerware

Lacquerware involves applying the refined sap of the lacquer tree to an object as a form of coloring and decoration. In the late Ming dynasty, Huang Ch'eng wrote *Catalogue of Lacquer Embellishment*, in which he listed more than a hundred techniques popular in the art of lacquerware at the time, including the major technique categories of carved lacquer, gold highlighting, filled lacquer, lacquer tracing, and mother-of-pearl inlay. However, most of the pieces of lacquerware in the collection chosen for transport to Taiwan are those of the Ming and Ch'ing dynasties.

The art of carved lacquerware involves applying layer after layer of lacquer sap onto an object until it reaches a certain thickness. Then a design is carved into the layers. A technique using only red-colored lacquer layers is called "engraved red", while that involving layers of different colors of lacquer is referred to as "engraved colors". The art of "engraved red" was especially popular in the Chia-hsing area of Chekiang in the Sung and Yüan dynasties, even spreading to Japan and Ryuku, where it gained a wide audience. During the Yung-lo and Hsüan-te reigns of the Ming dynasty, craftsmen who specialized in the technique of "engraved red" from the Chia-hsing reign were even admitted to the court as officials, showing just how strongly the court felt about this art form. Among the surviving pieces of lacquerware are red carved pieces with the inscription reading, "Produced in the Yung-lo Reign of the Great Ming". Many of the pieces have layers of lacquer that reach up to a hundred in number, featuring a date-red color and lustrous

shine with intricate details of floral decoration that flow over the surface as if alive. Those pieces with figures and buildings are arranged like that of a painting, the skill of the carving clear and graded naturally, being polished and rounded to perfection while concealing all traces of the knifework. Yung-lo pieces are generally referred to as works of the "Orchard Factory", which represented the highest level of achievement in the art of lacquerware at the time.

In the latter Ming during the Chia-ching and Wan-li reigns, the court workshops specialized in the production of engraved color lacquerware. Again, layers of lacquer, this time in different colors, were applied. Lines and patterns were then carved away to reveal a colorful effect that complemented the subject of the decoration, such as red blossoms and green leaves, or black stones and purple clouds, yielding a dazzling quality unmatched since.

Everywhere in the palaces during the Ch'ing dynasty were large pieces of engraved red lacquerware furniture and display pieces made in the form of cabinets, dragon thrones, and screens. Many of them were carved in Yangchow and submitted to the throne as tribute. Covered with dense decoration and carved with exceptional detail, they present another facet in the beautiful realm of Chinese lacquerware.

▲ **Cloisonné enamelware lotus-blossom box**
Ching-t'ai reign, Ming dynasty
Height: 6.3 cm, rim diameter: 12.4 cm

▼ **Cloisonné enamelware plate with dragon décor**
Wan-li reign, Ming dynasty
Height: 7.1 cm, rim diameter: 48.0 cm

▲ **Cloissonné enamelware duck-shaped burner**
Ming dynasty
Height: 24.0 cm, length: 25.0 cm

▼ **Covered painted enamelware lotus blossom bowl**
K'ang-hsi reign, Ch'ing dynasty
Height: 9.5 cm, cover diameter: 11.4 cm

2. Enamelware

Enamelware is the art of firing and melting glass-like material onto the surface of a metal vessel. The technique can be divided into different forms. The first involves the process of laying out and soldering a pattern of metal filaments onto the surface of vessel into a desired pattern. Then the enamel pigments are placed into the spaces and fired to melt them. The entire piece is then ground and polished to create an art form known as "cloisonné ". Another technique involves engraving and hammering the scrolling floral decoration, which is then filled with enamel pigments and fired, in what is known as "champlevé". Then there is another technique in which opaque glaze is fired onto the body of the vessel, on top of which is painted the desired pattern. Fired to complete the process, it is known as "painted enamelware". All three methods were originally imported from foreign sources, but they were incorporated into the arts of China to form their own unique niche.

Cloisonné enameled wares were originally popular in Byzantine cultural circles. In the Yüan dynasty, when China was part of the Mongol Empire, they were introduced and known as "Arabic wares", being highly appreciated for their golden hue decorated with many colors. The most admired of all the cloisonné pieces made in the workshops of the early

◀ **Dragon-handled painted enamelware vase**
Yung-cheng reign, Ch'ing dynasty
Height: 21.3 cm, base diameter: 8.8 cm

The body of this vessel is covered with painted depictions of an auspicious array of peonies (the "king of flowers"), peaches (associated with immortality), and bats (a synonym for good fortune). The colors are also rich and the forms outlined with exceptional detail, representing a masterpiece fusing Chinese painting styles and subject matter with imported Western enamelware techniques. Attached to the shoulders of the vase are two gilt dragon-head handles, giving the vessel an even greater sense of imperial majesty and splendor. The underside of the vase in engraved with the mark "Produced in the Yung-cheng Reign".

▲ **Glass-body painted enamelware spittoon with décor of Western women**
Ch'ien-lung reign, Ch'ing dynasty
Height: 7.8 cm, rim diameter: 9.2 cm, base diameter: 4.4 cm

▼ **Champlevé painted enamelware kettle with décor of Western women**
Ch'ien-lung reign, Ch'ing dynasty
Height: 19.9 cm, greatest width: 12.6 cm

Ming dynasty court were those produced in the Ching-t'ai reign, hence the term "Ching-t'ai Blue". Many later generations forged the Ching-t'ai reign mark, making it very difficult to distinguish authentic pieces from later imitations. However, generally speaking, the solid body, bright coloring of the glaze materials, dense decoration, and clarity of gilding are features of early Ming court productions. In the Ch'ing dynasty, cloisonné was made into large decorative display pieces to adorn the interiors of many palace buildings and temples.

The art of painted enamelware was brought into China in the 17th century by Western missionaries and merchants. Catching the eye of the K'ang-hsi Emperor, an enamelware workshop was eventually established at the court to research and develop this art form. By the late K'ang-hsi era, the art and technique had been perfected, and many Western colors, such as pink and pastel green were adopted and utilized by painters at the court to render delicate and fascinating scenes and decoration. Painted enamelware was developed and utilized on the porcelain, dark clay, and glass bodies of the vessels. In the reigns of the Yung-cheng and Ch'ien-lung Emperors, new colors were developed to give the painted decorations even greater beauty and liveliness. In addition to traditional bird-and-flower subjects, there were also Western-style figures and landscapes as well as shading and perspective techniques to produce a wide variety of decorative themes, bringing the art of painted enamelware at the Ch'ing court to the peak of its development in the history of Chinese arts and crafts.

3. Studio Objects

The implements used in writing are intricately related to the transmission of culture. Consequently, Chinese scholars since the ancient past have paid particular attention to the production of materials and objects related to their studios, especially brushes, paper, ink, and inkstones. Scholars likewise have developed the inscription and appreciation of these utilitarian objects into an art form for presentation as gifts and for collecting.

Chinese ink is made from the soot of pines and oil that is mixed with resin to form a material for writing. After the Han dynasty, ink was manufactured into solid cakes that could be ground with water to form liquid ink to do painting and calligraphy, lasting for centuries without fading. Ink cakes were often decorated with a pattern or characters impressed on them. From the middle of the Ming dynasty, great attention was paid to the technique of ink molding. Ink producers competed with each other in inviting renowned calligraphers or painters to design their ink cakes along with famous engravers to carve the molds, making ink cakes not just a utilitarian object for grinding to make ink, but also an object of beauty on a par with other art forms. During the Wan-li reign of the Ming, the famous ink shops of Fang Yü-lu and Ch'eng Chün-fang in Anhwei each edited catalogues of the ink cakes they had designed and made, inviting famous calligraphers to write prefaces and endnotes to give them even greater prestige. These were produced via woodblock prints into *Fang's Ink Manual* and *Ch'eng's Ink Manual*, serving as major book productions of the period while also spreading the art and beauty of ink designs and bringing this art form to a peak. The Ch'ing dynasty court continued in this trend of using ink. Ink cakes were designed directly by the court and produced along with custom cases made to hold them. Many of the best pieces were assembled into collections, forming another trend in this art form.

There are more than four hundred inkstones in the collection of the National Palace Museum, of both high quality and in many different forms. Among them, those in the *Hsi-ch'ing Manual of Inkstones* attracted the most attention. This book, composed of 24 chapters and compiled between 1778 and 1791, is a catalogue of ancient inkstones in the collection of the Ch'ing dynasty court, including research on the materials, inscriptions, and dating of individual pieces. These are also accompanied by masterful drawings and decoration rendered by court painters of the period. The catalogue includes a total of 240 inkstones, and the National Palace Museum still has 95

▲ Square inkcake illustrating
"The Boat of Painting and Calligraphy"
Ch'eng Chün-fang, Ming dynasty
Height: 1.7 cm, length: 10.4 cm, width: 9.8 cm

▼ Tuan inkstone of
"Sea and Sky Bathing in the Sun"
Ming dynasty
Height: 5.9 cm, lengthwise: 20.2 cm,
width: 13.9 cm

▲ **"Sung-hua" round inkcake**
Lo Lung-wen, Ming dynasty
Height: 1.4 cm, diameter: 9.6 cm

▼ **Refined clay "Stone Moat" inkstone**
Ch'ien-lung reign, Ch'ing dynasty
Height: 8.9 cm, edge length: 14.6 cm

of them, representing a grand overview of ancient inkstone forms and colors. Most of these famous inkstones entered into the collection also include ornate and elegantly decorated cases that often feature inscriptions of the emperor's poetry or verse composed by court officials in response, the cases accompanied by a yellow inventory label with explanatory text. This careful and methodical approach to the collection reveals the level of importance attached by the Ch'ing court to ancient objects, including inkstones.

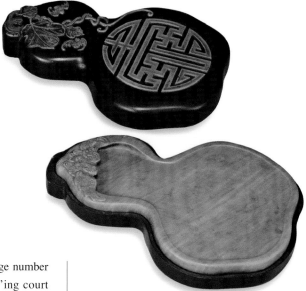

The National Palace Museum also has a large number of Sung-hua inkstones that were made in the Ch'ing court workshops. This type of stone of green, brown, or yellow coloring often occurs with layers of them together, through which the carver would engrave in order to produce multicolored patterns and designs. Since this stone is found in the Sung-hua River valley in the area of the homeland of the Manchus, rulers of the Ch'ing dynasty, it was quarried in limited amounts every year and submitted to the court as tribute to be made as imperial writing implements. Hence, very few ever made it outside of the court. The selection of designs for inkstone forms and patterns was elegant and upright, serving as a mirror of the qualities sought by the court.

▲ **Sung-hua gourd-shaped inkstone**
Yung-cheng reign, Ch'ing dynasty
Inkstone height: 0.9 cm, length: 12.6 cm, width: 8.9 cm

▼ **Cloissoné enamelware set of studio implements**
Ch'ien-lung reign, Ch'ing dynasty
Inkstone case height: 15.8 cm, brush-rest width: 22 cm

▲ **Carved bamboo brush holder with herding-horse scene**
Wu Chih-fan, Ch'ing dynasty
Height: 15.4 cm, diameter: 7.1 cm

▼ **Small ivory sculpture of figures in a landscape**
Feng Ch'i, Ch'ing dynasty (dated 1738)
Overall height: 6.8 cm, length: 5.8 cm, width: 9.7 cm

4. Small Carvings of the Ming and Ch'ing

Carvings of the Ming and Ch'ing dynasties often tended to be small decorative objects engraved or carved from pieces of bamboo, wood, ivory, horn, ivory, or even pit stones. As such, they could be intimately appreciated and even handled by the viewer.

The craft of bamboo carving stimulated the rise of important artist families in the southern Kiangnan region during the middle Ming dynasty. For example, there were the "Three Chu's of Chia-ting", three generations of artists comprised of Chu Sung-lin (Ho), Chu Hsiao-sung (Ying), and Chu San-sung (Chih-cheng). They carved brush holders, fan ribs, and hairpins from stalks of bamboo, also using the roots of bamboo to carve elegant water containers and brush rests. All of these became famous and were praised by connoisseurs at the time. These

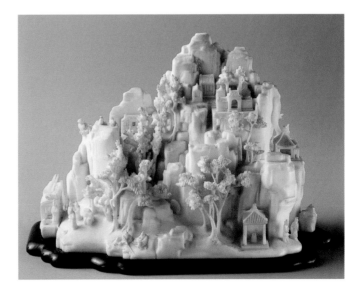

craftsmen were also gifted in poetry and painting as well, so their scholarly training also allowed them to become admired by officials and gentry of the period. This trend opened the door for this clan in the Chia-ting area for generations of artist-carvers.

The materials of ivory and horn became increasingly available in the 16th century due to the expansion of sea routes and use as a material in carving. Rhinoceros horn was often made into a cup for drinking wine, while ivory was carved into figures of immortals, cases, and ornaments. In addition to these trends, the warm and congealed quality of soapstone and the fine yet tough features of pits also led these materials to become arenas where carvers competed to demonstrate their skills.

▲ Carved bamboo washer in the shape of a lotus leaf
"San-sung" mark, Ming dynasty
Height: 7.2 cm, width: 15.1 cm

▼ Ivory openwork handled food case
Ch'ing dynasty
Height: 45.4 cm, length: 30.4 cm, depth: 21.6 cm

This handled case is comprised of three levels of thin pieces of openwork ivory, each of which is decorated with landscapes, buildings, figures, and animals. The ground of the pattern is done in openwork as fine as silk strands, giving the entire piece the feeling of being covered with a piece of silk gauze and making it a masterpiece of carving.

The court of the High Ch'ing sought gifted carvers throughout the land. Feng Ch'i and Shih T'ien-chang, for example, were both from Chia-ting, while Ch'en Tsu-chang and Huang Chen-hsiao were from Kwangtung. At the court, they produced carvings in a variety of materials and also specialized in meticulous and fine openwork carving, miniaturizing landscape and narrative scenes into the space no larger than your fist or fingertip. These miniature yet incredibly detailed sculptures make it hard to believe that such a large world could be squeezed into such small sizes.

▲ **Rhinoceros horn cup with landscape and figures**
Ming dynasty
Height: 13.1 cm, length: 18.2 cm,
width: 10.7 cm

▶ **Olive pit carving of a small boat**
Ch'en Tsu-chang, Ch'ing dynasty
(dated 1737)
Height: 1.6 cm, length: 3.4 cm

▼ **Carved "field-yellow" stone seal with knob**
Yang Yü-hsüan, late Ming to early Ch'ing
dynasty
Height: 5.6 cm, length: 4.4 cm, width: 4.3 cm

▶ **Wood carving of a lohan scratching his back**
Ch'ing dynasty
Height: 4.4 cm, width: 4.6 cm

5. Buddhist Implements

The Ch'ing dynasty court performed ceremonies with respect to the religions of Buddhism, Taoism, and Shamanism, but the imperial family obviously held Tibetan Buddhism with the highest reverence. On the one hand, this was for political considerations: "The rise of Yellow Sect (Tibetan Buddhism) was to pacify the Mongols". In order to win over the hearts and minds of the peoples in the regions inhabited by the Tibetans and Mongols, the Ch'ing court promoted the Yellow (Gelugpa) Sect of Tibetan Buddhism. On the other hand, many members of the imperial family were themselves devout followers of Tibetan Buddhism. In fact, the Yang-hsin Hall, the residence of the Ch'ien-lung Emperor, was equipped with Buddhist images and implements for use in ceremonies, perhaps suggesting that he himself had personally accepted the Tibetan Buddhist faith. For this reason, the political leader of the Yellow Sect, the Fifth Dalai Lama, had been invited to Peking in 1652, and in 1781 the Sixth Panchen Lama arrived in Peking to offer blessings for the emperor's birthday; both of them received the highest of honors. As a result, objects presented by Mongol and Tibetan monks and nuns flooded the court. The court workshops also produced various Buddhist images and implements, which were done with great skill and precision. Inlaid with precious materials, many were presented as gifts to Tibetan and Mongolian temples and members of the clergy.

In order to assure conformity to religious requirements, a number of Tibetan and Nepali craftsmen worked with Chinese, Manchu, and Mongol artisans at the Ch'ing court to produce implements and Buddhist images. This exchange of techniques and styles led to mutual influence. Combined with the input of the ruler, the fusion of Chinese and Tibetan styles became one of the distinctive features of Buddhist objects made at the Ch'ing court.

◄ **Vajra and bell**
Possessions of the Second, Third, and Fifth Dalai Lama from the Potala Palace in Tibet
Bell height: 18.2 cm, vajra length: 14.1 cm

▼ **Champlevé enamelware container inlaid with semi-precious materials**
Tibetan, 18th century
Height: 16.4 cm, rim diameter: 12 cm

Accompanied by a box, the inside of the cover includes an inscription that reads, "On the second day of the first lunar month of the forty-fifth year of the Ch'ien-lung reign (1780), the Emperor bestowed a gift upon the Panchen Lama, who in turn presented (this) covered enamelware container of precious materials along with red blossoms stored inside of it."

▶ **Gilt bronze sculpture of Tsong-kha-pa**
Ch'ing dynasty (dated 1781)
Height: 55.2 cm, width: 36 cm

Tsong-kha-pa is the founder of the Yellow (Gelugpa) Sect of Tibetan Buddhism, and this sculpture represents him as a manifestation of Manjusri (Bodhisattva of Wisdom). This 1781 sculpture was based on a Tibetan prototype and cast in bronze with gilding, the soft and flowing features of the body in contrast to the detail of the background bringing it more in line with Chinese aesthetic tastes.

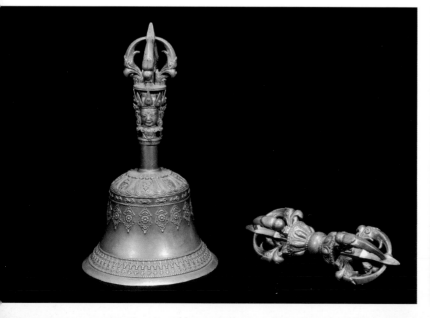

6. Clothing and Accessories

The collection of the National Palace Museum includes a large number of pieces of clothing and accessories associated with the imperial family, such as crowns and caps, imperial jewelry, fingernail guards, pouches, flint cases, and court belts. These were all produced according to the regulations set forth governing objects used by ruling clan in the Ch'ing dynasty. Different levels of officials and various occasions and ceremonies all required objects and materials of accordingly different colors, materials, and amounts, which were used to identify the ceremonial and ritual regulations. Take caps, for example. A high official of Rank One would use a ruby, Rank Two would use coral, and Rank Three turquoise. Absolutely no breach of etiquette could be allowed in changing their use. The type of pearl special to the Ch'ing court, known as the Eastern Pearl, was a freshwater pearl from the Northeast, the homeland of the Manchu rulers, and only members of the imperial family could wear them. A strand of 108 court pearls, although appearing similar to a strand of Buddhist rosary beads, includes another three pendant strings for fingering, for the back, and as drop beads. When wearing the strings, the back string would be draped behind, while the other two strands would be worn on the left for men and the right for women. Hairpins and accessories worn by women were even more resplendent. The flat square was a special curved *huang* hair ornament called a "two-head" in the Ch'ing dynasty, while fingernail guards were worn to protect the extra-long fingernails cultivated by ladies along with other lapel decorative accessories. These were all unique to the Ch'ing court. The gold- and silverwork was refined and pearls and jadeite used to create inlays, revealing the high skill and design capabilities at the court workshops.

◀ **Summer crown of the Ch'ien-lung Emperor Ch'ing dynasty**
Crown height: 14 cm, diameter: ca. 28 cm, finial height: 12.4 cm

The crown includes a yellow inventory label that states on one side, "One court crown made of cool down and tassels for the imperial use of the Pure Emperor, Kao-tsung (Ch'ien-lung)" and on the other, "Entered in the forty-third year of the Ch'ien-lung reign (1778)."

▼ **Fingernail guards Ch'ing dynasty**
Length: ca. 13.9 cm

▲ **Glass-body painted enamelware snuff bottle in the shape of a bamboo segment**
Ch'ing dynasty
Body height: 6.3 cm

▼ **Various snuff bottles**
Ch'ing dynasty
Heights: ca. 4.9 to 7.7 cm

7. Snuff Bottles

Snuff is made from an aromatic herb, the scent of which is used to lift the spirits. After it was imported into China in the early Ch'ing dynasty, it became popular among members of the imperial family and Tibetan and Mongolian peoples. The Chinese often repackaged large boxes of snuff into small bottles, which were originally small medicinal bottles commonly used for their convenience in carrying around. Later, all kinds of precious and exotic materials were used to make bottles specifically for snuff, including gold, silver, porcelain, jade, agate, and semi-precious gems, but the most favored type of snuff bottle in the Ch'ing dynasty was made of glass. The glass workshop at the Ch'ing court made various types of clear and colored glass, and they also developed techniques to combine layers of different colored glass, which could then be carved into beautiful patterns in an overlay technique known as "Peking glass". Painting with enamels was also done on lustrous white glass snuff bottles using fine brushwork. Accompanied by an ivory spoon and glass stopper, these are masterpieces of the palace workshops. By the late Ch'ing dynasty, a technique had even been developed whereby the inside of snuff bottles could be painted. This widely popular format was known as "inner painting".

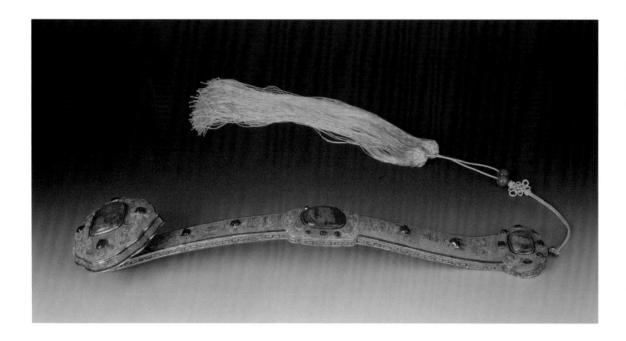

8. *Ju-i* Scepters

The *ju-i* is a kind of handle-shaped object held in the hand, the head of which is slightly curved like the palm of a hand. Similar objects can be traced as far back as the Warring States period, and by the Six Dynasties period, the term "*ju-i*" had appeared, this auspicious object becoming common among the scholar-gentry and Buddhists.

There are more than 120 *ju-i* scepters in the collection of the National Palace Museum, and most of them were made in the Ch'ing dynasty. Because of the auspicious connotations of the term "*ju-i*", it became a form of honored gift exchanged among members of the court during festivals and celebrations during the Ch'ing dynasty. The forms of decoration all deal with patterns and designs of auspiciousness, and among the more splendid ones are enlarged examples with inlays of various semi-precious materials such as jade. As much as the Chia-ch'ing Emperor tried to curb this extravagant trend in gift-giving, it continued unabated down to the end of the Ch'ing dynasty.

▲ ***Ju-i* scepter of the Eight Immortals with inlay and gilding**
Ch'ing dynasty
Length: 52.8 cm, head width: 13.6 cm

▼ ***Ju-i* scepter of jade with Nine Wishes and Bat of Fortune**
Ch'ing dynasty
Length: 30.0 cm, head width: 9.1 cm

▲ **Painted enamelware pocket watches with figures**
England, 18th century
Diameter: 6 cm, thickness: 3.8 cm

▼ **Champlevé enamelware timepiece in the shape of a *pipa* instrument**
England, 18th century
Length: 13.5 cm, width: 5.0 cm

▼ **Japanese *emaki-e* painted lacquerware boxes**
18th century
Height: 2.3 cm, length: 7.6 cm, width: 5.6 cm

▶ **Western champlevé enamelware makeup box**
18th century
Height: 7.2 cm, length: 7.1 cm, width: 5.2 cm

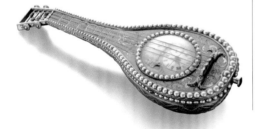

9. Tribute Objects

Throughout Chinese history, emperors have used tribute objects as a form of foreign diplomacy with neighboring states. Foreign emissaries would present tribute, often rare and precious local products of their homeland, to the court of China, which would then prepare a gift of some precious form of Chinese product in return. This exchange of gifts between states often involved objects of great value as a means of currying favor and reward. The Ch'ing dynasty court, for instance, presented gifts that included refined crafts of the Ch'ing court, such as *ju-i* scepters, enamelware, porcelain, embroidered pouches, and Sung-hua inkstones. The rare and exotic objects that foreign states would prepare for the Ch'ing court included crystal balls, ostrich eggs, telescopes, mechanical timepieces, Western enamelware, and Japanese lacquerware, all of which were arranged for display in various palaces at court. These objects were not only appreciated, they also simulated exchange and influence in terms of styles and techniques between East and West. For example, Chinese gold painted lacquerware was influenced by the *emaki-e* form lacquerware from Japan. Furthermore, the interest in enamelware and glassware objects on the part of the Ch'ing court was stimulated in part by Western tribute objects. Likewise, in the 17th and 18th centuries, the trend of chinoiserie (things Chinese) became increasingly popular in Europe as a result of exchange with China. Even the decorative elements of the Rococo style appeared not only in the court of Louis the 16th in France, but also that of the Ch'ien-lung Emperor in China during the 17th century.

10. Curio Boxes

Curio boxes (or, literally, "multi-treasure cabinets") are specially designed cases with different kinds of cabinets, levels, and drawers used to store many kinds of small art objects so that they can be transported conveniently. This kind of case has its origins in antiquity and derives from such cases used for brushes, studio objects, combs and accessories, travel, and perfume among the higher classes of society. Considerable effort was often paid to the design and production of such boxes so that they would complement the valuable contents contained therein. The greatest ingenuity and possibilities were sought to make the most out of the smallest of spaces. Often a single level would be divided into several, or a cabinet subdivided into several smaller ones. Sometimes a cabinet would hold drawers, and vice-versa. At other times, hidden compartments would be cleverly incorporated into the piece, requiring a special way of opening and closing. All sorts of manners for storage were involved to get at the objects contained inside, such as pulling, pushing, lifting, and unhooking. Indeed, curio boxes can be called the art of designing spaces, much like interior design, where almost

▼ **Gold-relief painted lacquerware curio box with dragon-and-phoenix décor (containing 43 curios)**
Ch'ing dynasty
Box height: 26.6 cm, width: 25.6 cm, depth: 17.4 cm

anything is possible. Compared to the makeup box of the West and inkstone case of Japan, there is much more that meets the eye when it comes to the curio boxes of China.

Although it is said that expert craftsmen in many places of the southern area of Kiangnan were already producing this type of curio box in the late Ming dynasty, many of the most beautiful curio boxes that we have today were made under the supervision of the Ch'ing dynasty court. On the one hand, the Ch'ing court focused on the appearance of the cases, instructing the use of carved sandalwood, porcelain inlay, bamboo applique, openwork mother-of-pearl, and even sometimes the use of lacquer, gold highlighting, and painting for decoration. At other times, ancient cases or Japanese lacquered boxes were converted into curio boxes, with the openwork window panels, moveable parts, and levels of complexity all becoming a part of the overall technical and aesthetic development of this art form. On the other hand, there are also the myriad works of small objects found inside of the curio boxes themselves. Ranging from antiquity down to the time the curio boxes were made, they include cleverly arranged Neolithic period jade ornaments as well as Western painted-enamel timepieces, small Japanese painted lacquerware, and Ch'eng-hua reign "competing colors" porcelains, all designed to show off their individual qualities. In the archives of the Ch'ing court are many references to the emperor's personal instructions as to which objects were to be placed in the boxes. He sometimes ordered craftsmen of the palace workshops to create miniature porcelains, bronzes, jades, and even scrolls and albums of paintings to fit into the boxes, making sure that more than a hundred pieces could fit together in a dazzling display of a myriad forms of colors and materials. Against the background of the aesthetically and cleverly designed boxes, they are indeed a "sight for sore eyes"!

The curio boxes in the National Palace Museum are from the former collections of the Yang-hsin Hall and Ch'u-hsiu Palace of the Ch'ing court. In other words, these were the places where the emperor and empress lived, meaning that they were some of the favorite objects that the imperial couple would take out and appreciate in their spare time. It is for this reason that curio boxes are sometimes referred to as the "toy chests of the imperial family". (Ts'ai Mei-fen)

▼ **Square sandalwood curio box (containing 30 curios)**
Ch'ing dynasty
Box height: 25 cm, length: 21 cm, width: 25 cm

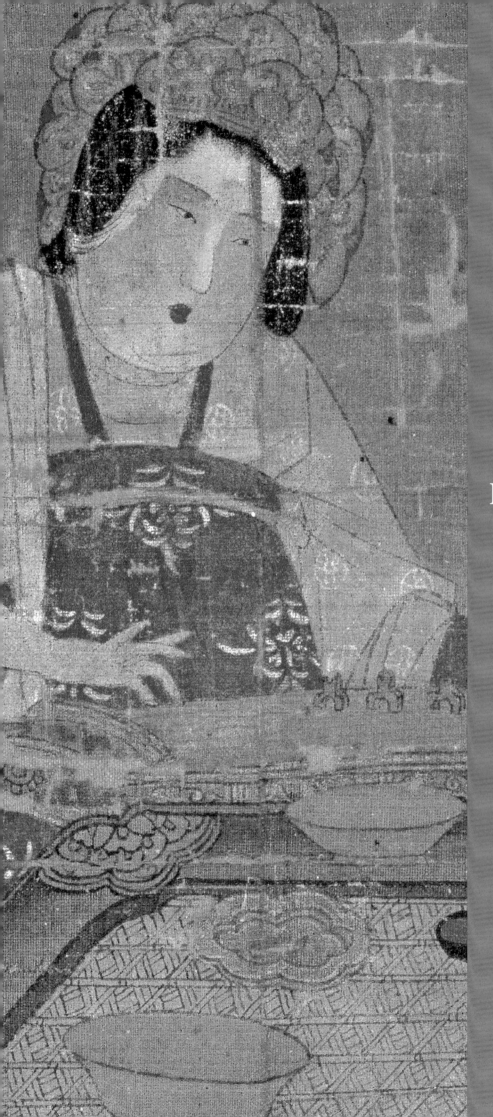

Wonders of
Ink and Color:

The Painting and
Calligraphy Department

1   2

Wonders of Ink and Color:
The Painting and
Calligraphy Department

The Collection

Many of the works of painting and calligraphy in the collection of the National Palace Museum originally were part of the treasures amassed by the Ch'ing dynasty court. However, as early as the 10th century in the early Northern Sung, the imperial collection had already achieved considerable scale and organization. Though additions and dynastic change resulted in vicissitudes for the collection, it reached a pinnacle by the 18th century, during the reign of the Ch'ien-lung Emperor. After a portion of the imperial collection was removed from mainland China by the Republican government to Taiwan, the National Palace Museum has continued to expand the field represented by the works while also developing the functions of a museum by actively pursuing the purchase of objects while also accepting donations of art from generous contributors. The result has been that the present collection exceeds the scope and quality of the former Ch'ing palace collection, further and more completely synchronizing with all the major historical developments that have taken place in Chinese art through the ages.

At present, the four types of objects (paintings, calligraphy, ink rubbings, and tapestries and embroideries) under the management and care of the Painting and Calligraphy Department represent a total of more than 10,000 individual items. Among them, those classified as "national treasures" and "important cultural objects" number more than 2,000, including such early masterpieces as "Clearing After Snowfall" by Wang Hsi-chih of the Eastern Chin, "Autobiography" by Huai-su of the T'ang, "Early Snow on the River" by Chao Kan of the Southern T'ang in the Five Dynasties, and "Blue Magpie and Thorny Shrubs" by Huang Chü-ts'ai of the Sung. These works are not only of exceptionally great artistic merit and value, they also include such important peripheral materials as early signatures, inscriptions, and seals that provide a detailed record of their transmission through private and court collections over the centuries. For researchers in the field of Chinese art history, this type of collection work provides no less than a miniature reflection of the transmission and history of one aspect of Chinese culture, making it even more precious.

Storage facilities of the Painting and Calligraphy Department are located in the solid and reinforced structure of the Museum basement, where the temperature is controlled and maintained under exacting conditions of a constant 19 to 22 degrees Centigrade and 55 to 60 percent relative humidity the year round along with a complete set of measures for pest prevention and eradication. Strict guidelines are in place for every staff member who accesses storage. To prevent the deterioration of materials, all works in handscroll, hanging scroll, and album leaf format are first protected in non-acidic cloth covers or wood boxes and then placed in wooden crates divided into separate levels.

Before each and every exhibition, staff members in charge of the collection first carefully examine the work scheduled for display to ensure that it is safe for presentation. Any creases or damage will be immediately handled for treatment and repair by the mounting section of the Department. Any repairs that cannot be handled in the short term must involve replacement by another work for display so that only optimal pieces are placed on exhibition for the aesthetic viewing pleasure of all visitors!

Exhibition and Research

Since works of painting and calligraphy done on paper and silk, if exposed for long periods to air and light, will easily suffer from advanced aging and deterioration, their display at the Museum is restricted without exception to no more than three months at a

3　　　　　4　　　　　5

1. A glimpse at the storeroom for painting and calligraphy.
2. The specially devised storage methods to protect the precious works of painting and calligraphy.
3. The unique design to the entrance of "Special Exhibition of Northern Sung Painting and Calligraphy".
4. Archive inventory of painting and calligraphy.
5. Work in the digital photography studio in the storeroom.

time. Furthermore, any works that have been on display must be placed in storage for at least 18 months before being taken out again for any reason. The purpose behind this is to provide an orderly system for the rotation of collection objects so that they can be appreciated by audiences today and to fulfill the Museum's historical mission of preserving and protecting these treasures for the future.

Over the decades, the exhibitions curated by the Painting and Calligraphy Department have covered a wide range of subjects and categories. Some have been planned in response to particular festivals, and others on the themes of seasons, animals, plants, architecture, and gardens. Other exhibits have probed the features of painting and calligraphy by individual artists, and some have analyzed the development of period styles. This provides an overview of the curatorial focus in the Department over the years.

With the beginning of a new century, several medium- and large-scale exhibitions at the Museum have combined the efforts of the Painting and Calligraphy, Antiquities, and Books and Documents Departments, making the display of the collection even more pluralistic and varied while also establishing a new trend for organizing exhibits at the Museum. Such exhibits include "Emperor Ch'ien-lung's Grand Cultural Enterprise", "Blossoming Through the Ages: Women in Chinese Art and Culture from the Museum Collection", and "Through the Prism of the Past: Antiquarian Trends in Chinese Art from the 16th to 18th Centuries", which all met with considerable praise and appreciation by scholars and general audiences alike.

In addition to exhibitions at the National Palace Museum, the exchange of loan objects with other renowned museums around the world has continued. Among the most representative exhibits are "Splendors of Imperial China: Treasures from the National Palace Museum (1996-1997, USA), "Mémoire d'Empire: Trésors du Musée National du Palais, Taipei" (1998-1999, France), and "Treasures of the Sons of Heaven" (2003-2004, Germany). In these large-scale special exhibitions, more than a hundred works through the ages selected by the Painting and Calligraphy Department have made the exhibits lauded and praised by many in the international art world.

To reinforce the National Palace Museum's responsibility to its social functions, starting from 2000, the Painting and Calligraphy Department has actively participated in the Museum's "Digital Archives" and "Digital Museum" projects. In doing so, it is hoped that the combination of various research efforts over the years will result in a large-scale storehouse of knowledge being constructed for all-around service in research on Chinese painting and calligraphy. At present, several Digital Museum projects have been completed, including "The Beauty of Sung Dynasty Album Leaves", "Treasured Painting and Calligraphy", "Age of the Great Khan", "Literary Images: Chinese Literature in Painting and Calligraphy", "Grand View: Painting and Calligraphy of the Northern Sung", and "The Calligraphic World of Mi Fu". Basic information (metadata) of the collection works is being expanded annually in the "Painting and Calligraphy Collection Management System". In time, regardless of whether one wants to just appreciate or study and research a particular field of Chinese painting and calligraphy, one can access the Internet and quickly search for and retrieve a great deal of information, presenting the pluralistic benefits of "art", "history", and "education and culture" of the masterpieces of painting and calligraphy at the National Palace Museum. (Liu Fang-ju)

Splendors of Calligraphy:
The Appeal of Brush and Ink

The National Palace Museum's collection of calligraphy includes masterpieces covering 1,300 years from the T'ang to the Ming and Ch'ing dynasties, most of which were either handed down through the ages by imperial courts or amassed by the Ch'ing emperors. These works were frequently cited in official and private catalogues, testifying to their legacy. Many of these masterpieces in the history of Chinese calligraphy serve as fine examples for the appreciation of the art and as models for the study of its development and transmission through the ages.

Wang Hsi-chih and Calligraphy of the High T'ang

By the Western Chin dynasty of the Three Kingdoms period in the 3rd century, the development of Chinese calligraphy had reached a level of maturity, as standard, semi-cursive, and cursive scripts became widely used. During the Eastern Chin period in the 4th century, written records and

▼ **Three Passages of Calligraphy: P'ing-an, Ho-ju, Feng-chü**
Wang Hsi-chih, Chin dynasty
Handscroll; ink on paper; 24.7 x 46.8 cm

▶ **Clearing After Snowfall**
Wang Hsi-chih, Chin dynasty
Album leaf; ink on paper; 23 x 14.8 cm

This piece of calligraphy was done mostly with rounded and centered brushwork concealing the tip, the forms being steady and regular. It therefore reveals a calm and leisurely manner that is neither too quick nor too slow. Later, in the Ch'ing dynasty, the Ch'ien-lung Emperor praised this as "without equal under the heavens, rare both now and before". One of the "Three Rarities" along with Wang Hsi-chih's "Mid-Autumn Modelbook" and Wang Hsün's "Po-yüan Modelbook", he treasured it in his "Three Rarities Hall".

連朝醞釀密
雲垂垂侵曉遽
立春將是朦
遠需拖是脹
宜時重樓千
二省毅玉世
墨三千遍被
聲拈筆欲吟
遠自問以差
何以若
天禧
庚寅新正三日
宓雪優霑杏
前延瑞田成
什書用志慶
御筆

天下無雙古今鮮對

羲之頓首快雪時晴佳想

安善未果為結力不次

羲之頓首

山陰張侯

君倩

slip documents were regularly rendered in semi-cursive and cursive scripts. Scholars and nobility of the time, in pursuit of literary refinement, became connoisseurs of calligraphy. The transmission of the style of Wang Hsi-chih (ca. 307-365), the "Sage of Calligraphy", offers an overview of this process.

Although no actual works by Wang have survived, the Museum has three important T'ang dynasty copies of his "Clearing After Snowfall", "Sending Regards to a Friend", and "Three Passages of Calligraphy (P'ing-an, Ho-ju and Feng-chü)". In addition, a Sung dynasty ink rubbing of "The Ting-wu True Version of the Preface to the Orchid Pavilion Gathering" is the earliest and most complete ink rubbing of the stone engraving of the "Preface to the Orchid Pavilion Gathering" by this master.

During the early and middle T'ang dynasty in the early 7th century, the calligraphy of Wang Hsi-chih was highly revered, as the court since the time of Emperor T'ai-tsung had actively collected, copied, and treasured his works. Calligraphic pieces from the latter half of the 7th century were all strongly influenced by Wang Hsi-chih. Imperial works, such as "Ode on a Wagtail" by Emperor Hsüan-tsung (685-762), and those of officials, such as "Essay on Calligraphy" by Sun Kuo-t'ing (ca. 648-703), reflect the stylistic trend of the time.

The New School of Calligraphy in the Mid-T'ang

In the middle of the 8th century, many calligraphers emerged from the common classes. The monk Huai-su (737-?) created an unrestrained, expressive style that captured the imagination of the northern scholarly class. Refinement was no longer considered the only measure of aesthetic beauty. Yen Chen-ch'ing (709-785), who modeled his work after Huai-su's "Autobiography", is representative of this new aesthetic current. Coming from an eminent family, Yen had experienced the ups and downs of a career as a government official for over fifty years, leaving behind a reputation as a loyal and sacrificing

▲ **Ode on a the Wagtail (detail)**
Emperor Hsüan-tsung, T'ang dynasty
Handscroll; ink on paper; 24.5 x 184.9 cm

▶ **Essay on Calligraphy (detail)**
Sun Kuo-t'ing, T'ang dynasty
Handscroll; ink on paper; 26.5 x 900.8 cm

Written in 687 and containing approximately 4,000 characters, this work is an appraisal of important calligraphers since the Han dynasty. It is also a summary of the styles, techniques, aesthetics, and theories of calligraphy from the Six Dynasties down to the T'ang. The brushwork is rendered naturally and without unnecessary flourishes, Sun having his own effortless cadence and rhythm as he lifted, turned, and pressed down the brush.

夫自古之善書者，漢魏有鍾張之絕，晉末稱二王之妙。王羲之云：頃尋諸名書，鍾張信為絕倫，其餘不足觀。可謂鍾張云沒，而羲獻繼之。又云：吾書比之鍾張

servant. The original "Draft of a Requiem for My Nephew" is written freely in cursive script, displaying his emotion and character quite naturally. Scholar-officials in the Northern Sung during the 11th century continued in this natural spirit, ushering in a new manner of spontaneity.

The Calligraphic Culture of Sung Literati and Scholar-officials

Following the chaos of the late T'ang and Five Dynasties period, the emperors of the early Sung dynasty promoted a revival of the old calligraphic methods of the Chin and T'ang dynasties. In the process of re-assembling the court collection, they established the "letters" tradition centered mainly on the Two Wangs (Wang Hsi-chih and his son Wang Hsien-chih). Many court calligraphers, officials, and recluse-scholars admired the beautiful and elegant running script of Wang Hsi-chih. Stele engravings, on the other hand, followed in the former manners of the High T'ang dynasty, mostly being done in the styles of Ou-yang Hsün and Yen Chen-ch'ing.

By the middle of the Northern Sung, the literati and scholar-official class had risen, and these literati with their broad learning and ultra-refined poetry, gave full expression to calligraphy and other artistic talents. They paved the way for artistic modes of expression and brought a deep understanding from ancient works of calligraphy. Calligraphy was used by them to announce their emotions, to become a form of artistic

▶ **Draft of a Requiem for My Nephew**
Yen Chen-ch'ing, T'ang dynasty
Handscroll; ink on paper; 28.2 x 75.5 cm

▼ **Autobiography (detail)**
Huai-su, T'ang dynasty
Handscroll; ink on paper; 28.3 x 755 cm

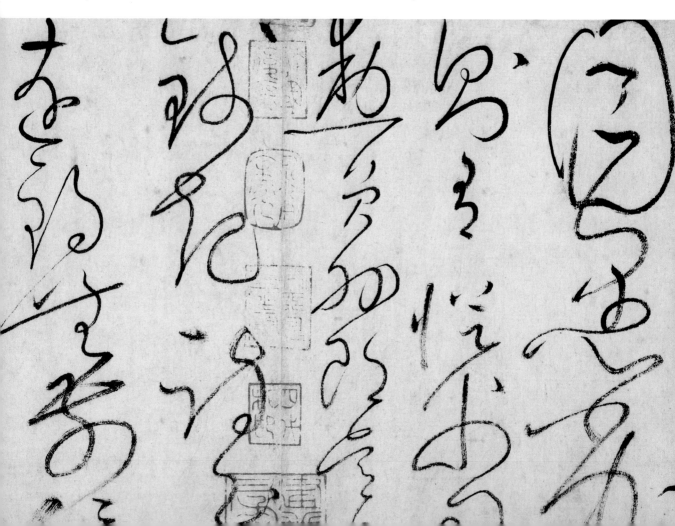

刺史上輕車都尉丹楊縣開國

男真卿以清酌庶羞祭子

□贈贊善大夫季明之靈曰

惟爾挺生夙標幼德宗廟瑚璉

階庭蘭玉每慰人心方期戩穀何圖逆賊間釁稱兵犯順

爾父竭誠常山作郡余時受命亦在平原

仁兄愛我俾爾傳言爾既歸止爰開土門土門既開凶威大蹙賊臣不救孤城圍逼父陷子死巢傾卵覆天不悔禍誰為荼毒念爾遘殘百身何贖嗚呼哀哉吾承天澤移牧河關泉明比者再陷常山攜爾首櫬及茲同還撫念摧切震悼心顏方俟遠日卜爾幽宅魂而有知無嗟久客嗚呼哀哉尚饗

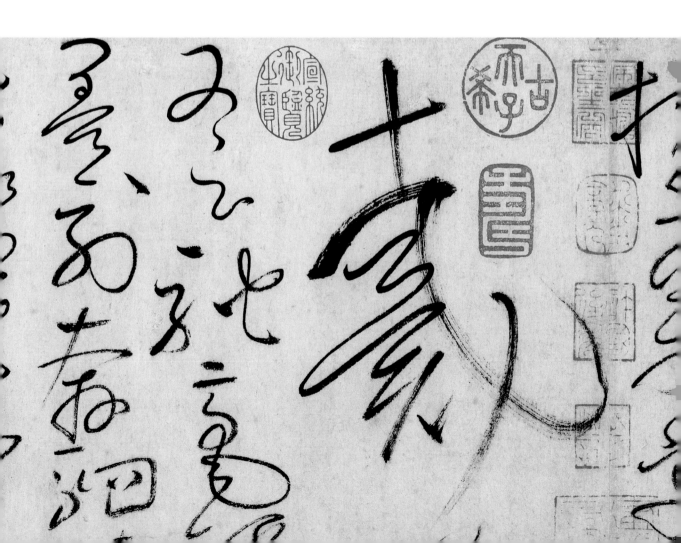

exchange with like-minded fellows, and to demonstrate their talents and knowledge. Many of their remaining works were done in semi-cursive script, each with their own unique and individual manner. Ts'ai Hsiang (1012-1067), Su Shih (1036-1101), Huang T'ing-chien (1045-1105), and Mi Fu (1052-1107) are celebrated as the Four Masters of Northern Sung calligraphy. They were court officials, poets, and art connoisseurs who eventually became representative figures in the development of Chinese literati art, and each was able to create a distinctive calligraphic style. Ts'ai modeled his work after Yen Chen-ch'ing's style but had a gentler manner. Su pursued natural refinement, describing his method as unrestrained and impromptu. Huang's slanted strokes exhibit great strength like a boatman pulling his oar. The force of Mi's calligraphy is swift as a sword and strong as a bow. The Museum boasts a rich collection of works by these four masters that includes literary compositions, letters, and inscribed colophons. "The Cold Food Observance" and "Ode on the Red Cliff" by Su Shih, "Poem on the Hall of Pines and Wind" and "Poem in Seven-character Verse" by Huang T'ing-chien, and "Calligraphy on Szechwan Silk" by Mi Fu are all masterpieces by them. In the later Northern Sung period, the "slender gold script" of Emperor Hui-tsung reproduced the exquisite taste of the imperial court at the time. The emperor's brushwork in "Poetry" is bold, incisive, and clear-cut, being the only surviving work in large-character running script by him. By the following Southern Sung period, the trend of the pursuit of classical elegance is represented in the works of Emperor Kao-tsung, Wu Yüeh, and Chang Chi-chih. The surviving works by the poet-calligrapher Lu Yu (1125-1209), Fan Ch'eng-ta (1126-1193), and Wu Chü (late 12th century) of the Sung, and Chao Ping-wen (1159-1232) of the neighboring Chin dynasty, reflect the legacy of the styles of Su Shih, Huang T'ing-chien, and Mi Fu. The work "Seven-character Truncated Verse" is further notable as the earliest surviving piece of calligraphy done in the hanging scroll format.

▶ **The Cold Food Observance (detail)**
Su Shih, Sung dynasty
Handscroll; ink on paper; 34 x 119.5 cm

▶ **Calligraphy on Szechwan Silk (detail)**
Mi Fu, Sung dynasty
Handscroll; ink on silk; 27.8 x 270.8 cm

▼ **Poem on the Hall of Pines and Wind (detail)**
Huang T'ing-chien, Sung dynasty
Handscroll; ink on paper; 32.8 x 219.2 cm

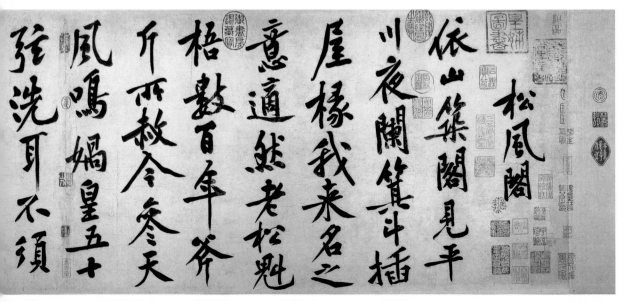

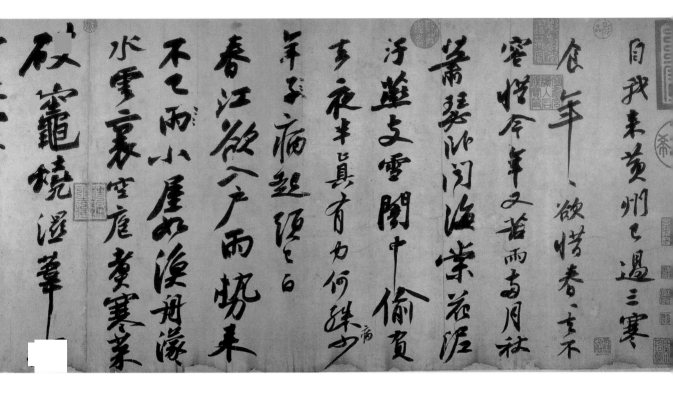

自我来黄州已過三寒
食年。欲惜春。春不
容惜今年又苦雨兩月秋
蕭瑟臥闻海棠花泥
汙燕支雪閉中偷負
去夜半真有力何殊少
年子病起頭已白
春江欲入户雨埶来
不已雨小屋如漁舟濛
水雲裏空庖煮寒菜
破竈燒濕葦

厭哉尾居似竹雨附心相
忘形魑鹤有冲霄心無
記誅種之是雲物相得
龜鹤年壽齊羽介雨
歳寒之
青松本無華安得蒨
吐子放鹤髪縮頸還
自立餘光射九之相見
蒋籍雲锦殷不墨不
連上松端秋花起烽烟
屈蟠種之出枝葉幸
青松勁挺姿凌雪恥
擬古

Transformation in Yüan Dynasty Calligraphy

The development of calligraphic expression characterized by the emphasis on ideas reached its zenith in the Southern Sung, and calligraphy by the Yüan dynasty was evolving once again. Calligraphers turned to the classical styles of the Chin and T'ang periods as models to create a trend of revivalism. The accomplished poet, writer, calligrapher, painter, musician, and official Chao Meng-fu (1254-1322) was the first to forge the new style and is regarded by many as the greatest calligrapher since the T'ang dynasty. Many Yüan and early Ming calligraphers were greatly influenced by the beauty and grace of his art. The wide gap in the brushwork of Hsien-yü Shu (1256-1301) from the tempered grace of that of Chao Meng-fu reveals that Hsien-yü Shu was strongly influenced by the strong and bold manner of T'ang dynasty calligraphers. It is said that after Ou-yang Shu (1266-1301) was enlightened to the ways of calligraphy after witnessing the way in which a cart driver pulled his wagon stuck in the mud. His "Calligraphing the Verse 'Water Curtain Cave' by a T'ang Poet" is bold and straightforward in its power and energy, integrating the vigorous manner of T'ang artists. Yüan dynasty calligraphy circles also witnessed multifaceted developments as the pace of calligraphers was not entirely consistent. "Seven-character Regulated Verse" by Chang Yü (1277-1350) and "Inscription on a Manual of Coins in Cursive Script" by Yang Wei-chen, for example, depart from the trend of revivalism at the time and boldly represent the notion of seeking change and individuality on the part of calligraphers.

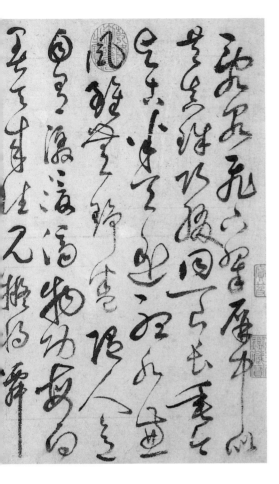

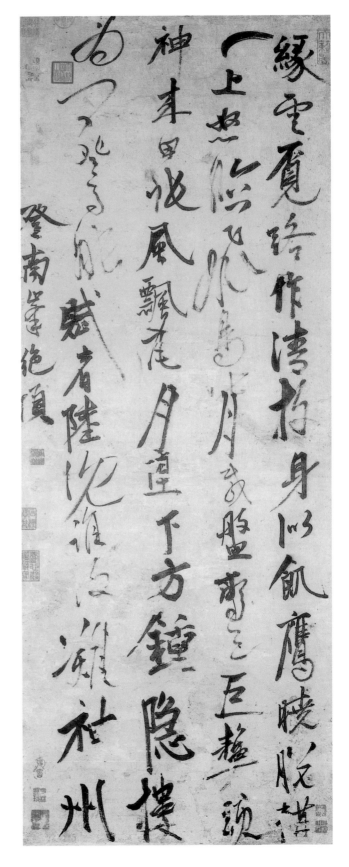

◀ **Two Odes on the Red Cliff in Running Script** (detail)
Chao Meng-fu, Yüan dynasty
Album of twenty-one leaves;
ink on paper; 27.2 x 11.1 cm

▲ **Calligraphing the Verse "Water Curtain Cave" by a T'ang Poet** (detail)
Ou-yang Shu, Yüan dynasty
Album leaf, ink on paper; 38.3 x 27.5 cm

▶ **Seven-character Regulated Verse**
Chang Yü, Yüan dynasty
Hanging scroll; ink on paper; 108.4 x 42.6 cm

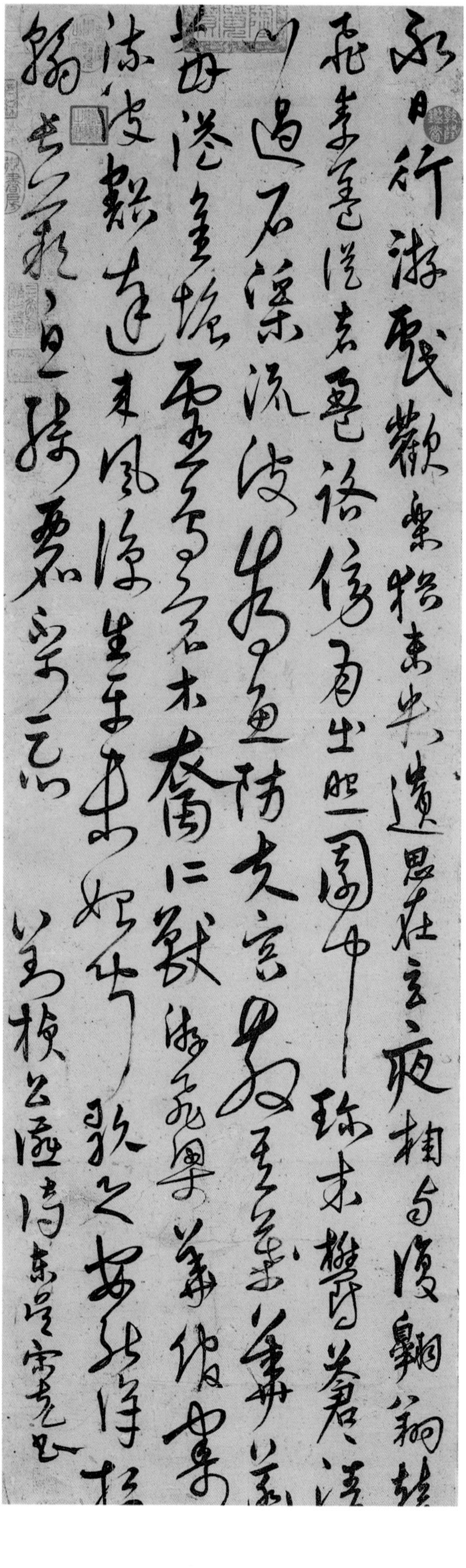

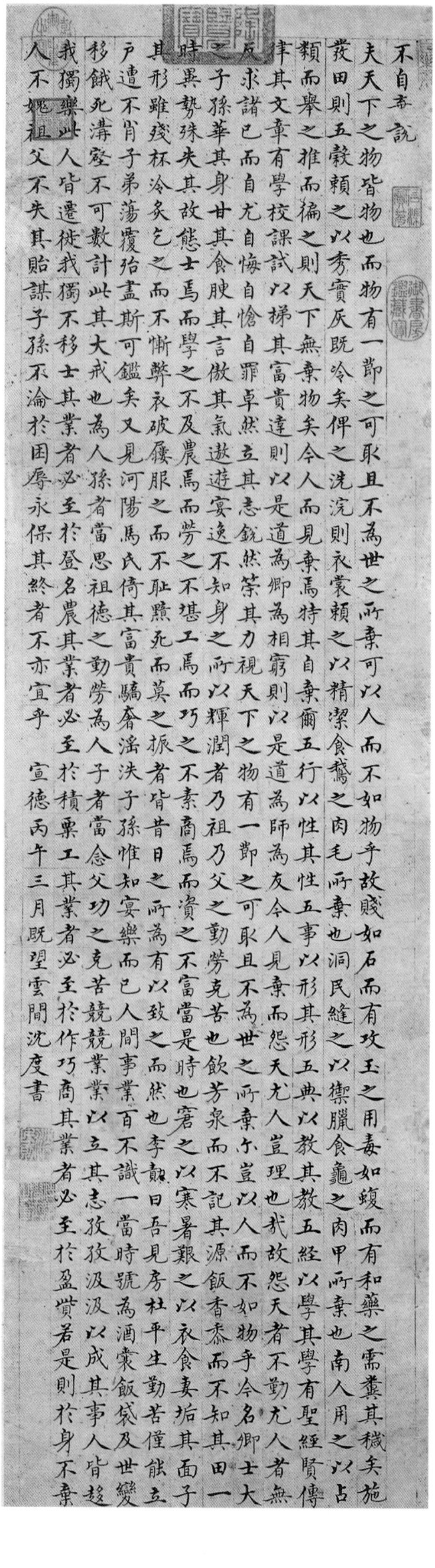

不自棄說
夫天下之物皆物也而物有一節之可取且不為世之所棄可以人而不如物乎故賤如石而有攻玉之用毒如蝮而有和藥之需糞其穢矣施
菑田則五穀賴之以秀實灰既冷矣俾之洗浣則衣裳賴之以精潔食鵞之肉毛所棄也洞民縫之以禦臘食龜之肉甲所棄也南人用之以占
類而舉之推而徧之則天下無棄物矣今人而見棄焉特其自棄爾五行以性其性五事以形其形五典以教其教五經以學其學有聖經賢傳
律其文章有學校課試以梯其富貴達則以是道為卿為相窮則以是道為師為友今人見棄而怨天尤人豈理也哉故怨天者不勤尤人者無
反求諸己而自尤自悔自懲自罪卓然立其志銳然策其力視天下之物有一節之可取且不為世之所棄尓豈以人而不如物乎今名鄉士大
夫之子孫華其身甘其食腴其言傲其氣遨遊宴逸不知身之所以輝潤者乃祖乃父之勤勞克苦也飲芳泉而不記其源飯香黍而不知其田一
時異勢殊失其故態士焉而學之不及農焉而勞之不堪工焉而巧之不素商焉而資之不富當是時也窘之以寒暑艱之以衣食妻垢其面子
其形雖殘杯冷炙乞之而不慚弊衣破屨服之而不耻黥死而莫之振者皆昔日之所為有以致之而然也李勣曰吾見房杜平生勤苦僅能立
戶遣不肖子弟蕩覆殆盡斯可鑑矣又見河陽馬氏倚其富貴驕奢淫泆子孫惟知宴樂而已人間事業百不識一當時號為酒囊飯袋及世變
移餓死溝壑不可數計此其大戒也為人孫者當思祖德之勤勞為人子者當念父功之克苦競競業業以立其志孜孜汲汲以成其事人皆趍
我獨樂此人皆遷徙我獨不移士其業者必至於登名農其業者必至於積粟工其業者必至於作巧商其業者必至於盈貲若是則於身不棄
人不媿祖父不失其貽謀子孫不淪於困辱永保其終者不亦宜乎
宣德丙午三月既望雲間沈度書

Refinement and Emotion in Ming Dynasty Calligraphy

From the Yüan into the Ming dynasty, calligraphers in general continued the trend of revivalism from previous generations. In the Yung-lo reign of Emperor Ch'eng-tsu, gifted calligraphers were called from various regions to the court to be selected for the tasks of calligraphing stelae inscriptions, imperial decrees, and transcribing texts. These calligraphers were selected for their skill in careful and precisely done regular script, and they also favored the archaic manner of draft cursive script that was popular in the Eastern Han dynasty and Three Kingdoms period of the third century CE. These calligraphers incorporated draft cursive methods into their works of cursive script, thereby adding a classically archaic atmosphere. Since their calligraphy paid particular attention to beautiful external forms and rigorous character structure, they tended to restrain their personal temperament and fall in line with the plain and classical style of writing favored by high officials of the court and in the academies at the time. As a result, this style became known as the "Academic Style". Classical examples of such in the Museum collection include Sung K'o's (1327-1387) transcription of "Liu Chen-yen Poetry" in semi-cursive script, Ch'en Pi's "Five-character Archaic Verse" in cursive script, Shen Tu's (1357-1434) "Discourse on Not Giving Up" in small regular script, and Shen Ts'an's (1379-1453) "Archaic Verse" in cursive script.

During the middle Ming period, cultural developments in the region south of the Yangtze River were accompanied by rising economic prosperity, as life of the literati increasingly centered around elegant gardens, appreciation of objects in the scholar's studio, the connoisseurship of painting and calligraphy, and

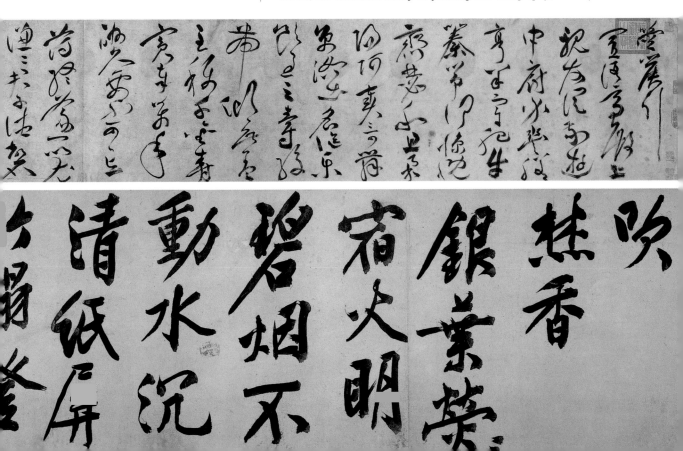

poetry exchanges among friends and like-minded associates. Such scholar-artists as Hsü Yu-chen (1407-1472), Shen Chou (1427-1509), Wu K'uan (1435-1504), Li Ying-chen (1431-1493), Chu Yün-ming (1460-1526), Wen Cheng-ming (1470-1559), and T'ang Yin (1470-1523) were all responsible for the flowering of a golden era in literati art and culture in the Soochow area. Chu Yün-ming was extremely knowledgeable and had studied a great range of calligraphic styles, the National Palace Museum having examples of his standard, running, and cursive script to show his multiple talents in this field. His cursive "Miscellaneous Calligraphy", which synthesizes the classical styles of the Han and Chin dynasties and loosens the columnar spacing of the characters, is most representative of his work in cursive script. Wen Cheng-ming was influenced by his teacher, Shen Chou, and in large-character script studied the manner of Huang T'ing-chien. The Museum collection includes "Calligraphing My Own Poetry", which was done at the lofty age of eighty. The handscroll includes two seven-character regulated verses and a six-character poem, revealing the peak of his poetic and calligraphic career in his late years.

In the transformation of the economy in China during the late Ming dynasty, trends in society became increasing extravagant. Ideas in the arts tended towards personal liberation and the pursuit of innovation and change. Starting from the middle Ming period, literati calligraphy gave birth to personal expression as modes for revealing in a straightforward way one's true nature became heralded. By emphasizing inner thoughts and spirit, adhering to the rules of calligraphy slackened. On the other hand, the "Modelbook School" also continued in the middle Ming, in which advances were made in the study of the ideas, practices, engraving, and connoisseurship of ancient calligraphy. Among these figures, Tung Ch'i-ch'ang (1555-1636) had the greatest influence on the development of calligraphy in the late Ming and early Ch'ing. Tung's path in his study of calligraphy traced back to the ancient Chin and T'ang traditions, collecting methods of ancient calligraphy into a grand synthesis. In his mind, imitating antiquity did not entail similarity in external form, but rather using it as a vehicle for personal expression, thereby injecting ancient calligraphic traditions with new life. His handscroll "Poetry on Immortal Lü" is a late work of his, and the calligraphic manner of the entire scroll is liberated and unbridled, skillfully fusing the spirited manner of both the poetry and calligraphy into an integrated whole.

▼ **Poetry on Immortal Lü (detail)**
Tung Ch'i-ch'ang, Ming dynasty
Handscroll; ink on paper; 24.7 x 293.1 cm

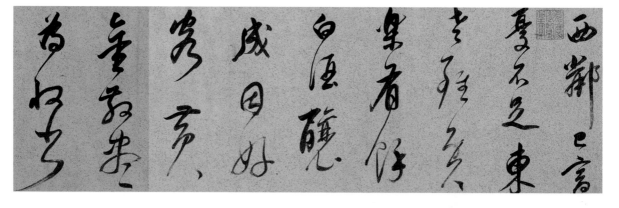

▼ **Small Scroll of Imitating Antiquity (detail)**
Liu Yung, Ch'ing dynasty
Hanging scroll; ink on paper; 75.2 x 29.9 cm

Donated by Messrs. Tann Po-yü and Tann Chi-fu

▶ **Seven-character Couplet in Regular Script**
Ch'ien Feng, Ch'ing dynasty
Hanging scroll; ink on paper; 164.5 x 36.7 cm

Donated by Messrs. Lin Tsung-i and Lin Ch'eng-tao

Old and New in Ch'ing Dynasty Calligraphy

Calligraphy of the Ch'ing dynasty can be said to have been blessed with numerous gifted practitioners. Archaeological interest in inscriptions on bronze and stone objects combined with the study of ancient writing became popular and thereupon opened completely new paths for development in calligraphy at the time. The ancient forms of writing known as seal and clerical scripts gradually became the mainstream of calligraphic circles, and achievements in these fields surpassed those in regular, running, and cursive scripts.

In the early Ch'ing dynasty, the K'ang-hsi Emperor (reigned 1662-1722) and Ch'ien-lung Emperor (r. 1736-1795) both were advocates of calligraphy, appreciating the styles of Chao Meng-fu and Tung Ch'i-ch'ang. For a while, cultivation in the trends of calligraphy not only advocated the manners of Chao and Tung, but also new directions in imitating antiquity, as the glory of traditional calligraphy once again took hold. Liu Yung's (1719-1804) "Small Scroll of Imitating Antiquity" represents a collection of characters imitated from the works of Wang Hsi-

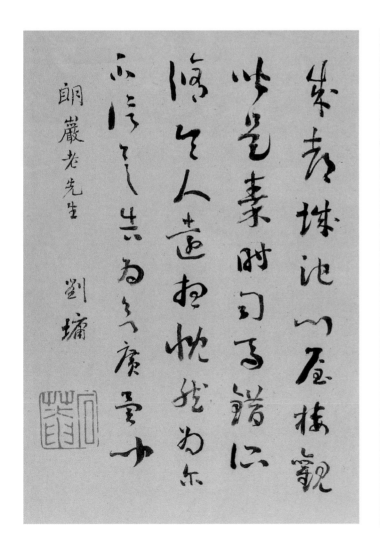

chih, Ts'ai Hsiang, and Su Shih. Following form to capture their spirit, this is a masterpiece of calligraphy that imitates antiquity while also giving vent to the personal and creative energies of the artist. Prince Ch'eng, also known as Yung-hsing (1752-1823), was diligent in his study and practice of calligraphy, and his "Seven-character Couplet in Regular Script" reaches the level of brush force achieved by T'ang dynasty regular script masters. In the early Ch'ing dynasty, only the regular script of Ch'ien Feng (1740-1795) attained both achievement and beauty in regular script.

After the Chia-ch'ing Emperor (r. 1796-1820), increasing numbers of objects were being unearthed, and this fragmentary record of the actual writings of the ancients gave rise to a turning point that gave prominence to the ancient forms of seal and clerical script calligraphy. Calligraphers increasingly turned to the archaic manners of the Ch'in-Han and earlier periods, injecting calligraphy with new vitality while also conveying the uniquely solemn force of ancient culture. Teng Shih-ju (1743-1805) instilled seal script with clerical script methods, creating an effect of making toughness soft. Ho Shao-chi (1799-1873), in his "Screen Format Clerical Script Imitating the Chang Ch'ien Stele," fused with the regular script calligraphic methods of Yen Chen-ch'ing to transcribe the expansive boldness of this Han dynasty stele. Lo Chen-yü (1866-1940), with this talents as both a scholar and calligrapher, copied the decrees of the Ch'in dynasty, interpreting the seal script of the Ch'in dynasty in a new, angular manner. In the transition of fusion and transformation, the tip of the brush combines both the beauty of ancient and modern written forms, revealing in many places the wisdom of the calligrapher while also paving the way for later followers to fathom the depths of traditional methods and to incorporate antiquity into modernity. Wu Ch'ang-shih (1844-1927) of the late Ch'ing and early Republican period, in his "Seven-character Couplet in Seal Script", plunged into antiquity to give rise to innovation, opening a new field for ancient seal script calligraphy. (Ho Ch'uan-hsing)

▼ **Seven-character Couplet in Seal Script**
Wu Ch'ang-shih, Ch'ing dynasty
Hanging scroll; ink on paper; both 132 x 33.4 cm
Donated by Mr. Ts'ai Chen-nan

▶ **Screen Format Clerical Script Imitating the Chang Ch'ien Stele**
Ho Shao-chi, Ch'ing dynasty
Four hanging scrolls; ink on paper;
each 124.6 x 31.2 cm

Ho Shao-chi was quite learned in the study of Chinese writing and characters found on ancient works of bronze and stone. With his foundation in calligraphy based on that of Yen Chen-ch'ing, he diligently studied ancient writing forms, seal-clerical, northern stelae, as well as stelae and brush writings of the Chin and T'ang dynasties, fusing elements of these to form his own style. This work is in imitation of the "Chang Ch'ien Stele" and was donated to the Museum by Messrs. Tann Po-yü and Tann Chi-fu.

孝武時有張騫廣通風俗開定
戎寇南邑八蠻西羅六戎北震
五狄東勤九夷荒遠既賓各貢

所育張是輔國世載其德爰既
於君盖其繼續我鴻緒牧守
相儵來殉高問孝弟於家中寒

於朝治京氏為兼麗權略蟄於
逆畋少為郡文隱練職位常在
股肋數為從事敢無細聞徵拜

郎中除巌城長蠻月业務求聞
四門臏正业燃休因歸賀八月
其民求順於郎　汩彬集

Radiating Splendors of Colors: The Lofty and Common Together in Painting

Chinese painting can be generally distinguished into two types: fine-line and sketched-brush manners. Artists have generally focused on capturing the spirit of the subject through form. Those especially talented in this art form are unrestrained by what the eye can see and flourish the ink-laden brush according to the mind's eye, being unhindered by nature but not quite departing from it completely. The focus of the compositional arrangement is to lead the viewers' eyes as if they were actually there.

Changing Styles: Multiplicity from the late T'ang and Five Dynasties to the Northern Sung

The Chinese paintings in the National Palace Museum truly represent a collection of treasures. As viewed from the history of Chinese painting, the classical period of figure painting was from the Six Dynasties period down to the T'ang dynasty (from approximately the third to ninth centuries). With the foundations laid by such masters as Ku K'ai-chih (ca. 344-405) and Wu Tao-tzu (ca. 685-758), the anonymous T'ang dynasty work "A Palace Concert" in the Museum collection represents the painting style of the late T'ang period. The standards of landscape painting formed approximately in the Five Dynasties period (about the tenth century) and incorporated features related to regional distinctions. Artists such as Ching Hao and Kuan

▼ **A Palace Concert**
Anonymous, T'ang dynasty
Hanging scroll; ink and color on silk; 48.7 x 69.5 cm

▶ **Travelers amid Mountains and Streams**
Fan K'uan, Sung dynasty
Hanging scroll; ink and color on silk; 206.3 x 103.3 cm

Fan K'uan (ca. 11th c.) used the "high distance" approach to portray the landscape of Northern China. The distant mountains are situated firmly in the center of the painting, taking up two-thirds of the composition. Its monumental appearance is quite imposing.

T'ung painted the landscape scenery of the north, while such masters as Tung Yüan and Chü-jan represented the water-filled landscapes associated with the Kiangnan region in the south. In terms of bird-and-flower painting, the Szechwan painter Huang Ch'üan and Hsü Hsi from Kiangnan also inaugurated two different models of rendition in this subject.

Culturally vibrant and flourishing, the Sung dynasty witnessed great advances in the study of nature and the application of technology. It was during this age that landscape and bird-and-flower painting became independent genres.

Li Ch'eng (916-967), Fan K'uan (ca. 11th c.), Kuo Hsi (fl. latter half of 11th c.), and Li T'ang (ca. 1049-after 1130) were Northern Sung masters of landscape painting and diligent observers of natural scenery. In fact, Fan had once lived in reclusion in the mountains and spent his days studying the surroundings and recording the craggy heights of the mountaintops with magnificent realism using vigorous brushwork. Kuo had also meticulously noted changes in the landscape at different times of the day and under varying atmospheric conditions. He used a variety of brush strokes and delicate layers of color to describe the rhythmic vitality of the land, such as the tranquil beauty of mountains in spring, the lush green of summer hills, the clarity of autumn days, and the desolation of winter.

Northern Sung landscape painters employed a "distant view with multiple focal points" to highlight the monumental power and grandeur of mountains. Peaks and foliage dominate

◀ **Wind in Pines Among a Myriad Valleys**
Li T'ang, Sung dynasty
Hanging scroll; ink and color on silk;
188.7 x 139.8 cm

▲ **Magpies and Hare**
Ts'ui Po, Sung dynasty
Hanging scroll; ink and color on silk;
193.7 x 103.4 cm

▶ **Early Spring**
Kuo Hsi, Sung dynasty
Hanging scroll; ink and color on silk;
158.3 x 108.1 cm

Kuo Hsi (fl. latter half of 11th c.) painted the mountain here as it would appear in early spring, as nature awakens from its hibernation. Using three modes of perspective (high, level, and deep distance), he has created a landscape in which viewers can be in, move through, or even reside in. "Early Spring" was done in 1072.

◄ **Ink Bamboo**
Wen T'ung, Sung dynasty
Hanging scroll; ink on silk; 131.6 x 105.4 cm

Wen T'ung was a bearer of the Presented Scholar ("chin-shih") civil service degree and a close friend of Su Shih. In this work, the bamboo stalk bending down from a cliff is done with brushwork that merges calligraphic and painting techniques. It is the earliest surviving example of bamboo painted in monochrome ink.

▼ **Chimonanthus and Birds**
Emperor Hui-tsung, Sung dynasty
Hanging scroll; ink and color on silk; 83.3 x 53.3 cm

the center of the composition. In Li T'ang's time during the late Northern Sung, however, perspective shifted to a closer view emphasizing detail. The texture of mountain rocks was expressed with greater detail, and the focal point tended to be simplified. In this perspective, fore-, middle-, and background closely overlap.

Huang Chü-ts'ai (933-after 993) was famous for his bird-and-flower painting in the early Northern Sung period. His work exhibits a gradual departure from the stylized forms of the bird-and-flower genre in the T'ang dynasty with an emphasis on decorative features, ushering in the age of "sketching from life". This means observing not only plants and animals but also their interaction in the environment. I Yüan-chi (fl. mid-11th century) was an artist who excelled in the depiction of monkeys and deer, and he even went to the mountains to observe the behavior of animals in their natural habitat. Another artist in this tradition was Ts'ui Po (fl. late 11th century), whose "Magpies and Hare" is characteristic of the Sung spirit of sketching from life.

The Sung emperor Hui-tsung (1082-1135) was fond of the arts and an excellent painter of birds-and-flowers in his own right. Infused with a poetic quality, his compositions are marked by pure simplicity and an emphasis on atmosphere. Concerned with the selection and cultivation of painters for the Imperial Painting Academy, Hui-tsung tested candidates for admission by requesting them to illustrate a line or two from a poem. In his time, not only was the scope of the Academy greatly expanded, a School of Painting was also established. Further, the *Hsüan-ho Catalogue* of Paintings was compiled during his reign, recording the paintings in the palace collection. A perusal of this book shows that bird-and-flower paintings were the greatest in number.

Slightly earlier, Wen T'ung (1018-1079), an artist known for his bamboo paintings in monochrome ink, Su Shih (1036-1101), and friends in their literary circle (such as Huang T'ing-chien [1045-1105] and Mi Fu [1052-1107]) had gradually formed a literati style of painting that had a great impact on the poeticism favored by Emperor Hui-tsung.

Chinese painting had originally centered on Buddhist and Taoist themes with its depiction of figures, but landscape and bird-and-flower subjects emerged later to take their place among the established genres. In the field of Buddhist and Taoist paintings, traditions of the T'ang dynasty continued into the Sung. The Sung spirit of a realistic approach, however, is also reflected in figure paintings, as well as landscape and bird-and-flower subjects, of the time. Portraiture and genre painting grew in importance, and their popularity spread from the gentry and literati to the common classes. The work "Along the River during the Ch'ing-ming Festival", for example, depicts the lives of commoners in Pien-ching, representing the vibrant scenery of the Northern Sung capital down to this day. (Lin Po-t'ing)

A Land of Mist and Water: A Turning Point in Southern Sung Painting

After the Sung court moved south, Emperor Kao-tsung (1107-1187) promoted the arts in the city of Lin-an, and Academy artists who had fled south joined his Shao-hsing Imperial Painting Academy. The political, economic, and cultural center therefore shifted to the region south of the Yangtze River. The geography there, vastly different from that of the Central Plains to the north, proved to be an inspiration for artists.

Northern Sung landscape painting featured stately and majestic monumental mountains, whereas scenery in the region around the Ch'ien-t'ang River during the Southern Sung was described by Li T'ang (ca. 1049-after 1130) as; "Villages in snow and smoke, and banks in mist: they are easy to enjoy, but difficult to capture." Views of snow or scenes shrouded in wisps of mist and haze create an atmospheric quality for a fresh and delicate contrast. In his words, "The river flows beyond the heavens and earth, the mountains appearing to fade in and out." Such a scene allows for the unlimited imagination of the viewer. Southern Sung artists relinquished the intricate and ponderous monumental landscapes for a misty, spacious stillness, using a one-sided compositional manner for further focus. Avoiding a distant view taking in the entire scene, artists turned to more intimate views and narrowed the focal point to a corner of the scene, concentrating on the exquisite beauty of the foreground. Such carefully planned compositions showcased the artists' advances in technique.

◀ **Temple at the Pass**
Chia Shih-ku, Sung dynasty
Album leaf; ink and color on silk; 26.4 x 26 cm

▶ **Pavilions on a Mountainside**
Hsiao Chao, Sung dynasty
Hanging scroll; ink and color on silk; 179.3 x 112.7 cm

One of the first impressions of this painting is the dark mountain towering up the left side. The trees, riverbanks, and distant mountains obscured by mists to the right are features not found in earlier landscapes. The main peak has been shifted from its former central, commanding position in the composition to the side.

Southern Sung landscape artists used this compositional mode to render complex scenes in a simple way, applying the concept of "less is more" to evoke the landscape of the south. Their suggestive, refined use of ink further established an elegant tone. The style is manifested in existing Southern Sung pieces in the form of small album leaves and fans. The reduced size brings focus on the most important and beautiful aspects of the scenery. The Sung interest in the objective study of nature led to the painting of animals and vegetation with particular attention to their natural interaction and environment. Realistic treatment thereby fused with ideal beauty. Using the form of a bird on a branch tip, for example, a painter could create within the confines of a small painting a world that allows the mind to enter the scene and go on a fanciful flight.

The Northern Sung tradition of detailed realism was followed by Southern Sung Academy artists in their figure

▼ **Conversing with a Friend by the Pine**
Hsia Kuei, Sung dynasty
Album leaf; ink on silk; 27 x 39 cm

▶ **The Knick-knack Peddler**
Li Sung, Sung dynasty
Album leaf; ink and color on silk; 25.8 x 27.6 cm

▶ **Immortal in Splashed Ink**
Liang K'ai, Sung dynasty
Album leaf; ink on paper; 48.7 x 27.7 cm

paintings. Moralistic narratives and stories formed the main subject matter, such as historical tales and myths. They were done with great precision and meticulous detail. Towards the middle and late Southern Sung, figure painting became more refined and elegant, as in the new developments of landscape painting at the time.

Apart from artists of the Imperial Painting Academy, painters in the Southern Sung also included officials, literati, and monks. Their theories of painting reflected a grounding in Confucianism and Buddhism. Whether they subscribed to the bold and free "sketching ideas" manner of painting or the meticulous realism of the "fine line" approach, literati painters sought refinement and natural elegance in their works and chose to express themselves in ink, a tradition passed down from the Northern Sung. They painted landscapes, withered trees, and bamboo and rocks with concise strokes. Plum blossoms, orchids, and narcissi were symbols of moral virtue, viewers understanding them immediately as emblematic of the artists' own attitudes and ideals. The convergence of various non-academic styles eventually became the mainstream in the Yüan dynasty.

While literati painters worked from knowledge, their Ch'an (Zen) Buddhist counterparts relied more on intuition. They were keen on condensing observed phenomena into simplified forms, allowing viewers to experience a sudden reaction to painting. Works of Ch'an painting were particularly popular in Japan. (Wang Yao-t'ing)

Mountains by the Riverbank: Literati Painting of the Yüan Dynasty

Unable to participate in government during the Yüan dynasty under control of the Mongols, many literati turned their attention to art and literature. Instead of following tradition, they sought to give expression to their inner thoughts, and their innovative styles brought literati painting to a new pinnacle.

Yüan painting is generally characterized by its unrestrained simplicity and preference for monochrome ink. Notable examples include the ink bamboo paintings of Li K'an (1245-1320), such as "Peace in the Four Seasons" and "Twin Pines", and the ink plum blossom painting "The Earliest Plum Blossoms of Spring" by Wang Mien (1287-1359). These works exhibit elegant and unconventional brushwork and are representative of the plant-and-flower painting at the time. Outline painting in ink (known as "*pai-miao*") reached a peak in figure painting, with Chao Meng-fu (1254-1322) the most prominent of its practitioners. Other important painters include Chang Wo (fl. mid-14th century) and Wei Chiu-ting (fl. 14th century), who were noted for their pliable and fluid brushwork as well as dignified and elegant forms. Wang Chen-p'eng (fl. 1280-1329) was foremost in fine "ruled-line" painting. His "Dragon Boat Race" is precise and refined without relinquishing its spiritual expressiveness.

Yüan painting encompasses a wide range of subject matter but still generally focuses on the landscape. Important landscape painters include Ch'ien Hsüan (1235-after 1303) of the early Yüan period, who studied the "blue-and-green" technique of Chao Po-chü and painted with an elegant simplicity and plainness. Chao Meng-fu combined the styles of the T'ang and Five Dynasties painters Tung Yüan and Chü-jan and the Northern Sung artists

▶ **The Earliest Plum Blossoms of Spring**
Wang Mien, Yüan dynasty
Hanging scroll; ink on silk; 151.4 x 52.2 cm

▼ **Dragon Boat Race (detail)**
Wang Chen-p'eng, Yüan Dynasty
Handscroll; ink on silk; 30.2 x 243.8 cm

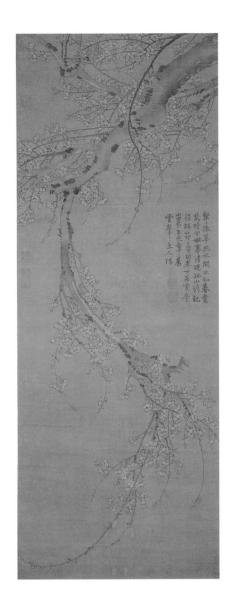

Li Ch'eng and Kuo Hsi. Kao K'o-kung (1248-1310) inherited the tradition of painting misty forests and cloud-covered mountains from the style of Mi Fu and his son, using it to create his own approach. Other followers of Li Ch'eng and Kuo Hsi included Ts'ao Chih-po (1271-1355) and Chu Te-jun (1294-1365). Huang Kung-wang (1269-1354) and Wang Meng (1308-1385), two of the Four Masters of the Yüan Dynasty, were influenced by Chao Meng-fu and harkened back to Tung Yüan and Chü-jan to create their own distinctive styles.

As Ch'ien Hsüan, Chao Meng-fu, Ts'ao Chih-po, Chu Te-jun, Sheng Mou, T'ang Ti (ca. 1287-1355), and the Four Yüan Masters were all active in Wu-hsing, Soochow, and Hangchow, the scenery south of the Yangtze River naturally became the subject of their works. In fact, the charm and elegance with which they depicted the watery region set the tone for the refined manner of Yüan landscape painting and shifted the focus from lofty mountains to the distant spaciousness of the watery regions. In Chao Meng-fu's "Layered Rivers and Tiered Peaks", for example, a boat traveling along the river is seen passing an open expanse of reedy banks. Huang Kung-wang's long scroll "Dwelling in the Fu-ch'un Mountains" depicts the Fu-ch'un River in Chekiang with low-laying forests and villages by the water interspersed among the banks, the tranquil scene done with fluid brushwork. Likewise, "Fisherman" by Wu Chen (1280-1354) also exhibits a sense of rich fullness, while "The Jung-hsi-chai Studio" by Ni Tsan (1301-1374) is a work of spare austerity and "Playing the Zither Beneath Trees" by Chu Te-jun is a fine example of a pure and refreshing atmosphere. While these works were done in various styles using different techniques, they all depict the compositional formula of two banks separated by a stretch of water. Yüan artists replaced the "deep distance" composition of

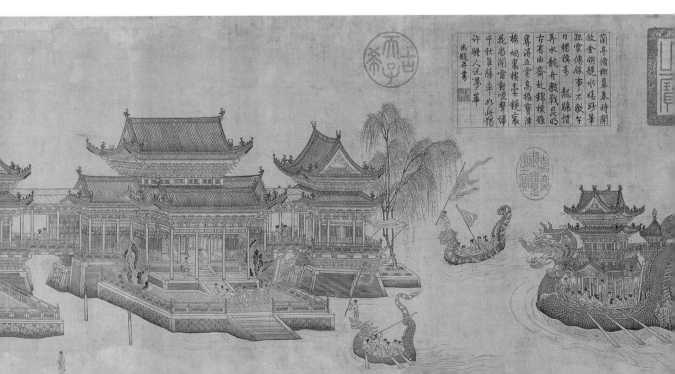

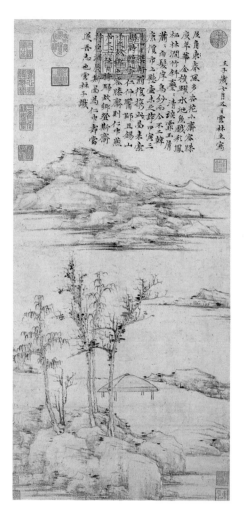

◀ **Fisherman**
Wu Chen, Yüan dynasty
Hanging scroll; ink on silk; 176.1 x 95.6 cm

▲ **The Jung-hsi-chai Studio**
Ni Tsan, Yüan dynasty
Hanging scroll; ink on paper; 74.7 x 35.5 cm

▲ **Playing the Zither Beneath Trees**
Chu Te-jun, Yüan dynasty
Album leaf; ink on silk; 144.9 x 58 cm

▼ **Layered Rivers and Tiered Peaks**
Chao Meng-fu, Yüan dynasty
Handscroll; ink on paper; 28.4 x 176.4 cm

Sung painters with "vast distance." Mountains are set into the background on the far side of the riverbank, and the middle of the painting is divided by a stretch of water, juxtaposing solid and void and thereby imbuing the painting with a rich sense of spaciousness.

Whereas Northern Sung painters were known for their monumental mountain and Southern Sung artists were skilled at the one-corner compositional approach to depict atmospheric, misty scenes, Yüan landscape painters focused on presenting riverbanks. By describing the beauty and charm of villages in the region south of the Yangtze River, Yüan painters created a new view in the genre of landscape. Many of the Yüan painters renowned today were literati, who combined elements of literature and calligraphy in their painting for a style that gradually moved from realism to expressionism. The elegant beauty of Yüan landscapes with their scenes of solitude and tranquility, depicted with suggestive artistry, embodies a purity that captivates the viewer time and again. (Hsü Kuo-huang)

Beyond Brush and Ink: New Horizons in Painting of the Ming

By the time Chinese painting developed in the Yüan dynasty (1271-1368), the two different traditions associated with professional and literati painting had formed. The history of painting in the Ming dynasty saw the ebb and flow of these two painting manners as they followed intertwining but often divergent paths.

Painting in the Hung-wu and Yung-lo eras (from 1368 to 1424) at the beginning of the dynasty mainly followed the tradition of literati painting of the Yüan dynasty. When Emperor Ch'eng-tsu of the Hung-wu reign assumed the throne, he moved the capital to Peking and established a painting academy at court. In the early years, due to the taste of the Ming imperial family, classical and beautiful bird-and-flower subjects as well as narrative scenes involving interesting figural themes were generally favored. Masterpieces by such famous painters of the time as Lin Liang (flourished 1457-1487) and Lü Chi (fl. 1439-1505) can be found in the Museum collection. In addition, since many of the court painters came from the southern Kiangnan region, the moist ink style associated with the Southern Sung court painting academy also found favor and became popular at the time. Court taste trickled down to the Kiangsu and Chekiang areas

◄◄ **Hawk in Autumn**
Lin Liang, Ming dynasty
Hanging scroll; ink and color on silk;
136.8 x 74.8 cm

◄ **Egrets and Hibiscus in Autumn**
Lü Chi, Ming dynasty
Hanging scroll; ink and color on silk;
192.6 x 111.9 cm

▲ **Layers of Snow in Wintry Mountains**
Wu Wei, Ming dynasty
Hanging scroll; ink on silk;
242.6 x 156.4 cm

▶ **Returning Late from a Spring Outing**
Tai Chin, Ming dynasty
Hanging scroll; ink and color on silk;
167.9 x 83.1 cm

女几山前野路橫
松督偏解合泉聲

靜裏閒傾耳便覺冲然道氣生

李父母大人先生

治下唐寅畫呈

to spur the formation of the so-called "Che School". Tai Chin (1388-1462) and Wu Wei (1459-1508) were two famous painters of this tradition.

Later, in the Chia-ching era (1522-1566), dynastic power waned and court painting also gradually went into decline. The low point of the Che School occurred as painters let go of the brush with almost complete abandon, which came to be looked down upon by people as debased. During this period, commerce in the Soochow area of Kiangnan witnessed a marked rise, and the favorable economic conditions provided a boost to developments in the arts. Painters such as Shen Chou (1427-1509) and Wen Cheng-ming (1470-1559) advocated the gentle and cultivated styles of Tung Yüan and Chü-jan of the Five Dynasties as well as those of the Four Yüan Masters. These developments quickly came to the attention of painting circles at the time, harking the rise of the so-called "Wu School" of literati painting and marking its presence therein. Beginning with the theory of "Northern" and "Southern" schools of painting promoted by such painter-theorists as Tung Ch'i-ch'ang (1555-1636) and Ch'en Chi-ju (1558-1639), increasing distinction came to be made between the forms of expression and methods of painting by artists. As a result, landscape painting was divided into two main streams, the Southern School of orthodox painting represented by such artists as Wang Wei, Tung Yüan, and Huang Kung-wang firmly establishing the status of literati painting.

Despite the conflicts that continually occurred between professional and literati artists in painting circles during the Ming dynasty, these two traditions also often influenced each other. For instance, the Wu School painter T'ang Yin (1470-1523) had once studied under the professional painter Chou Ch'en (ca. 1455-after 1536). By the late Ming dynasty, the distinction between these two traditions became increasingly blurred. For example, Ch'en Hung-shou (1599-1652), who came from a well-to-do family, did illustrations to be engraved for the printing of such popular literature at the time as *The Water Margin* and *Romance of the Western Chamber*. Exhibiting personal qualities and seeking innovation and novelty became social trends starting from the middle Ming period. The development of this regional school that inherited from the previous generations but also sought something different can be seen as one of the unique achievements of Ming dynasty painting. Furthermore, these apparently contradictory and complex phenomena also highlight the Ming dynasty as one of the greatest movements in the musical score of Chinese painting. (Lee Yü-min)

◄◄ **Sound of Pines on a Mountain Road**
T'ang Yin, Ming dynasty
Hanging scroll; ink and color on silk;
194.5 x 102.8 cm

◄ **Cold Trees and Wintry Waterfall**
Wen Cheng-ming, Ming dynasty
Hanging scroll; ink and color on paper;
194.1 x 59.3 cm

▼ **Sixteen Views of Living in Reclusion**
Ch'en Hung-shou, Ming dynasty
Album leaf; ink and light color on paper;
21.4 x 29.8 cm

The Ancient as New: The Legacy and Innovation of Ch'ing Dynasty Painting

Although the establishment of the Ch'ing dynasty marked a change in the ruling house in China, painting in the early Ch'ing could not completely cut itself off from the tradition of literati painting of the late Ming dynasty. In particular, the orthodox style of Tung Ch'i-ch'ang (1555-1636) continued in the development and legacy of the Four Wangs. In the political situation of the period, there was also a group of "leftover" artists from the previous dynasty, and their paintings express alienation from the political climate of the day as well as a sense of loss, their works serving as a vehicle for expressing emotions. On the other hand, although there was no painting academy by such a name under the K'ang-hsi (r. 1661-1722) and Ch'ien-lung (r. 1736-1795) emperors, an institution of court painting existed in fact as a result of the promotion of the arts by these two rulers. Court painters of the period, with opulent and precise painting manners as their foundation, made exquisite records of various court activities. The influence of these three main trends led painting of the early to middle Ch'ing period.

The Four Wangs of the Early Ch'ing considered themselves as upholders of the Orthodox School. Led by Wang Shih-min (1592-1680), the other three included Wang Chien (1598-1677), Wang Hui (1632-1717), and Wang Yüan-ch'i (1642-1715). Among them, one of the most creative was Wang Hui, who followed the manners of such earlier masters as Huang Kung-wang (1269-1354) and Wang Meng (1308-1385). With brushwork adapted from the calligraphy of Yüan dynasty masters and using the painting style of such Northern Sung painters as Chü-jan, Fan K'uan (ca. 11th century), and Yen Wen-kuei (967-1044), he was able to reinterpret the style of monumental landscape painting. His texture stroke method was arranged in orderly fashion, and the churning rise and fall of landmasses in his paintings form a kind of grand energy and presence. This kind of composition came to be called "dragon veins", allowing him to break through the constraints of copying and imitating antiquity and thereby use personalized brush and ink to revolutionize literati painting styles.

Among the so-called "leftover" painters from the Ming dynasty, Kung Hsien (1618-1689) and Tao-chi (also known as Shih-t'ao, 1642-1707) were two of the most famous. Kung Hsien did not favor the forms of literati painting popular in the late Ming period, but instead used a painting method involving a dry brush to express simple and solidly filled landmass forms to recreate not only a volumetric effect but also the grand energy of the landscape. Tao-chi, on the other hand, often used calligraphic lines to create a painting style marked by its uniqueness and infinite change.

◄ **Red Trees Among Mountains and Streams**
Wang Hui, Ch'ing dynasty
Hanging scroll; ink and color on paper;
112.4 x 39.5 cm

▶ **Streams, Mountains, and Trees**
Kung Hsien, Ch'ing dynasty
Album leaf; ink on paper; 23.5 x 33 cm

▼ **"Peonies" in a Cooperative Album of**
Flowers and Landscapes
Yün Shou-p'ing and Wang Hui,
Ch'ing dynasty
Album leaf; ink and color on paper;
28.1 x 43.1 cm

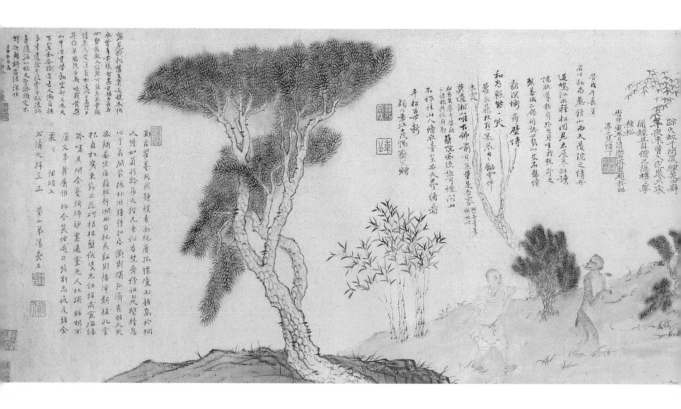

▲ **Small Self-Portrait Planting Pine Trees**
Shih-t'ao, Ch'ing dynasty
Handscroll; ink and color on paper;
40.3 x 170 cm

Donated by Mrs. Lo Chia-lun
(Ms. Chang Wei-chen)

◄ **Hundred Steeds (detail)**
Lang Shih-ning
(Giuseppe Castiglione), Ch'ing dynasty
Handscroll; ink and color on silk;
94.5 x 776.2 cm

Among court painters, Leng Mei (fl. late 17th c.-early 18th c.), Chiang T'ing-hsi (1669-1732), and Lang Shih-ning (Giuseppe Castiglione, 1688-1766) used brilliant colors and realistic techniques to record and illustrate activities and subjects associated with the imperial family. Giuseppe Castiglione, also known by his Chinese name Lang Shih-ning, was one of the most influential at the time. A missionary from Italy, he became a Jesuit noviate at the age of 19 and learned painting and architecture. He arrived in China at the age of 27 to conduct missionary work and came to the attention of the court for his artistic skills. He was gifted at painting figures, birds and flowers, and especially horses. In landscape painting, he mixed in Western painting techniques, resulting in the volumetric effect of the landmasses, trees, and buildings he rendered and making them different from traditional Chinese painting methods.

During the Ch'ien-lung era of the Ch'ing dynasty, commercial developments in the city of Yangchow led to the rise of taste in art dictated by the market. Among the individualistic artists who emerged there at the time, some of the most representative were Huang Shen (1687-1766) and Cheng Hsieh (1693-1765). They emphasized the influence of thought, personal taste, learning, and talent in creating artworks. Paintings often tended to focus on flowers, but there were also landscapes and figures. Following the "sketching ideas" tradition of the Sung and Yüan dynasties, they broke away from the orthodox constraints of the painting circles and developed scene-based "sketching from life" and emotionally charged works, giving Ch'ing painting new life in the legacy of trends that it had inherited. (T'ung Wen-o)

Wonders of Silk: The Beauty of Tapestry and Embroidery

Chinese silk textiles were famous as early as the first and second centuries CE, China itself being known as the "Country of Silk." Tapestry, one of many kinds of silk weaving, appears like other silk products but is made with a different technique. In most textiles, weft threads are woven all the way through the set of warp threads. Tapestry, however, is woven with discontinuous weft threads, meaning they do not create a continuous horizontal line across the warp threads. Instead, the different colored weft threads go through the warp only within the confines of the pattern and then are turned back. This creates the design of a tapestry. The unwoven warp threads are then done with different colored weft threads to suit the pattern. The points where the weft threads turn back mark the contour of the pattern. The serrated gaps left between the weft threads have the appearance of being cut, which is why it is sometimes mistakenly called "cut silk (*k'o-ssu*)". In fact, the character "*k'o*" used for tapestry means the weft of the woven fabric, referring to the fact that the pattern depends solely upon the weft threads.

Chuang Ch'o and Hung Hao of the Sung dynasty noted in their *Miscellaneous Notes* and *Records of Observances in Sung-mo* that the technique was brought to China in the early Southern Sung period by the Uighurs. Examination of existing works shows that the technique had already been perfected by the Southern Sung. However, archeological excavations have yielded remnants of wool and silk textiles from the Northern and Southern Dynasties done with a discontinuous weft tabby weaving technique. Such findings show that the tapestry techniques were already employed at this early stage.

Sung dynasty tapestry compositions are realistic and characterized by their simple style and elegant colors. Weavers created natural forms with consummate skill, striving to be loyal to the original draft. This was the golden age of Chinese tapestry. In the Yüan dynasty, gold thread was woven into tapestries, resulting in a stunning and unique style. Unfortunately, few Yüan dynasty pieces exist today. Tapestry products of the early Ming dynasty were often copies of Sung dynasty works. By the mid-Ming period, however, a unique style featuring vivid compositions and superb techniques had emerged. In the Ch'ing dynasty, tapestry techniques had reached the pinnacle of development in terms of precision and fineness. Prolific, large-scale patterns were produced with brilliant colors. Extremely fine or complicated sections of the design were done with a brush, creating a new style merging tapestry and painting.

Embroidery, on the other hand, was applied to a variety of silks, including plain woven, twill woven, satin, and brocade. It was done using a needle and colored threads to create a raised design on the fabric, differing from patterns woven into the silk that were flat.

▶ **Kingfisher and Lotus Blossom**
Anonymous, Ch'ing dynasty
Album leaf; embroidery; 32.9 x 29.8 cm

▼ **Abode of Immortals (detail)**
Anonymous, Sung dynasty
Album leaf; tapestry; 28.1 x 35.7 cm

Set against a light brown weave, cranes and
phoenixes fly around a building in the land
of the immortals with the landscape dimly
visible in the mist. The colors are crisp, and
the threads extremely fine and closely woven,
bringing out every detail. The centrally
symmetrical composition is full of life, this
being an exquisite example of Sung period
tapestry.

Early embroidery was made to meet requirements in clothing, daily necessities, and decoration, being taken as symbolic of the owner's status. The subject matter for designs was drawn from contemporary socio-political, genre, and daily life themes. The popularity of painting and calligraphy in the Sung and Yüan dynasties gave birth to highly artistic embroidered pictures. A succession of famous weavers brought embroidery to its peak of development, elevating it from practical origins to the realm of art. The National Palace Museum's collection of embroideries is composed of the latter type. The craft of textile dyeing was highly developed by the Ming dynasty, and embroidery carved out new territory as the technique was refined. The "Ku-style" embroidery of the Lu-hsiang Garden was particularly famous. During the Ch'ing dynasty, embroidered works for imperial use were meticulously and beautifully done, while popular styles of embroidery emerged in such regions as Soochow, Szechwan, Hunan, and Kwangtung, each with its own unique weaving techniques and use of stitch and thread. Known as the "Four Great Styles of Embroidery," these extremely fine works, with skillfully matched colors, have earned a reputation throughout the world.

The arts of tapestry and embroidery both require extremely fine and precise skill as well as the expertise of an artist. The compositions of many works in the National Palace Museum collection capture the essence of painting and calligraphy. In fact, their artistic value is so great that when mounted, viewers often mistake them for works of painting and calligraphy. (Hu Sai-lan)

◀◀ **Plum Blossoms, Bamboo, and Wild Birds**
Anonymous, Sung dynasty
Hanging scroll; embroidery; 130.8 x 54.5 cm

◀ **Swallows and Apricot Blossoms in Spring**
Anonymous, Yüan dynasty
(after a painting by Ts'ui Po)
Hanging scroll; tapestry; 104.8 x 41.5 cm

▲ **The Peach of God of Immortality**
Wu Ch'i, Ming dynasty
(after a painting by Shen Chou)
Hanging scroll; tapestry; 152.7 x 54.6 cm

▶ **Poetic Sentiment on the Lo-shou Hall**
Made at the imperial decree of the
Ch'ien-lung Emperor, Ch'ing dynasty
Hanging scroll; embroidery; 92.7 x 61.5 cm

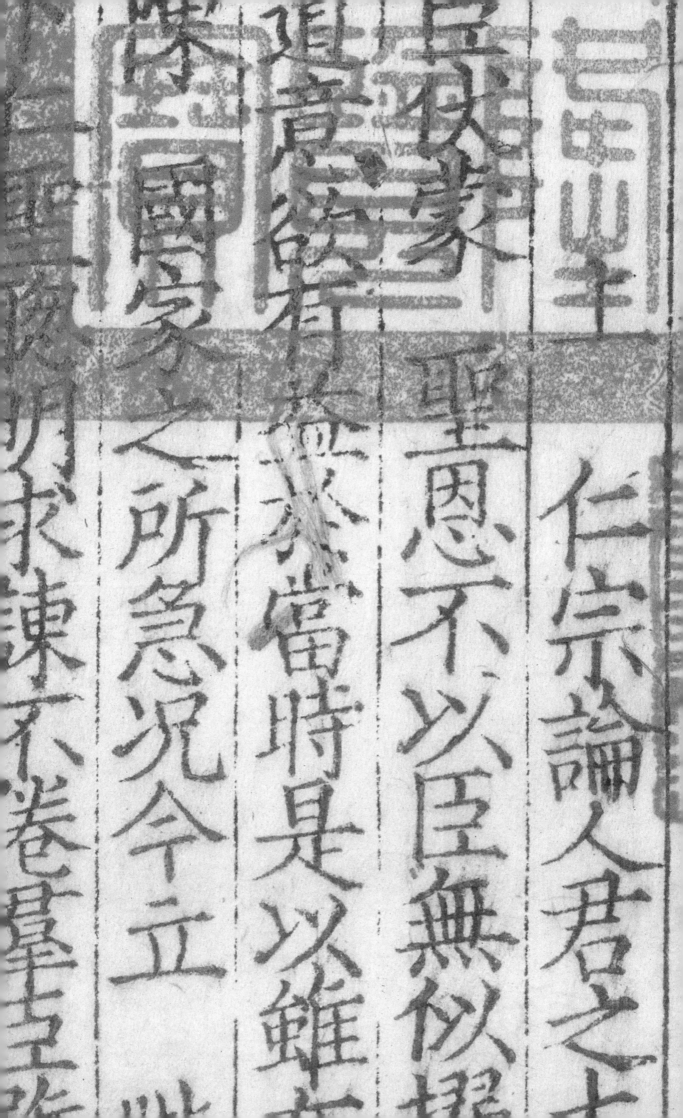

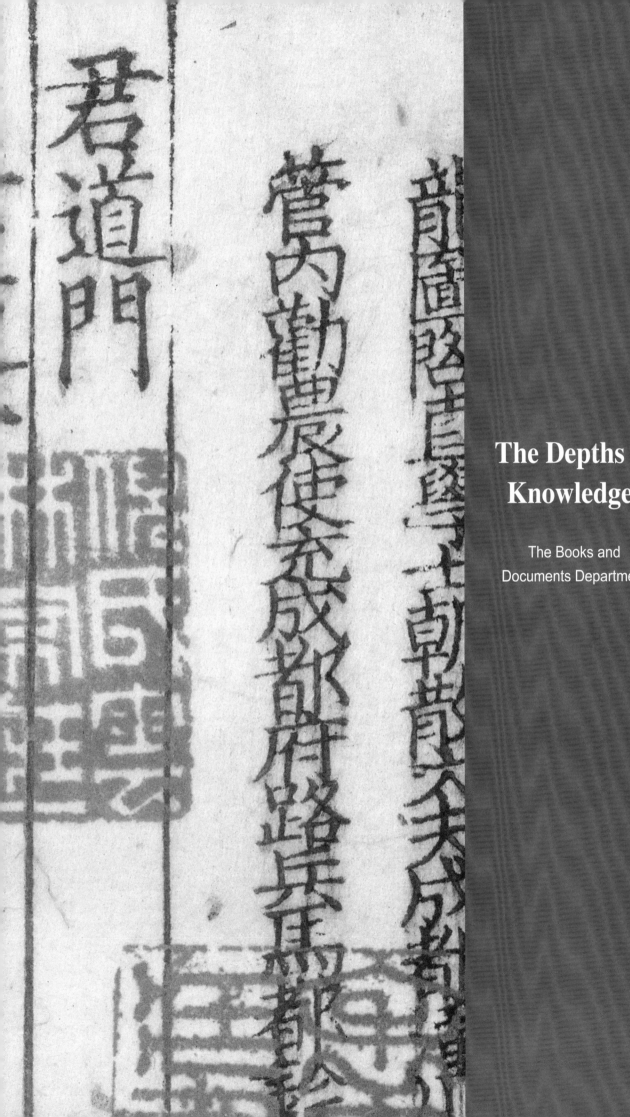

The Depths of
Knowledge:

The Books and
Documents Department

1 2

The Depths of Knowledge: The Books and Documents Department

Books represent information that has been compiled and written into a set format and often printed for dissemination. Documents refer to files or independent pieces of information. Both of these represent invaluable records of the ancients and are known as writings or texts.

In 1925, soon after the Palace Museum was established, there were two halls devoted to antiquities and books, with the latter divided into the two categories of books and documents. In 1928, after the national government assumed direct control, the departments in charge of managing artifacts were divided into the halls for antiquities, books, and documents. In 1965, the Executive Yuan passed the "Provisional Organic Regulations of the National Palace Museum", and the artifacts were divided into antiquities as well as painting and calligraphy. At that time, books and documents were the responsibility of the Painting and Calligraphy Department. In 1968, the provisional regulations were revised to add the Books and Documents Department. At that time, the antiquities as well as painting and calligraphy sections were also formally upgraded in status to departments. From that time, the Books and Documents, Antiquities, and Painting and Calligraphy Departments have been the three main research and archival divisions of artifacts in the collection of the National Palace Museum. In June of 1985, the Books and Documents Department held its first special exhibit entitled "Historical Materials on the Revolutions Prior to the Founding of the Republic of China in the Museum Collection". Afterwards, the task of rotating permanent exhibitions became one of the functions of the Books and Documents Department, and the four primary functions of the Department (collection, research, exhibition, and service) finally were complete.

The Books and Documents Department is renowned around the world for its wealth of Ch'ing dynasty court archives and rare books under its care. Of these two divisions, that of Ch'ing court archives can be further separated as follows: palace archives (158,535 memorials in Manchu and Chinese from the court), Council of State archives and volumes (including 190,837 archived memorial copies and 6,218 archive volumes of the Council of State, which can be further divided into catalogues, edicts, special cases, memorials, records, and telegrams). These archives are composed mainly of archive volumes and memorials, representing documents compiled and edited by the Historiography Institute,

compilations of state documents, and state documents of the Ch'ing court. The total of 395,544 items makes this one of the most important first-hand sources for information in researching the history of the Ch'ing dynasty.

In terms of rare books, the Books and Documents Department has a vast collection of Ch'ing dynasty and pre-Ch'ing woodblock-carved prints, movable-type prints, editions proofread and commented by famous figures of the time, manuscript editions, transcript versions, and even a few print and handwritten editions from Korea and Japan. For example, when Juan Yüan served as Provincial Education Commissioner of Chekiang, he searched for books, which he presented as tribute to the court as the "Wan-wei Collection". Known as one of the most complete collections is the *Complete Library of the Four Treasuries* that was stored in the Wen-yüan Pavilion as well as the *Abstracted Contents of the Complete Library of the Four Treasuries* housed in the Ch'ih-tsao Hall. There are also more than fifty thousand volumes that cover nearly all of the teachings, plans, poetry, and memorials produced and published by the Ch'ing court over the years. "Imprints of the Wu-ying Palace" themselves comprise more than 1,200 series. In addition, the revision of the *Unified Gazetteer of the Great Ch'ing* represents a collection of all the local gazetteers at the time. Together, these rare books were once part of the former Ch'ing court collection or have been transferred into the collection of the National Palace Museum.

In addition to books from the former Ch'ing court and those transferred from other collections into the National Palace Museum, there are also other sources for the books in the collection under the care of the Books and Documents Department. They include the Kuan-hai Collection of books from Yang Shou-ching of the late Ch'ing dynasty, books formerly in the collection of the original Peking Library, and purchases and donations to the Museum in recent years.

The Kuan-hai Collection of books was purchased by Yang Shou-ching when he was in Japan. After he passed away in 1915, the newly established Republican government purchased his collection, which he had named Kuan-hai ("Views of the Sea"). The Palace Museum managed part of his collection at the time. The number of books from the Kuan-hai Collection in the National Palace Museum number more than fifteen hundred, including

3   4   5

1. Installation of an exhibition by the Books and Documents Department.
2. Storage facilities for Ch'ing palace archives.
3. Storage facilities for the rare books.
4. Packing a rare book during inventory.
5. Taking inventory of the Ch'ing palace archives.

15,491 volumes. Among them are many rare editions, such as *Classified Collection of the Imperial Library* that had been printed by the Wan-chüan ("Ten-thousand Volume") Hall of Yü Jen-chung of Chien-an during the Sung dynasty. Of particular note is that Yang Shou-ching's collection contains more than four hundred treatises on traditional medicine, many of which had been in the former collection of Messrs. Kojima and Tamba in Japan and are extremely rare editions with considerable historical value.

In 1909, two years before the fall of the Ch'ing dynasty, the Library of the Directorate of Education was changed to the Capital Library, becoming the predecessor of the Peking Library. During the Second Sino-Japanese War (War of Resistance Against Japan, 1937-1945), the most precious parts of the collection of the Peking Library along with 60,000 volumes of rare books were transported south and stored for safekeeping. In 1940, following the full-scale eruption of World War II, the Library Director at the time, Mr. Yüan T'ung-li, received the consent of the US government and had more than 20,000 of the most precious volumes shipped in 102 crates along with 18 crates of maps to the Library of Congress in the US for safekeeping. In 1965, the books were returned to the Republic of China in Taiwan. In 1985, the Ministry of Education thereupon entrusted the National Palace Museum with the care of these books. Although this collection includes only 20,785 volumes, they comprise as many as 214 precious editions from the Sung and Yüan dynasties. There are also rare volumes from the Yung-lo encyclopedia of the Ming dynasty, rare editions of local gazetteers from the Ming dynasty, illustrated plays and novels, and Ming dynasty literary collections, demonstrating the outstanding quality of the collection.

The National Palace Museum has also made purchases and accepted donations over the past few years, accounting for a new major source of books in the collection. In May of 1983, for example, the Ministry of Defense transferred a collection of rare books and gazetteers in its collection to the National Palace Museum. Among them are 118 Ming and Ch'ing dynasty books in 8,362 volumes and 1,100 local gazetteers in 9,261 volumes.

In recent years, the National Palace Museum has been fortunate to have no less than thirty occasions for the donation of rare books to its collection. These include such local notables as Hsü T'ing-yao, General Huang Chieh, Ch'en Chih-mai, and Lo Chia-lun, all of whom had rare books in their collections transferred or donated to the National Palace Museum. The more notable of these are as follows: Mr. Hsü T'ing-yao donated a total of more than 200 books in 2,406 volumes of Ming and Ch'ing dynasty imprints, and Mr. Shen Chung-t'ao donated his "Yen-i Tower Book Collection", including 90 rare books in 1,169 volumes. After researching and cataloguing Shen's collection, it turns out that there are 32 Sung dynasty editions, eighteen Yüan editions, one Sung edition with Yüan additions, 31 Ming editions, three Ch'ing editions, two manuscript texts, and three transcribed editions. Though not outstanding in quantity, this collection is extraordinary in quality.

Over the years, the National Palace Museum has also made purchases of rare books to augment its collection, numbering more than three hundred texts in 2,968 volumes. The more notable of these are as follows: Sung editions of the *Shan-t'ang Index*, *Dharini Sutra*, *Dharini Sutra of the Great and Powerful One*, *Biography of T'ung Hsi-i*, and *Literary Collection of Hou-ch'un Chü-shih*. There is also a Yüan dynasty edition of *The Four Books Propagating the Way*. Among Ming dynasty editions are *Letters to Ch'i Piao-chia*, *Letters for the Next Generation*, *Su-huan san-tuan*, and *Complete Writings on Defending the City*, compiled or written by Ch'i Ch'eng-yeh. Ch'ing dynasty handwritten editions include the *Overall Compilation of the Four Treasuries from the San-yü Hall*, part of the *Complete Library of the Four Treasuries* of the Wen-yüan Pavilion, and *Imperial Collection of Poetry and Prose by the Ch'ing Emperor Shih-tsung* and *Complete Fukien Poetry* from the *Complete Library of the Four Treasuries* of the Wen-tsao Pavilion. Finally, there is also a "Handscroll Map on the Canal between the Capital and Hangchow" painted on silk.

The collection of rare books in the National Palace Museum is not only significant for its quality and importance for research, but also in that it serves as testimony to the course of developments that took place in the history of Chinese printing and book production. They also are invaluable for checking against later editions, in which case the sole surviving editions and copies in the National Palace Museum become even more important. The preservation for future generations of this collection presenting the art of Chinese book production serves as an invaluable guide for research that speaks for itself. (Lin T'ien-jen)

A Treasure Trove of Information: Ch'ing Dynasty Memorials and Archives

State papers are documents used by government institutions and agencies in dealing with government affairs. In order to serve as a record and as documentation in further work, these documents were later assembled for verification and consciously preserved together as a group. These documents form what are known as archives. In 1925, the Palace Museum was preparing to open, and the precious antiquities and objects amassed deep with the palaces over the centuries became the cultural heritage belonging to the public. Among them, the dusty court records and files that had been stored for so many years were also protected to prevent them from being destroyed or dispersed. Many secrets of the Ch'ing dynasty court and details of the imperial family have come to light as a result of the study of these documents, providing invaluable sources for understanding Ch'ing dynasty history.

The collection of the National Palace Museum includes at present nearly 400,000 items of Ch'ing dynasty court archives, all of which are rare and valuable documents. They can be divided into the following four major categories: 1) palace archives, 2) Council of State archives, 3) archives of the various halls and ministries under the Grand Secretariat, and 4) archives of the Ch'ing dynasty Institute of Historiography and the Republican Institute of Ch'ing Historiography. On the basis of format and features, the archives can also be divided into the three divisions of memorials, archive volumes, and official writings, such as mandates and proclamations.

1. Memorials

The memorials in the collection of the National Palace Museum include the two main categories of palace archives from the Ch'ing dynasty court rescripted in vermilion ink along with archive copies from the Council of State. All together, they number more than 340,000 and comprise four-fifths of the Ch'ing dynasty archives in the Museum collection. From these holdings, we can understand the extensive and universal practice of using memorials as a form of official documentation in the Ch'ing dynasty.

The imperially rescripted palace memorials in vermilion ink in the National Palace Museum collection date from the reigns of nine emperors of the Ch'ing dynasty, starting with the K'ang-hsi Emperor (r. 1662-1722). Comprising more than 150,000 in number, they were mostly submitted by high civil and military officials to the Ch'ing court with regard to various matters. They were either personally commented upon by the ruler in red ink or by high officials of the Council of State entrusted to respond to the memorial writers. Early in the reign of the Yung-cheng Emperor, it was ordered that, after the sender of the memorial received the memorial with court instructions, they be sent back to the court. These returned memorials were in both Manchu and Chinese, being stored in various places at court, such as the Mao-ch'in and Ching-jen Palaces. After 1925, more than a decade after the establishment of the Republic of China,

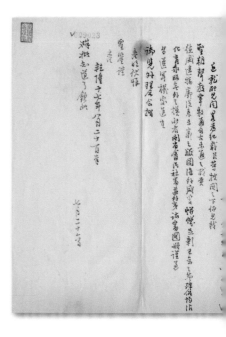

▲ **Copy of a memorial by Karjišan, Gover general of Fukien and Chekiang**

Dated to the 21st day of the eighth lu month of the 17th year of the Ch'ien-Emperor (1752), Ch'ing dynasty

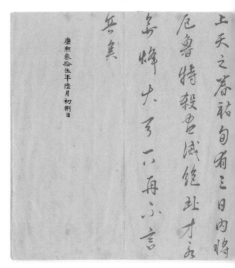

▼ **Memorial by Ts'ao Yin, Silk Manufact Supervisor of Kiangning, wishing emperor well and congratulating his vic in quelling the rebellion of the Zung founder Dga'-ldan**

Dated to the 8th day of the 6th lunar mo of the 35th year of the K'ang-hsi Emp (1696), Ch'ing dynasty

10 x 20.5 cm (5 folds)

the Documents Department of the Palace Museum began the task of organizing this massive collection of Ch'ing documents. At the time, they were known as "archives from various palace locations", which was abbreviated to "palace archives", becoming the precious first-hand historical materials valued so highly by historians of the Ch'ing dynasty today.

The use of memorials began in the reign of the K'ang-hsi Emperor. According to the contents reported in the memorials, they can be divided into the four general categories of "memorials wishing the emperor well" (of a congratulatory or commemorative nature), "memorials of gratitude" (presented in gratitude for a gift from the emperor), memorials reporting on matters, and confidential memorials (the latter differentiated on account of the secretive nature of their contents). Memorials for wishing the emperor well, as the name suggests, are more like formal greeting cards in nature. In order to express reverence and respect, the cover was usually covered in yellow silk or paper to signify their imperial nature. This was the highest standard of memorial at the time. The attention and detail placed in the production of these memorials, even if not very long, would even include illustrations of a double-dragon spewing-pearl, plum blossoms and crackled ice, or floral-mass and brocaded-flower designs, further heightening the decoration effect of these documents. For memorials dealing with public or confidential matters, the use of yellow silk was therefore forbidden by precedent.

The "wishing-well" memorial was therefore a means of private communication between privileged high officials and the emperor. This being the case, they did not pass through the hands of other officials and were presented directly to the emperor, being the most confidential in nature. The emperor, who resided deep within the Forbidden City, used the system of memorials to take more personal control over the administration of the government and reinforce authority, top officials at court and throughout the land serving as his eyes and ears. Thus, court documents known as memorials were important channels for carrying out policies and quickly dealing with issues, especially those in local areas, providing the emperor with a personal grasp over the goings-on in the entire country.

The memorial system was marked by a set of standard procedures regulating everything from the writing to the packaging, presentation, commenting, return, and storage of these documents. After an official had written the contents of a memorial, it would be inserted into a casing and sealed, then placed within a leather or wooden case provided by the court. It would thereupon be locked and the keyhole sealed before finally being placed within a yellow silk wrapping. In the early years of the delivery system, subordinates or others entrusted by the memorial writer were delegated with the task of delivering the memorial. During the K'ang-hsi reign, special permission was given to first and second rank officials to use the system of courier horse relay. Depending on the urgency of the matter reported in the memorial, a certain speed was specified for its delivery, anywhere from 300 to 400, 500, 600 or even 800 *li* per day. After the memorial reached the capital, it was sent to the memorial office at the Ching-yün Gate, and the grand eunuch dealing with memorial matters would present it to the emperor for perusal and comment. In the reign of the Yung-cheng Emperor, after the establishment of the Council of State, all memorials that had been rescripted in vermilion ink by the emperor were first transcribed by the memorial office at the Council of State as a copy and then sent back to the original memorial writer.

In the collection of the National Palace Museum, there are even more of these copies of memorials from the Council of State than those of palace memorials, numbering more than 190,000.

After the founding of the Council of State, the memorials that had been rescripted by the emperor in red ink and first sent to the Council of State for copying became known as "memorial copies". These transcribed memorials were divided by month and stored in packets that became known as "monthly packets of the Council of State". Memorial packets included not only memorials, but also other official documents, such as notes, memoranda, forwarded documents, notices, summons, public postings, petitions, contracts, telegrams (starting later in the 19th century), and correspondence. These, too, were all divided by month, thereby reflecting the plurality of the documents that eventually were stored in these monthly packets of the Council of State.

In addition to the collection of memorials in the National Palace Museum collection, there are also all types of attachments included with the memorials themselves. When Ch'ing dynasty officials wrote memorials, they would use clear, concise, and detailed descriptions in reporting on matters to the emperor. They might also attach illustrated explanations, lists, or inventories as supplementary materials. These include lists of grain prices, topics in the provincial civil service examinations, listings of tax revenues, inventories of confiscated properties, records of the amount of rainfall, illustrated river construction projects, and illustrations of city walls and mountain passes, battle plans, and routes for imperial inspection. Generally, after a memorial had been rescripted in vermilion ink by the emperor, it was sent back to the original writer, but most of the attachments were retained or submitted to the Council of State, where they were kept with the copies of the memorials and placed in the packets. This is why there are many more materials dealing with memorials and attachments in the monthly packets from the Council of State than the imperially rescripted palace memorials in vermilion ink.

2. Archived Volumes

The archives of the Council of State include not only the above documents known as memorials, but they also comprise various types of handwritten processed documents divided according to the month and year and bound as volumes. This system continued unbroken up until the end of the Ch'ing dynasty. Archived volumes were compiled every five years in Manchu and every three years in Chinese, with a handwritten copy ordered by high officials of the Council of State to prevent any mistakes. There are more than thirty series of archived volumes from the Council of State in the National Palace Museum collection comprising more than 20,000 volumes. Based on their format, they can be divided into the categories of catalogues, imperial decrees, special cases, memorial matters, memoranda of events, and telegrams, mainly representing classified transcriptions of archived volumes of the Council of State dealing with matters of the state.

▲ **Sketch map of sieges by bandits in th** **Chiayi County area**
32.5 x 84 cm

▼ **Veritable Records of the Lofty Emperor T'ai-tsu (Nurhaci) of the Great Ch'ing (red edition)**
For the 1st to 6th lunar months of 1616
23 x 37.5 cm

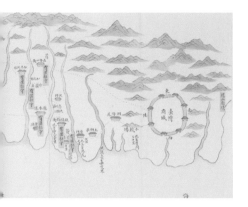

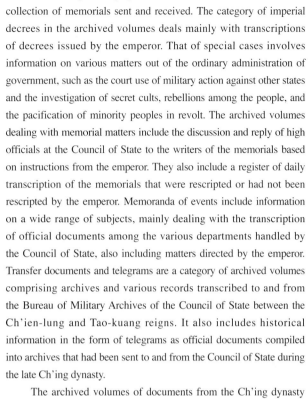

The catalogue category of archived volumes is a record of the collection of memorials sent and received. The category of imperial decrees in the archived volumes deals mainly with transcriptions of decrees issued by the emperor. That of special cases involves information on various matters out of the ordinary administration of government, such as the court use of military action against other states and the investigation of secret cults, rebellions among the people, and the pacification of minority peoples in revolt. The archived volumes dealing with memorial matters include the discussion and reply of high officials at the Council of State to the writers of the memorials based on instructions from the emperor. They also include a register of daily transcription of the memorials that were rescripted or had not been rescripted by the emperor. Memoranda of events include information on a wide range of subjects, mainly dealing with the transcription of official documents among the various departments handled by the Council of State, also including matters directed by the emperor. Transfer documents and telegrams are a category of archived volumes comprising archives and various records transcribed to and from the Bureau of Military Archives of the Council of State between the Ch'ien-lung and Tao-kuang reigns. It also includes historical information in the form of telegrams as official documents compiled into archives that had been sent to and from the Council of State during the late Ch'ing dynasty.

The archived volumes of documents from the Ch'ing dynasty include not only the compiled materials from the Council of State but also the archived volumes of diaries of daily matters from the Grand Secretariat.

The majority of the archived volumes from the Grand Secretariat in the collection of the National Palace Museum are comprised of the *Histories* of the Six Offices of Scrutiny, including a total of 235 volumes dealing with the Ministries of Personnel, Revenue, Rites, War, Justice, and Works. These mostly involve information in abstracts transcribed by officials in the Six Offices of Scrutiny under the Grand Secretariat, which was collected into books and then stored in the Grand Secretariat so that they could serve as references for court historiographers. As for the archived volumes of transcribed imperial decrees in the Registry Office for official documents under the Grand Secretariat, there are the *Registry of the Secretariat* and *Registry of His Majesty's Decrees*. Officials in the outer provinces, after receiving memorials back from the throne, would comply with orders and have their records stored for reference in the *Registry of Outside Events*. The important archived volumes of memorial subjects and matters transcribed by officials in the various ministries and offices were collected into *Archives of Presented Memorials* and *Archives of Memorialized Matters*. In addition, the official documents issued by the Council of State were catalogued and entered into the *Archives of the Council of State*. These registers and volumes total more than nine hundred. Although not as great in number as the archived volumes of the Council of State, they nonetheless provide important clues for understanding the daily working of the Grand Secretariat and the nature of documentation in the Grand Secretariat during the Ch'ing dynasty.

Among the archived volumes of documents from the Ch'ing dynasty, the National Palace Museum has more than forty monumental volumes of the *Archives in Old Manchu*, the only surviving set anywhere in the world. After this set of archived volumes was reorganized and transcribed in the Ch'ien-lung reign back in the 18th century, it was stored away deep in the court, where few people knew of its existence. It was not until the early 20th century that it was rediscovered in the storerooms of the Grand Secretariat, making this one of the four greatest discoveries of historical materials in the modern era. The contents represent important historical information for historians of the ancestors of the Ch'ing dynasty Manchu rulers in terms of legends of their origins, beginnings of the Eight Banner System, and customs of Manchu society, their economic system and lifestyle, tribal developments, and relations with other states and tribes. It also provides invaluable material on the development of the Manchu language, having been written in an older system.

In addition to the archived volumes from the Council of State and the Grand Secretariat are materials from the Historiography Institute under the jurisdiction of the Hanlin Academy during the Ch'ing dynasty. There are also compiled and transcribed drafts of archived volumes edited into the *Draft of Ch'ing History* written by the Ch'ing Historiography Institute established by the government of Yüan Shih-k'ai in 1914. These materials were later transferred for management by the Palace Museum, representing important materials for the research of scholars on the history of the Ch'ing dynasty. The Historiography Institute had been officially established and followed the traditional historiographical conventions of dividing materials into annals, treatises, tables, and biographies. The collection of the National Palace Museum currently contains more than 23,000 volumes of archives of transcribed compilations of annal drafts, treatise collections, annual table transcriptions, draft biographical materials, and long drafts. There are also more than 3,500 packets of archived materials compiled by members of the Historiography Institute in their preparation for writing biographies of notable figures.

The materials in these biographical packets are especially valuable, because they not only preserve transcriptions of the drafts for these biographies of important figures by official historians, they also contain the original historical information in volumes related to the life and events of the person involved as well as (according to the person) a list of facts, family background, political achievements, resume of office, various events, military achievements, historical sketches, stele inscriptions, family register, education, Banner distinction name, filial achievements, memorial drafts, chronology, literary writings, and narratives. Many of these sources would have been lost forever had they not been stored and preserved for use in the official biographies.

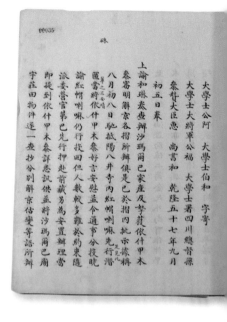

▲ Gorkha archives
For the 9th and 12th lunar months of the 57th year of the Ch'ien-lung Emperor (1792), Ch'ing dynasty
27.4 x 29.4 cm

▼ **Contents of the biographic packet for Tseng Kuo-fan**
Ch'ing Historiography Institute

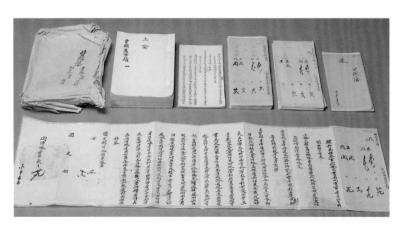

3. Mandates and Official Documents

The collection of mandates and other such imperial documents in the collection of the National Palace Museum includes proclamations issued by the Grand Secretariat, such as edicts, patents, and decrees. These are generally referred to as "imperial directives". So-called "mandates" were official documents promulgated when a major national event took place so that all the people of the country, from the highest officials down to the common folk, would know of it. Such events included the ascension to the throne of a new emperor, a major imperial marriage, the appointment of an imperial regent, the death of the emperor, inheritance of the throne, imperial removal, reform of the highest laws of the land, or a catastrophic event, and they would all be announced to the country in the name of the emperor. There are fifty mandates in the collection of the National Palace Museum, such as "Edict Proclaiming the Removal of Prince Regent Dorgon and his Mother from the Imperial Shrine", "Edict on the Ascension of the T'ung-chih Emperor", "Edict on the Regency of the T'ung-chih Emperor", and "Edict on the Peaceful Inheritance of the Great Tradition".

Decrees were written in a certain way and followed a set format. The text would start with the phrase, "The Emperor, who governs with the Mandate of Heaven, declares that..." and would end with one meaning, "Proclaimed to all under the Heavens, let it be known" or "Proclaimed to all the states, let it be known" (depending on the intended audience). The contents of the event would come in between these two phrases. After the full contents were finalized by the Grand Secretary, the mandate would be submitted to the emperor for final review. It would then be written in Manchu and Chinese on a large sheet of yellow imperial paper with Manchu on the left and Chinese on the right, proclaiming the contents of the event for all in the country. The final mandate was known as a "yellow mandate", and after the announcement ceremony, it would be sent to the Ministry of Rites to be copied or converted into a print edition, which would then be distributed throughout the land. Handwritten copies of mandates were known as "handwritten yellows", while those distributed as prints was known as "rubbing yellows". Most of the imperial mandates in the collection of the National Palace Museum belong to the handwritten type.

As for patents and decrees issued to officials, they were mostly used in ceremonies commemorating or bestowing noble rank on meritorious officials and their ancestors or descendants. Officials of the rank of five or above as well as those who could

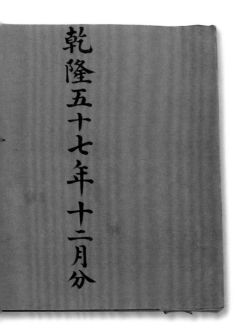

▼ **Edict on the peaceful inheritance of the Great Tradition of the throne**
Dated to the 5th day of the 12th lunar month of the 13th year of the T'ung-chih Emperor (1874), Ch'ing dynasty
79 x 226 cm

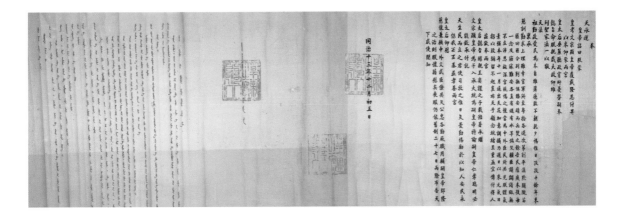

bequeath posthumous title to following generations would be issued a "patent" by the emperor. Those of the rank six or below were issued a "decree". Of the patents and decrees in the Museum collection, the ones bestowing inheritable title are the most representative. They are often quite large and long, leaving ample space for later descendants to fill in their names and the titles that they assumed. A fine example of this type of document is "Imperial Patent Bestowing Posthumous Title on Shen To", which was issued in 1744 but also includes additions dating up to 1888.

Other Ch'ing dynasty official documents include veritable records, sagacious instructions, notes of the imperial diary keeper, and annals of the dynasty that were ordered for compilation by the Historiography Institute by the emperor as well as the histories, treatises, tables, and biographies submitted for their composition. These materials include a vast collection of books both printed and handwritten, consisting of archived volumes that are extremely important for researchers on the political history of the Ch'ing dynasty. The veritable records throughout the reigns of the Ch'ing emperors in the National Palace Museum collection were made in three versions of Chinese, Manchu, and Mongolian, numbering more than 4,000 volumes. Sagacious instructions representing the writings of the emperor, dating from the first Manchu Ch'ing ruler Nurhaci up to the T'ung-chih Emperor, appear with Manchu and Chinese side by side in both handwritten and print editions. The notes of the imperial diarist refer to the compilations of sayings uttered by the emperor and recorded by the diary keeper that were compiled into archived volumes. The Ch'ing dynasty volumes of the imperial diarist in the Museum collection appear in both Manchu and Chinese, encompassing more than 7,700 volumes. Starting with the establishment of the Imperial Diary Office by the K'ang-hsi Emperor until the end of the dynasty, the work of the diarist continued unbroken and their contents were quite detailed. This information can be used to fill in lacunae found in other official documents and to provide a valuable and direct form of historical evidence for understanding the lives of the Ch'ing dynasty rulers as well as how they carried out politics of the court.

The archived volumes of the Historiography Institute in the collection of the National Palace Museum not only narrate the contents of aforementioned drafts of various historical materials, such as annals, treatises, tables, and biographies, but they also include many official imperial yellow versions submitted by the Institute starting from the rule of the Ch'ien-lung Emperor. The contents that they comprise are concise with the abstracted annals of the emperor's rule, clear categorization of historical treatises, complete overall chronology tables, and the biographies of figures of fame and ill-repute contained therein. All of these writings presented by the Historiography Institute are carefully edited and written in a strict and precise manner representing a systematic order that be regarded as a form of official document.

4. Local Records and Land Deeds

The collection of Ch'ing dynasty documents in the National Palace Museum derive mostly from the Ch'ing court, including a variety of documentary materials from the central and provincial government levels. As a result, documents of a local character, both

▼ **Certificate from She-hsien, Hui-chou Dated to the 5th year of the Hsien-feng reign (1855), Ch'ing dynasty**

▼ **Mortgage contract for Chan Te-mu, et al. Dated to the *keng-shen* year (1860) of the Hsien-feng reign, Ch'ing dynasty**

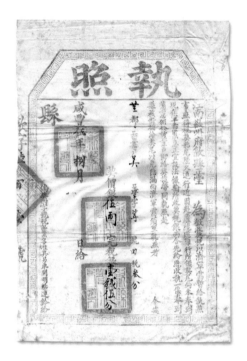

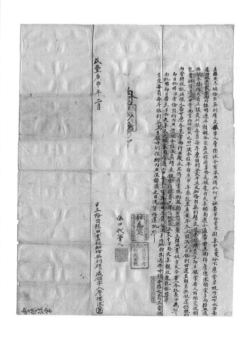

public and private in character, are quite limited in the Museum collection. Over the past few years, however, the National Palace Museum has begun focusing on strengthening its collection of local archives and documents. Through purchases by the Museum and donations from generous benefactors, the scope and range of the collection of Ch'ing dynasty documents has increased considerably.

In 2004, for example, the National Palace Museum made its first purchase of a group of Ch'ing dynasty archival documents from the collection of Mr. Liu Chin-i, including many documents related to the various prefectural, circuit, and county government offices that fall under the administration of the provincial governments. These include interdepartmental documents, submissions, petitions, letters, posted instructions, regulations, certificates, postal deliveries, receipts, shipping contracts, warrants, and household registrations. These materials assist in our understanding and learning about the various types of local documents that were used in the Ch'ing dynasty.

Furthermore, in 2005, Ms. Liu Chin-yi generously donated a batch of more than a hundred land deeds and documents pertaining to the Chan family of the Tung-shih area in Taichung County in central Taiwan. The dates of these documents extend from the Chia-ch'ing reign of the Ch'ing dynasty down to the early Showa era of the Japanese colonial period. The materials include originals for contracts dealing with the sale of houses and land, rentals of tilling fields, mortgages, subletting, entrustments, agreements, and receipts of loans. This group of contracts and documents are not only complete and orderly, they also reflect the commercial relations between clans in central Taiwan during the early period of its development. They also represent the traditional tenant relationships that existed in the past as well as the features of inheritance and property rights distribution among these clans, filling in the gaps found in the record of official documentation.

Official files from the Ch'ing dynasty can be called a treasure trove of information right under our noses and have been known to many a scholar in the field. The National Palace Museum will continue to strive and make this vast collection of materials open to the public for all to share and learn, not just restricted to scholars. By digitizing the materials and arranging exhibitions for people to come and view, this treasure of historical information can become even more renowned and appreciated. (Cheng Yung-ch'ang)

▼ **Sublet contract for cultivation by P'an Mao-ko**
Dated to the 21st year of the Tao-kuang reign (1841), Ch'ing dynasty

▶ **Household registration for Pao-chia, She-hsien**
Dated to the 26th year of the Kuang-hsü reign (1900), Ch'ing dynasty

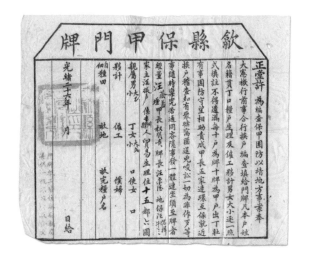

Books of Renown:
A Treasure Trove of Rare Books

The collection of rare books in the National Palace Museum numbers almost 200,000 volumes, making it one of the most important holdings of ancient publications in the Taiwan region. This collection of books ranges in date from the Northern Sung dynasty down to the late Ch'ing and includes volumes in the four traditional Chinese classifications of the Classics, histories, philosophy, and literary writings. These books come from a variety of sources, including the former collection of the Ch'ing court, the Kuan-hai Hall collection of books, and new purchases by the Museum as well as donations and entrustments by generous supporters. Among the most notable rare books in the collection are a set each of the *Abstracted Contents of the Complete Library of the Four Treasuries* from the Ch'ih-tsao Hall and the *Complete Library of the Four Treasuries* from the Wen-yüan Pavilion. These can be found only in the National Palace Museum, making them treasures unmatched anywhere else in the world. Also in the Museum collection are books from the *T'ien-lu lin-lang* and palace imprints of the Wu-ying Palace, as well as local gazetteers and Buddhist scriptures. These all form the precious contents of rare books in the Museum collection. As for the collection of books from the Kuan-hai Hall of Yang Shou-ching, most were purchased by him when he was in Japan during the Kuang-hsü era of the Ch'ing dynasty. Many are books that are extremely rare in China today, especially the more than four hundred rare books on traditional Chinese medicine, which are invaluable. As for purchases by the Museum and donations and entrustments, the greatest in terms of quantity and quality are represented by those that had been earlier entrusted from the National Peking Library. There are also more than 10,000 volumes of local gazetteers transferred to the National Palace Museum from the Ministry of Defense. Finally, generous donations of rare books by individuals have enriched the Museum collection, benefiting all of society.

The collection of rare books in the National Palace Museum is actually quite varied as well as immense. For those who wish to capture a glimpse of this collection, or do not know quite how to approach it, this introduction offers an opportunity to learn more about this invaluable assembly of knowledge and craft in the form of Chinese books. Here, they are arranged chronologically by dynasty, from the Sung down to the Yüan, Ming, and Ch'ing dynasties, presenting the beauty and importance of these rare texts along with their unique features. People can not only come away with an understanding of these

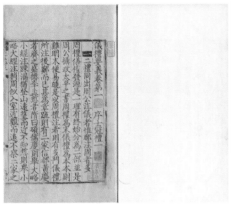

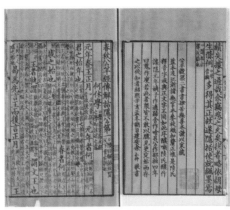

▲ **Principal Meaning to the Book of Etiquette and Ceremony**
Written by Wei Liao-weng, Sung Dynasty
1252 Sung imprint by Wei K'o-yü of Hui-chou as part of "Principal Meanings of the Nine Classics"

▶ **Kung-yang's Commentary on the Spring and Autumn Annals**
Written by Ho Hsiu, Han dynasty
1191 Sung imprint by Yü Jen-chung of Chien-an

▼ **Illustrated Text of the Hsüan-ho Emissary to Korea**
Written by Hsü Ching, Sung dynasty
1167 Sung imprint by Hsü Ch'an of the Chiang-yin District School

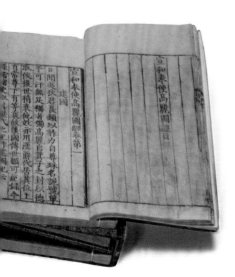

precious books, but also understand how to appreciate them, entering into a fascinating world of China's past with books. The collection of rare books in the National Palace Museum is actually quite varied as well as immense. For those who wish to capture a glimpse of this collection, or do not know quite how to approach it, this introduction offers an opportunity to learn more about this invaluable assembly of knowledge and craft in the form of Chinese books. Here, they are arranged chronologically by dynasty, from the Sung down to the Yüan, Ming, and Ch'ing dynasties, presenting the beauty and importance of these rare texts along with their unique features. People can not only come away with an understanding of these precious books, but also understand how to appreciate them, entering into a fascinating world of China's past with books.

Infatuation for Priceless Sung Editions

Among the immense holdings of books in the collection of the National Palace Museum, the fewest in number but greatest in value are the rare editions dating from the Sung dynasty. Not only are they the oldest books in the collection, but due to the extreme rarity of Sung editions, they are often found nowhere else in the world. The Sung editions in the Museum collection are nowadays considered as either national treasures or important cultural objects, thus reflecting their unusual rarity and preciousness.

The Museum collection of Sung editions numbers approximately two hundred books in a total of 2,452 volumes. These Sung editions were not only stored deep in the collection of the Ch'ing dynasty emperors, some of them also come from the Peking Library, the Kuan-hai Hall collection, as well as purchases and donations to the Museum. Many of them are also the sole surviving copies, such as the *Illustrated Text of the Hsüan-ho Emissary to Korea* now in the Museum collection that was originally carved and printed in 1167, during the Southern Sung. This copy has been passed down through the ages for more than eight hundred years, it also being precious for the fact that it is the earliest surviving record by a Chinese author on the customs and lifestyles in Korea. There is also *Principal Meaning to the Books of Etiquette and Ceremony* that was printed in 1252, later in the Southern Sung. More than twenty years after the book was published, the original woodblocks for the printing were destroyed, resulting in the present copy in the National

Palace Museum being the only surviving one in the world.

Sung dynasty editions have always been treasured by book collectors throughout the ages. Take, for example, *Kung-yang's Commentary on the Spring and Autumn Annals* that was printed in 1191 during the Southern Sung. It was published by the famous bookshop owner Yü Jen-chung, and the style of the characters were engraved with great precision and clarity, making it even more rare among the rarities. This rare book passed through the collections of such bibliophiles as Chi Chen-i, Chiang Tsung-hai, Huang P'i-lieh, Wang Shih-chung, and Ch'ü Yung during the Ch'ing dynasty, the end of the book also including a handwritten inscription by Huang P'i-lieh. In it, he wrote that the book was something he had to acquire at any cost, money being of no importance. In between these lines, he reveals the age-long passion for Sung dynasty books shared by many book collectors. There is also *Memorials by Officials of the Dynasty* that was printed in 1250 during the late Sung dynasty in Fuchow. Due to the age of the imprint, the characters are slightly worn, but nevertheless notable for the very dense feature of the printing. The numerous ownership and appreciation seals impressed on it testifies that this edition had passed through the hands of such noted book collectors of the Yüan and Ming dynasties as Chao Meng-fu, Ni Tsan, Yüan Chung-che, Lu Shui-ts'un, Chu Ta-ch'ung, Wen Cheng-ming, and Hsieh Chin, who cherished this book before it finally entered the Ch'ing court collection.

What was so valuable about Sung editions that led to such a craze among Ming and Ch'ing book collectors? First of all, Sung dynasty editions represent some of the oldest surviving books in China's history, being equal in value to an estate or comparable to the beauty of a beloved one. For example, there are stories in the Ming dynasty of how Wang Shih-chen parted with his manor and Chu Ta-shao with his cherished concubine in order to get their hands on Sung dynasty books. Even Huang P'i-lieh took the name "Master Flatterer of Sung [Editions]," showing just to what extent book collectors would go in their passion and frenzy for acquiring Sung dynasty books. Second, the paper and ink used in the printing of books in the Sung dynasty was usually of the highest quality, and the carving of the woodblocks was often quite meticulous as engravers frequently emulated the styles of such famous T'ang dynasty calligraphers as Ou-yang Hsün, Yang Chen-ch'ing, and Liu Kung-ch'uan. The characters are generally large and clear, their evenly and orderly arrangement enhancing the aesthetic quality and attracting the eyes of connoisseurs through the ages. For example, *New Revised Imprint of Tu Fu's Poetry with Annotations* was printed in 1225 and marked by its exceptionally high artistic quality. Finally, from an academic point of view, the level of editing among authors in the Sung dynasty tended to be quite strong, which is why they were so highly valued by Ch'ing textual historians. In fact, in the pursuit of historical evidence by scholars of textual criticism in the

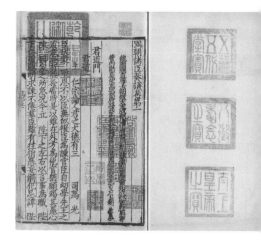

▲ **Memorials by Officials of the Dynasty**
Edited by Chao Ju-yü, Sung dynasty
1250 Sung imprint by the Fuchow Circuit Superintendent Shih Chi-wen

▶ **New Revised Imprint of Tu Fu's Poetry with Annotations**
Written by Tu Fu, T'ang dynasty
Annotations by Kuo Chih-ta, Sung dynasty
1225 Sung imprint by the Transport Commission of Kwangtung

▼ **Dynastic Regulations for Sagacious Rule of the Great Yüan**
Anonymous, Yüan dynasty
Yüan imprint

Ch'ien-lung and Chia-ch'ing reigns of the Ch'ing dynasty, many of them were also book collectors themselves. With the high level of editing and proofreading found among Sung editions, it is no wonder that they became the object of praise and admiration by Ch'ing dynasty bibliophiles.

Rare and Valuable Yüan Editions

The Yüan dynasty was relatively short, which is why the quantity of books printed during that era was less than that of the Sung. However, the books of this period are not only marked by their rarity and value, but also for the features that they reflect of the period in which they were made. The collection of Yüan dynasty books in the National Palace Museum collection numbers 304 for a total of 3,667 volumes. Compared to the number of Sung editions in the Museum collection, this is still quite considerable, and many of these Yüan editions are also very rare or sole surviving copies themselves, making them even more important to scholars. Among the books are *Dynastic Regulations for Sagacious Rule of the Great Yüan*, which was printed in 1320. Even as early as the Wan-li era in the Ming dynasty, this book had survived only in fragments. Although there have been later reprintings, they are filled with many errors that make them all but unusable from a scholarly point of view. Not only does this partial copy in the Museum collection come from the original printing, it is also the sole surviving one in the world, thereby making it exceptionally valuable in academia for proofreading later editions. The book also bears the marks of the Ming dynasty book collector Mao Chin, indicating that it was once part of his renowned Chi-ku ("Drawing from Antiquity") Pavilion. The quality and importance of this book thus goes without saying.

Generally speaking, printings were done in the Yüan dynasty around the capital of Ta-tu as well as P'ing-shui, Hangchow, and Chien-yang. The Supply and Printing Office of the Yüan government was established in the capital, and among the imprints made in Ta-tu, many were government ones, such as the edition of *The Comprehensive Mirror for Aid in Government* that was printed by the Supply and Printing Office that is now in the Museum collection. P'ing-shui (modern P'ing-yang County, Shansi Province) was the center of printing in the previous Chin dynasty, and this trend continued into the Yüan dynasty. The rare surviving books printed at the time are marked by their exceptional quality, such as the compilation of Taoist scriptures in the Museum collection entitled *Seven Slips from the Satchel of the Clouds* that was printed in 1244 by the Mongol empress Naimajin Töregene. Although only three volumes of this imprint made in the P'ing-shui region now survive in the Museum collection, its rarity speaks for itself in terms of preciousness. Since most surviving editions of *Seven Slips from the Satchel of the Clouds* are Ming and Ch'ing dynasty imprints or transcriptions, this Yüan dynasty version is even more important. This edition in the Museum collection thus provides crucial information for research among scholars of textual criticism who wish to compare later versions with this one.

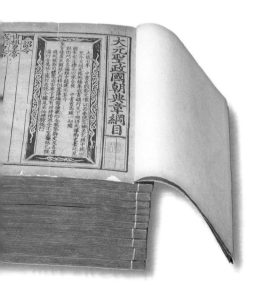

In addition, the Museum's collection of Yüan dynasty editions also includes numerous bookshop imprints. These private printings comprise editions from famous bookshops of the Chien-an region, such as the Wu-pen Hall of the Yü clan, the Ts'ui-yen Studio of the Liu clan, the Kuang-ch'in Hall of the Liu clan, the Tsung-wen Hall of the Liu family, the Jih-hsin Hall of the Liu clan, and the Ch'in-yu Hall of the Yü family. These imprints from renowned bookshops are mostly printed in the elegantly rounded manner of characters associated with the Chao (Meng-fu) style of calligraphy. Although the engraving of characters is not as refined, it has an enchantingly simple and archaic quality.

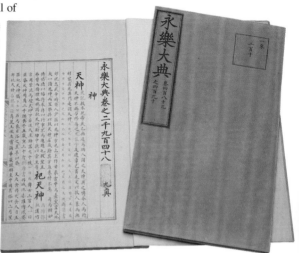

Handcrafted and Printed Ming Editions

The collection of Ming dynasty books in the National Palace Museum is exceptionally rich as well and also marked by its high quality. Among the more famous handwritten Ming dynasty editions is the re-transcription by the Ming inner court of the *Vast Documents of the Yung-lo Era* dating from the Chia-ching and Lung-ch'ing reigns. *Vast Documents of the Yung-lo Era* is a large-scale collectanea that was compiled on the order of Emperor Ch'eng-tsu (also known as the Yung-lo Emperor). It was completed in the sixth year of the Yung-lo reign (1408) and comprised 11,095 volumes, representing the culmination of the search for and transcription of up to seven or eight thousand texts and documents dating from the previous Sung and Yüan dynasties. In the Ming dynasty, during the reign of the Chia-ching Emperor, it was almost destroyed in a fire. The emperor, fearing that it would be lost in a future incident, ordered that a handwritten copy be made, and it was finally finished in 1567. The transcribed copy made during the Yung-lo era (the original) was kept at the Wen-yüan Pavilion. Unfortunately, in the last years of the Ming, the Wen-yüan Pavilion caught fire and the original was completely consumed in the flames. As for the copy made during the Chia-ching and Lung-ch'ing reigns that was stored at the Imperial Histories Institute, it survived into the following Ch'ing dynasty, but large portions were either destroyed or scattered during the Anglo-French Allied Invasion of the mid-nineteenth century and the invasion of the Eight-Power Alliance in 1900. This resulted in the survival of only 300 volumes, which were scattered in both domestic and foreign collections as well as private hands. Of the very few volumes of the *Vast Documents of the Yung-lo Era* that survive, the National Palace Museum has 62 of them in its collection, making it the largest such holdings of this important text in the Taiwan region. Despite the losses that occurred in the past, we are fortunate to have these few precious volumes for study and appreciation.

The books printed by the government in the Ming dynasty are comprised mostly of those from the Directorate of Ceremonial and very high in quality. For instance, the Imperial Household imprint of *On the Five Relationships* that was printed in 1448 is quite large in size and also spacious in arrangement,

◀ **Vast Documents of the Yung-lo Era**
Written on imperial order by Hsieh Chin, Ming dynasty
Re-transcribed Ming court copy of the Chia-ching (1522-1566) to Lung-ch'ing (1567-1572) reigns

▲ **Chang Shen-chih's Revised Edition of the Romance of the Western Chamber with Northern Melodies**
Written by Wang Shih-fu with additions by Kuan Han-ch'ing, Yüan dynasty
Illustrated by Ch'en Hung-shou and engraved by Hsiang Nan-chou, Ming dynasty
Late Ming imprint

▼ **On the Five Relationships**
Written by Emperor Hsüan-tsung, Ming dynasty
1448 Ming Imperial Household imprint

featuring high quality paper and ink as well as refined binding. As such, it fully reflects the attention of the imperial family devoted to the art of printing and binding of books as found in inner court imprints. This edition features sixty-two books that describe the ideal relationships in society in descending order as that of ruler and officials, father and son, husband and wife, elder and younger brothers, and among friends. In addition to serving as a textbook for the Directorate of Education, it was also promulgated throughout the land in the court's hope of promoting social harmony.

The features of books privately printed in the Ming dynasty mainly reflect the trend of using illustrations that had become popular at the time. In the middle and late Ming, the woodblock printing industry reached new heights as literary works also greatly increased in number, thereby spurring the development of books dealing with drama and novels that came into such great demand then. With increasing competition and pressure to produce ever more innovative and appealing books, the key to attracting new audiences gradually rested on the inclusion of illustrations. In order to increase profits and get the upper hand, bookshops and publishers competed with each other in paying for the best painters, illustrators, and engravers that they could find, in the hopes of creating publications that would appeal to audiences at the time. This trend continued until the late Ming as the illustrations in books became increasingly refined and the techniques of engraving ever more detailed. This marked one of the greatest features of private Ming dynasty imprints and brought the art of illustrated book production into a golden era. The National Palace Museum collection includes many finely illustrated woodblock printed books, most of which had been formerly in the collection of the Peking Library. Take, for example, *Chang Shen-chih's Revised Edition of the Romance of the Western Chamber with Northern Melodies* that had been printed in the late Ming. It features illustrations originally painted by the famous late Ming artist Ch'en Hung-shou and carvings by the renowned engraver Hsiang Nan-chou, serving as one of the most refined editions produced of *Romance of the Western Chamber*, a classic Chinese novel.

The realm of illustrated books in the Ming dynasty included not just dramas and novels, but also other genre of publications as well. There is, for example, *Ch'eng's Garden of Inkcakes* that was published by the Tzu-lan Hall in the Wan-li era of the Ming dynasty. This book was published as a catalogue to promote the inkcakes produced by the artisan Ch'eng Chün-fang. The illustrations cover a wide range of inkcake designs also accompanied by supplementary text, and the famous artist Ting Yün-p'eng had been commissioned to do the paintings. This type of arrangement in which prints are done based on illustrations by a renowned artist not only raised the level of direct participation by both the artist and engraver, it also continued into the following Ch'ing dynasty, becoming an established mode in the production of books in the private sector.

Exquisite Printing of Ch'ing Editions

The rare books in the National Palace Museum come mostly from the former collection of the Ch'ing dynasty court, which is why many of them are Ch'ing editions. Though perhaps not as old, many of these Ch'ing books are rare and beautifully bound editions. Of particular note and importance among the Ch'ing dynasty books in the Museum collection are the two series entitled *Complete Library of the Four Treasuries* from the Wen-yüan Pavilion and the *Abstracted Contents of the Complete Library of the Four Treasuries* from the Ch'ih-tsao Hall. In 1773, the 37th year of the Ch'ien-lung Emperor's reign, the emperor ordered the compilation of the *Complete Library of the Four Treasuries*. Not until nine years later was the first copy produced, comprising more than 3,400 books bound in more than 360,000 volumes. In all, seven copies were transcribed, and the project was finally completed in 1787. The copies of *Complete Library of the Four Treasuries* that were stored in the Wen-yüan, Wen-chin, and Wen-su Pavilions were the most complete, while that from the Wen-lan Pavilion was incomplete. Of these surviving copies, that of the Wen-yüan Pavilion now in the Museum collection is the most complete and also the most refined. As for *Abstracted Contents of the Complete Library of the Four Treasuries*, this series, as the title indicates,

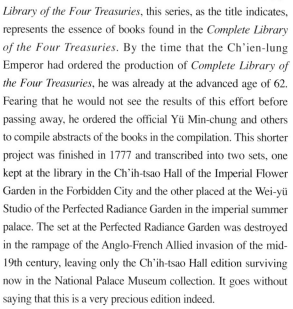

represents the essence of books found in the *Complete Library of the Four Treasuries*. By the time that the Ch'ien-lung Emperor had ordered the production of *Complete Library of the Four Treasuries*, he was already at the advanced age of 62. Fearing that he would not see the results of this effort before passing away, he ordered the official Yü Min-chung and others to compile abstracts of the books in the compilation. This shorter project was finished in 1777 and transcribed into two sets, one kept at the library in the Ch'ih-tsao Hall of the Imperial Flower Garden in the Forbidden City and the other placed at the Wei-yü Studio of the Perfected Radiance Garden in the imperial summer palace. The set at the Perfected Radiance Garden was destroyed in the rampage of the Anglo-French Allied invasion of the mid-19th century, leaving only the Ch'ih-tsao Hall edition surviving now in the National Palace Museum collection. It goes without saying that this is a very precious edition indeed.

In any discussion of the quality of books produced during the Ch'ing dynasty, one cannot overlook those made by the Ch'ing court. These so-called "palace imprints" refer to books that were made by the Wu-ying Palace at court, including those produced with woodblock as well as movable type printing techniques. The Wu-ying Palace had been established in 1680 under the K'ang-hsi Emperor and served as the office for the most important printings of the court, being the representative

▲ **Abstracted Contents of the Complete Library of the Four Treasuries**
Transcription of the Ch'ien-lung reign, Ch'ing dynasty

▶ **Imperially Approved Complete Library of the Four Treasuries**
Ordered by the Ch'ien-lung Emperor, Ch'ing dynasty
Wen-yüan Pavilion handwritten copy of the Ch'ien-lung era, Ch'ing dynasty

▶ **Completed Collection of Graphs and Writings of Ancient and Modern Times**
1726 Wu-ying Palace movable bronze type imprint, Ch'ing Dynasty

government printing office of the time. The imprints produced in the K'ang-hsi era at the Wu-ying Palace are marked by fine printing on *k'ai-hua* and *pang* paper. Exceptionally pleasing to the eye, these high quality imprints have been treasured by book collectors. Among them is *Completed Collection of Graphs and Writings of Ancient and Modern Times* produced under Ch'en Meng-lei from 1706 to 1716. After the K'ang-hsi Emperor personally reviewed the draft, he ordered that the Wu-ying Palace print it using movable bronze type. This edition was begun in 1720 and completed in 1726, under the following Yung-cheng Emperor, representing the most famous set done in movable bronze type by the Wu-ying Palace.

In fact, of the Wu-ying Palace imprints preserved in the National Palace Museum collection, many are exceptionally fine examples of the art of book production. Most carry prefixes to their titles of imperial authority and backing, such as "Imperially Produced", "Imperially Selected", "Imperially Annotated", "Imperially Commented", and "Imperially Endorsed", demonstrating without doubt the mark of court approval. Many of these books are of even greater value for the fact that they were actually approved, reviewed, or personally written by the emperor himself. Examples include *Imperially Produced Poems on Agriculture and Sericulture with Illustrations* printed in 1696, *Imperially Approved Complete Poetry of the T'ang* from 1707, *Imperially Approved K'ang-hsi Dictionary* completed in 1716, *Imperially Approved Compilation of Legends in the Book of History* from 1730, and *Illustrated Edition of the Book of Odes* handwritten by the Ch'ien-lung Emperor himself. Among the most highly prized in this type of book are *Imperially Produced Poems on Agriculture and Sericulture with Illustrations* and *Illustrated Edition of the Book of Odes*. Of particular note is the fact that *Imperially Produced Poems on Agriculture and Sericulture with Illustrations* is adorned with the calligraphed poetry of the K'ang-hsi Emperor. The court painter Chiao Ping-chen then did the illustrations, which were engraved by the Soochow master Chu Kuei. *Illustrated Edition of the Book of Odes* represents a personal transcription by the Ch'ien-lung Emperor himself, which was then sent to the Painting Academy for illustration. Both of these editions are marked by their large format and refined, classical manner of illustration and engraving. Not only do they reflect the lofty status of the imperial hand behind their production, they also represent the pursuit of perfection in the art of book production by the court. (Hsü Yüan-t'ing)

Gems of Religion: Buddhist Scriptures, Pattra Leaf Sutras, and the *Qu'ran*

Buddhist Scriptures

Buddhism was introduced to China in the Han dynasty, and Chinese translations of Buddhist classics explaining the doctrines of Buddhism gradually circulated among the populace. These books also became part of the tradition of books in China, treasured by many people. However, for Buddhists, they were also a source of religious devotion and piety. Buddhist classical texts, known as sutras in the Indian Sanskrit language, became referred to in China as "Treasures of the Buddhist Law", and they were one of the three "treasures" of Buddhism that devotees revered and supported. Some Buddhist texts also recorded that the transcription, printing, and support for the production of sutras could help the individual acquire considerable merit. This was widely publicized by monks, and their influence reached far and wide. Buddhist texts were not ordinary books, but sacred objects possessing great powers. As a result, the production of Buddhist sutras over the ages, involving the writing of the text and the carving, printing, and binding of the books, was different from those of other books, in both materials chosen and craftsmanship. The devotion to the production was meant to convey the respect and reverence for Buddhist beliefs. Among the books in the National Palace Museum collection, Buddhist texts in terms of production and selection of materials, the bindings and mountings used to protect them, and the casings used to store them, all involve the utmost refinement of quality and presentation as testimony to the devotion of those involved in their production.

The National Palace Museum collection of Buddhist classics is quite extensive. Composed mainly of texts written in Chinese, they come in a variety of editions that can be divided into handwritten manuscripts, woodblock prints, tapestry editions, and embroidered versions. Among the manuscript versions, transcriptions of *The Diamond Sutra* are undoubtedly the most numerous. The full name of *The Diamond Sutra* in Sanskrit is *Vajracchedika Prajnaparamita Sutra* (*The Diamond*

Perfection of Wisdom) and has long been known to people of all walks of life throughout China. It still remains as one of the most widely read of the Buddhist scriptures, with its teaching so sharp and to the point as to "cut like a diamond", presenting all with a guide to eradicating the notion of self and attachment on the path to achieving enlightenment into the universal Buddha nature. There are altogether six editions of the Chinese translation, the most common being the one translated by Kumarajiva.

Of the handwritten transcriptions of *The Diamond Sutra* in the National Palace Museum collection, two are masterpieces meticulously done by famous calligraphers of the past. The earlier one is by Chang Chi-chih (1186-1266), one of the most important and representative calligraphers of the Southern Sung period. His transcription of *The Diamond Sutra* in his incomparable brushwork is a treasure of calligraphy in its own right. This album was once in the possession of the Ming dynasty collector Hsiang Tu-shou, and it later entered the Ch'ing dynasty court collection, being stored at the Ning-shou Palace. Both before and after the calligraphy are impressions of ten collection seals of the Ch'ien-lung Emperor, such as "Treasure of the Ning-shou Palace" and "The Son of Heaven at Seventy Years of Age at the Hall of Five Fortunes and Five Generations". These seals show just how much the emperor treasured this sutra edition.

The other calligraphed edition of *The Diamond Sutra* is by the renowned scholar-artist Tung Ch'i-ch'ang (1555-1636) of the Ming dynasty. The frontispiece and endpiece of this handscroll version of the sutra includes illustrations in gold ink on *tz'u-ch'ing* paper of the Buddha preaching the Law and the protective deities. The actual text itself was done in small regular script on sutra paper, the characters being very refined, dense, and powerful in structure. The spacing between the characters and lines is relatively expansive, forming a spacious arrangement that creates an incomparable beauty in the contrast between the dense brushwork of the characters and the spacious blank space of the paper. The gradations of the tones and warmth of the ink has a simple yet spacious manner that suggests the meaningful and eternal qualities of this Buddhist classic.

▲ **The Diamond Sutra**
First translated into Chinese by Kumarajiva (344-415), Later Ch'in dynasty
Handwritten edition by Tung Ch'i-ch'ang (1555-1636), Ming dynasty

◀ **The Diamond Sutra**
First translated into Chinese by Kumarajiva (344-415), Later Ch'in dynasty
Handwritten edition by Chang Chi-chih (1186-1266), dated 1253, Sung dynasty

In addition to sutras in Chinese, the National Palace Museum also has a variety of sutra texts written and printed in minority languages. Among the two most precious ones are *The Dragon Tripitaka* and *The Complete Tripitaka in Ch'ing*. The full title of *The Dragon Tripitaka* translated from Tibetan is *The Dragon Tripitaka in Tibetan Inlaid with Gems on Blue Paper in Gold Ink Respectfully Ordered for Repair by the Supreme Empress*. The Supreme Empress here refers to the grandmother of the K'ang-hsi Emperor, nee Borjijite, who was a devoted follower of Buddhism. According to the "Imperial Preface" in Manchu and Tibetan in the first volume by the K'ang-hsi Emperor, which perfectly matches the rest of the *Tripitaka*, she made her rounds in the palaces and storerooms one day in 1669 and discovered part of the "Kanjur" in Tibetan written in the Ming dynasty. Damaged over the years, she instructed the K'ang-hsi Emperor to have it imitated by hand, hence the origin of the repair and reconstruction of this Tripitaka.

The binding of *The Dragon Tripitaka* is in the "Indian pleated-leaf binding" format, the entire set stored in 108 boxes. Each box has upper and lower red lacquered protective planks decorated with gold pigment. The surface of the planks is engraved with the six-character Sanskrit incantation of "om ma ni pad me hum". Inside the protective sutra plank is a blue sutra board, the cover of the upper sutra board written and painted in gold pigment with the Buddhist phrase and illustration of Tibetan Buddhist auspiciousness reading "rnam bcu...dbang ldan". The bottom includes five layers of sutra blinds in yellow, red, green, blue, and white, which are each embroidered in color with Tibetan letters and patterns of the Eight Treasures. The reverent inscription of "prostrating before the Three Gems of the Buddha, Dharma, Sangha" on the lower sutra blind is flanked on either side by a painting of a bodhisattva. The borders are rimmed with dozens of semi-precious materials, such as inlaid pearls and pieces of coral and agate. The lower sutra plank

◄ **Protective sutra board of** *The Dragon Tripitaka* **in Tibetan**

◄ **Upper sutra board of** *The Dragon Tripitaka* **in Tibetan**

▲ **Various parts of The Dragon Tripitaka in Tibetan**
1. **Red-lacquered protective board**
2. **Sutra leaf**
3. **Sutra binding cord**
4. **Yellow silk wrapper**

is generally like the upper one, but the cover is painted and inscribed with three sets of "intersecting *vajra*" patterns, the lower cover sutra blind changed to a painting of five deities protecting the Buddhist law. Between the upper and lower sutra boards are the actual sutra leaves with transcribed texts. The protective and sutra boards were all designed to protect these sutra leaves, which are dark blue and 87.5 centimeters wide by 33 centimeters tall. The texts were written in the regular script of Tibetan known as "Dbu can", transcribed horizontally and read from left to right, one side containing eight lines. The writing is elegant yet powerful, and the gold pigment against the blue background greatly increases the eye-dazzling opulence. Each box has more than 300 to more than 500 leaves. The sutra leaves are orderly and neat, their borders painted with patterns of the Eight Treasures in gold pigment for reverence and protection. Finally, the outside of the sutra leaf protective board was bound in sutra string and then wrapped in yellow silk to form the contents of a single box.

The contents of this *Tripitaka* are the "Kanjur ('bkav vgyur')" in *The Tripitaka in Tibetan*, which means "translated version of the Buddha's religious decrees". This corresponds to the collection of sutras and regulations in *The Tripitaka in Chinese*. The entire *Tripitaka* is divided into six major sections based on the different contents of the texts: the exoteric (*rgyud*), prajna (*shes phyin*), treasures (*dkon brtsegs*), Hua-yen (*phal chen*), sutras (*mdo sna tshogs*), and regulations (*vdul ba*) sections, encompassing more than a thousand texts.

The full name of *The Complete Tripitaka in Ch'ing* is *Imperial Production in the Ch'ing Language of the Translation of the Complete Tripitaka (Manju hergen i ubaliyabuha amba*

in Manchu. The "Ch'ing language" here therefore refers to Manchu. After the Manchu people established the Ch'ing dynasty in China, they took the form of writing known as "Manchu" belonging to their group and established it as the official written language of the land, becoming known as "Ch'ing language" or "Ch'ing writing". In China, the gathering of all books on Buddhism is known traditionally as a "Great Sutra Collection" or "Tripitaka", also going by the names "All Sutras", "Collected Sutras", and "Great Collection". However, there is no name known as the "Complete Tripitaka", which must have been a creation of the Ch'ien-lung Emperor. He believed that the Tripitaka originally included only a collection of translations in Tibetan, Chinese, and Mongolian. With the translations now also finished in Manchu, it was deemed as the "Complete Tripitaka in Four Languages", hence known as the "Complete Tripitaka". Consequently, *The Imperial Production in the Ch'ing Language of the Translation of the Complete Tripitaka* refers to the emperor's order to use the Manchu translation of the compendium of Buddhist sutras and texts.

Two reasons lie behind the value of these two *Tripitakas.* On one hand, they are valuable as cultural objects, both being the only surviving copies domestically. The precision of the woodblocks to the opulence of the binding and beautiful production all represent a pinnacle in printing and book production in the Ch'ing dynasty. On the other hand, they are also of great documentary value. *The Dragon Tripitaka* can be used to proofread other versions of *The Tripitaka in Tibetan,* and the Buddhist terminology in *The Complete Tripitaka in Ch'ing* can be used to fill gaps in Manchu over the ages. (Hu Chin-ts'ai)

▲ **Sutra leaf from** *The Complete Tripitaka in Ch'ing*
Printed in red ink, the frame is composed of a single line around the text. To the left is Manchu text and to the right is Chinese.

▲ **Lower sutra board of** *The Complete Tripitaka in Ch'ing*
The four female protective deities of the Buddhist faith, here from left to right, are "dung ma", "dpal bevu ma", rgyal mtshan ma", and "vkhol lo ma".

▼ **Vinayana of the Tripitaka (Khandaka, abridged version)**
Handwritten in 1926
Pattra leaf sutra, 57 x 6.5 cm

Donated in 2005 to the National Palace Museum by Mr. Lu Chung-hsing, collector of pattra leaf sutras.

Pattra Leaf Sutras

"Pattra leaf sutras", a format of Buddhist scripture and a type of writing with origins more than two thousand years ago in India, was spread to South and Southeast Asia as well as Yünnan in China. This vibrant form of sutra with distinct regional characteristics is regarded nowadays by nearly every major Western museum and library as one of the representative texts of Asia. The triple layer "pattra leaf sutras" in the collection of the National Palace Museum in the Burmese language of Pali include several volumes of the Manimanjusa, Vinayapitaka (Khandaka, Culavagga), and the Ganthabharana in Pali grammar. The dates of the carving and transcription of the former are unknown, that of the Vinayapitaka is from 1926, and the latter is from 1873. The pattra leaves are complete and in fine condition, and this state of preservation offers a general understanding of the type of decoration and binding that was used in these sutras.

Of the three texts mentioned above, the contents of the Manimanjusa (also known as the Abhidamma) represent one of the three discourses of Buddhist scriptures found in the Tripitaka compilation, dealing with the rites and ceremonies of the religion. The Vinayapitaka is recorded in the Pali language and includes the upper transmission of the rules section of the Tripitaka from Sri Lanka (also known as the *Gilded Vinayana* and *Vinayana of the Southern Transmission*). The Vinayana represents a collection of proscriptions and conditions that Buddhist monks and nuns were intended to follow. This version in the Museum collection in Pali belongs to the "abridged version" of the "Khandaka". The external appearance of these two scriptures have their own unique characteristics. The protective sutra boards of the Manimanjusa volumes are made of teak wood and are simple and unadorned, the two ends of

the long leaves being adorned with cinnabar in the middle and the rest being decorated with gold foil. The protective boards and leaves of the Vinayana Buddhist scripture are all decorated with gold lacquer.

The Holy *Qu'ran*

Two new additions to the National Palace Museum collection are sixteenth-century versions of the *Qu'ran* (also romanized as *Koran*), the central religious text of Islam. One volume is from Iran and the other is an annotated version from Bihar in India. These fully reflect the basic religion belief system of the *Qu'ran* and represent the artistic style of books produced in these regions at the time. Their art of calligraphy, ornamentation, and mounting are all fastidious, each representing the extraordinary art of the book in Islamic culture and the devotion of Muslims.

The Art and Splendor of Iranian Books

During the fifteenth and sixteenth centuries, the military, economic, and political power of the Islamic world was at its peak. Those involved in the art of producing books, such as calligraphers and decorators, received the full support and patronage of rulers, each vying to produce opulent versions of the *Qu'ran* to present to each other as gifts. The Iranian version of the *Qu'ran* in the collection of the National Palace Museum, judging from its inscription, was produced in the Savafid Empire (1502-1736) in Iran for the Turkish ruling family of the Ottoman Empire (1299-1923). The Damascus chief Hüseyin Pasha was the patron behind its production, representing the peak of development in the art of the *Qu'ran* at this time.

The more than three hundred pages of this version of the *Qu'ran* are all handwritten and calligraphed in the delicate and flowing Arabic Naskh style, and segments of the text are also accompanied by notes and pronunciation guides written in red and black ink. One of the most eye-catching features of this text is the incredibly beautiful binding and ornamentation, its format both large and splendid. The binding format of the book preserves the original appearance of Iranian production at the time, while the cover of the book was done in leather that was inlaid with delicate filaments of gold and silver appearing among the red, blue, and green colors for an opulent

▲ Iranian *Qu'ran*
Handwritten paper edition, ca. 1560
40.7 x 26.6 cm

This format of binding preserves the original appearance of production in Iran at the time, the opening of the book being one of its characteristics. At the same time, this book also has an opulent manner of decoration that reflects the features typical of the Safavid Shiraz style in Iran. The two symmetrical six-petal large floral patterns of the opening pages as well as the medallions in the frames complement the colorful decorative arrangement of the framing and marking of the text within.

Religious Texts | 153

▼ **Indian *Qu'ran* with grammatical explications**
Handwritten paper edition, ca. 1500
30 x 21.5 cm

The use of Bihari script in calligraphing the *Qu'ran* was short-lived. In 1398, after Timur (1336-1405) conquered northern India, it was used until the early sixteenth century in the Muslim territory of northern India to transcribe the *Qu'ran*. As a result, in the West it is known as the Bihari *Qu'ran*. This style features more vertical and elongated strokes along the lower level of the characters.

and dazzling effect. Appearing mainly in gold and blue, the arabesque vines and the symmetrical balance of the decoration are beautifully revealed here. The main decorative spaces of the entire book take the form of opulent floral scroll patterning as well as a cloud pattern originally from China that fills the background. The fullness of the gold and blue represents the majesty of the ruling family, and the floral scrolls and gold background among the rolling clouds on some of the pages of this holy text fully reflect the great attention paid to the production of the *Qu'ran* at this time as well as the maturity of the arts and crafts involved.

The Pure and Beautiful Styles of Indian Books

The Indian version of the *Qu'ran* with grammatical explications in the Museum collection is composed of more than 660 pages and is a work of the early Mughal dynasty (1526-1857). Due to the climatic and political circumstances of the area in which it was made, very few complete handwritten versions have been preserved, making this large-scale version of the *Qu'ran* even more rare among the surviving editions around the world today.

This version of the *Qu'ran* was written in the calligraphic script known as Bihari, which was an offshoot of the Arabic Naskh style. Gold, black, and blue ink intersperse among the lines of the handwritten text, forming a unique and innovative manner of writing. Outside of the Naskh calligraphy in the frame are explications of the grammar, this part of the writing being done in zigzagging angular rows along the edge of the pages, presenting a unique manner that is both functional and decorative. In addition, the ornamentation of the book is quite appealing, the text beginning on the left-hand page and the header being done in ornate and delicate multilayered colored frames. Each chapter is titled in a framework of gold, orange, and blue, a medallion decorating the outside of the frame. This is then complemented by pointed extensions from the page of winding and floral forms. The poetic lines are marked with floral gold decoration with red and blue dots for the petals of the flowers. This book reflects the unique coloring and decoration of Indian books, leaving its impression on Islamic culture in northern Indian as well as the eyes of viewers today. (Yeh Shu-hui)

A Microcosmic World: Ancient Maps of the Ming and Ch'ing Dynasties

Ancient maps generally refer to maps that were made in the days before modern precision instruments were used to survey the geographical features of the Earth, thereby resulting in the great differences in terms of proportion, bearing, and geometry when compared to those found in modern maps. Long before the invention of writing systems, prehistoric peoples of China used simple lines and symbols to express information about the features of the land and their surroundings, creating primitive "maps" in the process. With advances in civilization, the techniques of producing maps has become increasingly sophisticated and their contents all the more encompassing. The variety of maps also multiplied, so that by the Ming and Ch'ing dynasties, there were not only general maps, but many different specialized maps produced in quantity and quality as well. In the history of Chinese cartography (mapmaking), these documents underwent unique and major developments. Most importantly, however, is the fact that many of them have fortunately survived to the present day, offering us a glimpse at the legacy and knowledge of cartography in the past.

The collection of maps in the National Palace Museum is divided into three major categories based on their point of origin: the former collection of the National Peking Library (NPL for short), attachments to copies of archived memorials at the Council of State of the former Ch'ing dynasty, and illustrations found in rare books.

The maps from the former NPL collection total 273 with more than 800 individual pieces. Most of them are Ming and Ch'ing dynasty maps selected from the red editions in the storage of the Grand Secretariat from the Ch'ing dynasty court, and a small portion represent later purchases. Many are officially drawn maps or those presented as tribute. As a result, they are of exceptional quality. They include printed and painted versions as well as those on paper and silk, and they also come in many sizes with contents that are even more varied. In

▼ **Maps of Taiwan with the Pescadores Archipelago (detail)**
Made from 1723 to 1727, Ch'ing dynasty
Handscroll, ink and colors on paper, 62.5 x 663.5 cm (+93 cm)

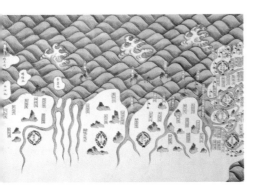

addition to overall administrative maps (general maps), there are also specialized maps of coastal regions, border defenses, waterways, river construction projects, cities, palaces, roads and neighborhoods, and postal stations.

Administrative maps generally outline the position of rivers and mountains in relation to administrative localities, including those on both a national and a local level. Of the former, the most representative national map is the "Imperial Map of the Ch'ien-lung Reign" (which was completed in 1748), while those of the latter include mostly provincial maps covering Chinese territory other than that of Tibet and Sinkiang.

As for coastal maps, there are two kinds. One is devoted to coastal defenses, while the other defines the features of the coastline. The former depicts the location and facilities of defenses maintained by those units entrusted with naval protection. For example, there is a Ming dynasty "Map of Four Fortifications of the Sea at Ning Seen from Mt. Chin" painted on paper and the "Map of the Sea" painted in the Ming dynasty, also on paper. The latter type of map describes the features of the land, paying close attention to the various islets, islands, sand banks, submerged reefs, and bays along the coast. Of these, two of the most notable are "Complete Map of All Provincial Coastal Passages" painted by Ch'en Mei in colors during the Tao-kuang reign (1821-1850) during the Ch'ing dynasty and "Complete Map of the Coast" painted on paper in the Ch'ing dynasty.

Maps of border defenses generally refer to the more vulnerable northern territories, paying particular attention to the illustration of such military facilities as beacons and fortresses along the Great Wall. These mainly depict the nine defense borders along the north and northwest, and many of them were either painted or printed in the latter half of the Ming dynasty or the early Ch'ing. Of the more important ones are the woodblock printed editions in ink of the "Nine Borders Map", "Map of the Four Fortifications of Shensi", "Sketch Map of Fortifications and Battle Defenses in Shensi", "Sketch Map of Fortifications and Battle Defenses in Kansu", and "Sketch Map of Fortifications and Battle Defenses of Ninghsia" that were done in the late Ming period, between 1597 and 1643.

Many of the maps on waterways deal with the Yellow River, followed by the Huai River and the Yangtze River. Among the more notable of such maps in the Museum collection is "Map of the Yellow River" painted on a handscroll of silk, the beginning of which shows the Yellow River emptying into the sea and the end revealing its source at Dragon Gate (Lung-men)

▲ **Map of the Sea (detail)**
Made between 1562 and the end of the Ming (1644), Ming dynasty
Handscroll, ink and colors on paper,
30.5 x 2081 cm

▼ **Map of the Canal between the Capital and Hangchow (detail)**
Made between 1698 and 1723, Ch'ing dynasty
Handscroll, ink and colors on paper,
78.6 x 2050 cm

▶ **Sketch Map of Fortifications and Battle Defenses in Kansu**
Made 1544 to 1545, Ming dynasty
Album leaf, ink and colors on paper,
each leaf 90 x 52 cm

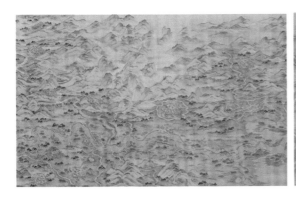

in Shansi. The map covers the entire length of the Yellow River, including related waterways, mountain ranges, fountainheads, lakes, dams, river dikes, and the prefectures and localities through which it runs, as well as historic and scenic sites. Another map is "Geographic Map of the Yangtze River", painted in the Ch'ing dynasty on silk. With south at the top and north at the bottom, it portrays the military facilities along the lower reaches of the Yangtze River in the area between Chiu-chiang and Chen-chiang. Shown on the river are blockade river cables, blockade bamboo rafts, and battle ships, along with smoke beacons, wooden buildings, cannon sites, and high-tide camps indicated. There are also markings for the distances between high and low tide.

The Ch'ing court also paid considerable attention to the maintenance of the Grand Canal and the Yellow River. All major projects involving these waterways were the responsibility of certain officials, who had to prepare maps in reporting to their superiors, thereby accounting for the large number of construction maps for waterways. Such maps as "Construction Map of the Yellow River from its Source through Each Area to Honan Province", "Condition Map for Construction on the Yellow River in Each Locality Through Which It Passes in Kiangnan", and "Map of the Yellow River from Beginning to End" all start from the right at the Constellation Sea (referring to its legendary source among the stars) and ending at the left as the Yellow River empties into the sea. These maps show dike and lock dam construction on either bank in considerable detail along with flood prevention controls indicated in writing along the river, tidal areas marked with lines, and dikes. Special attention was paid to the important construction projects involving flood basins and canals as well as the areas where the mouths of rivers converged.

Maps of cities and palaces are comparatively few, however, with "Map of the Completed Restoration of the City Wall of the Provincial Capital of Shensi" being a typical example. The

▼ **Map of the Pontoon Bridge over the Yellow River at Lanchow**
Made between 1839 and 1867, Ch'ing dynasty
Handscroll, ink and colors on silk, 213 x 120 cm

provincial capital of Shensi refers to the city of Hsi-an, the map showing the city walls and streets, government offices, bureaus, schools, temples, and archways within the city. Most significant is the use of yellow labels attached to the map showing basic information, such as names and measurements, of the towers that were renovated in Hsi-an, providing invaluable information on the history of repairs that took place in that city. The Ch'ing dynasty painted "Map of the Palaces and Halls of the Imperial City" is confined to the imperial city in Peking, recording in detail the streets, palaces, gardens, government offices, warehouses, temples, shrines, and princely residences within the imperial city along with waterways and lakes.

Maps of roads and neighborhoods were used by the Ch'ing emperors when they went on "inspection" tours of various regions, serving as guide maps. For example, "Detailed Maps of the Stations to and from the Capital" was presented by Emperor Te-tsung to the Empress Dowager Tz'u-hsi for the trip to and from the Eastern Imperial Tombs that took place from the 15th to the 23rd day of the second intercalary lunar month of the sixteenth year of the Kuang-hsü reign in the Ch'ing dynasty, correlating to the year 1890. Postal station maps refer to the routes for transportation used by couriers riding on relay horses, the Museum collection of such maps all being fairly similar in color, style, and format. "Postal Station Map from Nanking to Kansu", for example, starts with Nanking at the beginning of the handscroll and ends with "City of Sha-chou (Sands)" in Turfan far to the west. The courier route is marked in brown lines, with markings along the way for cities, temples, famous sites, mountains, waterways, bridges, and checkpoints. It also includes markings for the post stations, emergency relay stops, and relay transport offices, along with those for such military facilities as wall defenses, smoke beacons, and blockades.

Maps are also found scattered in rare books in the National Palace Museum collection, so numerous as to be difficult to calculate. It is especially common to find maps in printings of local gazetteers, where most of these are located. For example, *Gazetteer of Shensi* includes an illustration of "People and Places of the Western Regions", presenting a map east from the Ming-chia Valley Pass that includes a record of various natural phenomena and peoples in China's western regions, making this the finest Ming dynasty edition describing China's "Western Regions". In addition, thematic maps also appear in various specialized texts. For example, the famous "Overview of River Flood Prevention" is found in the book Overview of River Flood Prevention, and the entire contents of Matters for River Management include extraordinary color paintings of the entire course of the Yellow River and the Grand Canal.

Maps are the product of a culture at a particular time and place. Things change over the years, and so does the land. Different renderings of the features found in ancient maps are like a bridge from the present, allowing us to engage in a dialogue with the past. (Lu Hsüeh-yen)

▲ **People and Places of the Western Regions**
Made in 1542, Ming dynasty
Book, ink printed on paper,
each half leaf 23 x 16 cm

▲ **Geographic Features of Hsi-hsia**
Made in 1885, Ch'ing dynasty
Book, ink printed on paper,
each half leaf 20.3 x 4.5 cm

Visual Freeze Frames: Exhibitions of the Books and Documents Department

The exhibitions in the Books and Documents Department may lack the dazzling and awe-inspiring "stars" of Chinese antiquities, such as bronzes, jades, or porcelains, and neither do they usually reflect the high art of such forms as painting and calligraphy for the personal or period artistic styles of which they are a part. What the displays in the Books and Documents Department do present, however, are the art of preserving and disseminating knowledge in Chinese culture, social changes that took place over the ages, and the political ups and downs in the dynasties throughout history. These all can take the form of books and documents. With the changes that took place over time, the vernacular of the past became the classical language of the present. Modes of language and communication transformed continually, sometimes making it difficult for people of the present day to understand the forms and contents of these books and documents from the past. With that said, however, books are still in a form that we readily understand, preserving the legacy of experiences and knowledge passed down through history. Documents also take the form of those forms we readily see as texts, which record the internal and external means of communication of the government at the time. From the viewpoint of history, the contents of these writings represent the continual chain of tradition over the ages. Only by understanding events and ideas from the past can we learn how to deal with our thoughts and experiences in the present and future. This perhaps is one of the additional benefits of the Books and Documents Department presenting the wisdom of the ancients to people of the present through these exhibitions.

Over the years, the Books and Documents Department has held different regularly scheduled special exhibitions on a

▼ **The 2007 display of "Grand View: Sung Dynasty Rare Books".**

▲ **The Essence of Government in the Chen-kuan Era**
Written by Wu Ching, T'ang dynasty
Compilation by Ko Chih, Yüan dynasty
1473 Imperial Household edition,
Ming dynasty
Display in the "Gems in the Rare Books Collection" exhibit.

variety of themes. Sometimes they have focused on a particular period, or dealt with a specific format, and sometimes they were meant to accompany major exhibits held by the other two departments in the National Palace Museum, such as "The Ch'ien-lung Emperor's Cultural Enterprise", "Age of the Great Khan", and "Prism of the Past", all of which went on to win considerable acclaim from general audiences and scholars as well. In terms of short-term special exhibitions, there was the recently held "Thou Art Understood: Ch'ing Court Communication as Reflected in the Palace Memorials", which was a successful example of this type of display. Because the emperor in traditional China was the pinnacle of power and authority, he was surrounded by an aura of mystery and awe. However, when we see memorials that were actually brushed in imperial red ink by the emperor, we can view the emperor's personal actions and what he thought, offering a fascinating glimpse into the mind of this almighty person in Chinese history. Then there was also the exhibition entitled "The Buddha Light Illuminating All: Masterpieces of Buddhist Scriptures and Paintings from the Museum Collection", which was another fascinating display attracting many different kinds of audiences. Especially in terms of devoted Buddhists, many were awestruck upon encountering these dazzling and majestically ornamented Buddhist scriptures and works from the Chinese and Tibetan traditions.

With the completion of the new makeover of the National Palace Museum, the Books and Documents Department now has a permanent exhibition gallery on the first floor of the East Wing of the Main Building. From a macroscopic point of view, this area will on the one hand present the course of development in the production of books in traditional China. It will deal with these books from their contents to the methods of printing and binding them, the traditional Chinese bibliographic categories being the Classics, histories, philosophies, and literary collections. Developments also took place from the writing of books down to the techniques of woodblock printing and movable type printing. This exhibition hall also introduces the various binding formats, such as the traditional ones of handscroll, album leaf, and pleated sutra mounting, as well

as the wrapped-back and stitched bindings that more closely resemble those of modern books. The point is to demonstrate to audiences the great variety of traditional Chinese books. Likewise, the delicately carved woodblocks that render the characters as well as the wrapped-back bindings that spare nothing in terms of opulence reveal different aesthetic standards of those who made them in the past. This is why the exhibition is called "Gems in the Rare Book Collection". On the other hand, there are documents that have been left to us from the former Ch'ing dynasty court, and they are on display in Gallery 103 of the East Wing in an exhibition entitled "Heaven-Sent Conveyances: Treasures Among Ch'ing Historical Documents". Also a permanent exhibition with rotating displays, audiences can come to understand the means by which the government operated in the Ch'ing dynasty. In addition to internal edicts issued by the emperor, there were also diplomatic credentials exchanged with other states, documents by which the ruler and officials exchanged opinions, records of how the central government agencies put the imperial orders into effect, how policies were enacted, and even what the emperor did during the day. All of these were recorded, often in great detail, and they are presented here in clearly understood terms offering explanations to viewers, who may sometimes be somewhat confused by the bewildering array of information from the past and its means of dissemination. As such, these historical documents are not just static reminders of the past, but records of life and thought in the Ch'ing dynasty. Being here in Taiwan, we also cannot overlook the importance with which the Ch'ing court paid to Taiwan during its rule over the island, including local customs of its indigenous peoples, their food and objects of daily life, habitat and lifestyle, and other facets of living. In fact, the National Palace Museum has an abundance of historical materials and maps from the Ch'ing court dealing with its rule over Taiwan. These have also been developed into a permanent exhibition with rotating objects entitled "Early Dwellers of Taiwan: Illustrated Historical Documents in the Collections of the National Palace Museum," presenting an informative and interesting display of official documentary materials produced in the Ch'ing dynasty concerning Taiwan.

▲ Record of Taiwan aborigines in the *Complete Library of the Four Treasuries* **from the Ch'ing court.**

Display from the "Early Dwellers of Taiwan: Illustrated Historical Documents in the Collections of the National Palace Museum" special exhibition.

▼ *The Lotus Sutra*

Translated by Kumarajiva, Later Ch'in dynasty

Sung imprint of a Su Shih handwritten edition

Displayed in the 2007 "Grand View: Sung Dynasty Rare Books" exhibition.

In addition, to complement the full re-opening of the National Palace Museum following its renovation, the Books and Documents Department has cooperated with the Painting and Calligraphy as well as the Antiquities Departments to present a special exhibition of "Grand View: Sung Dynasty Rare Books", presenting some of the finest and rarest examples of ancient books from this epochal period in the production of books in Chinese history. The exhibition was divided into the following categories: "Seeking Antiquity and Learning: Imprints by the Government", "All in the Confucian Family: Printed Books by Scholars", "On the Bestseller List: Bookshops and Printing for Profit", and "Spreading the Faith: Fundraising to Print Buddhist Scriptures". These sections presented the most important facets of book production in the Sung dynasty. In the exhibition itself, discussion was presented on the details of the layout design, the names of officials in charge, the importance of taboo characters, the different styles of character print, the trademarks of printing houses, the impressions of seals by book collectors, and examples of illustrated woodblock printing, all presented together to highlight the innovative and paradigmatic significance of Sung dynasty rare books in the Chinese bibliographic history. As with all exhibitions in recent years at the Museum, if you did not catch an exhibition, a condensed version is always available online on the Museum website.

On the first floor of the West Wing of the NPM Main Building is a special exhibition gallery for displays on different themes, presenting various features of books and documents from the past. The first installation in this gallery in 2007 is entitled "Treasures of the Forbidden City: Palace Imprints of the Ch'ing Dynasty", which deals specifically with publications that were produced by the central government in the Ch'ing period, introducing how a ruling outside minority people (the Manchus) used the editing and printing of books to present and reinforce their notions of political authority and culture over China. The exhibit is divided into two major sections. The first shows how the contents of books were used by the Manchu Ch'ing rulers to pursue the goals of social cultivation and military success. Based on the actual printing and binding of books, the other section deals with the glorious achievements in the art of bookbinding during the Ch'ing dynasty. Book titles were prefaced with "imperially produced" and "imperially endorsed," for example, to imply the power and prestige of the Ch'ing rulers, and publications with an "imperially produced foreword" were also printed. These all formed a series of publications that differed markedly from government books printed in previous dynasties, forming one of the greatest features of "palace imprints" of the Ch'ing dynasty.

Exhibitions are a form of visual language, and in the transformation of documents into exhibit objects, one finds that their limitations are sometimes significant. How to supplement and present these objects to allow audiences to glimpse at the periods, places, and people behind them is one of the greatest challenges that faces the Books and Documents Department. (Wu Pi-yung)

A World of 0s and 1s: Establishing the Books and Documents Databanks

The Books and Documents Department manages a huge collection of Ch'ing dynasty archives and rare books. In order to more fully preserve them and expand the range of its academic services, the Department has since 1996 set aside an annual budget to digitize the Ch'ing archives, photographing the "Council of State archived memorials" being its first mission. Starting in 2001, the Department has also been part of the five-year national digital archives program, continuing in the production of the "Council of State Archived Memorials Digital Databank". The Department is also cooperating with the Institute of History and Philology at Academia Sinica in establishing standardized formulae for the cataloguing of Ch'ing dynasty archives while also mutually creating the "Ch'ing Dynasty People's Name Authority Files". In addition, starting in 2003, the Department has also participated in another five-year national digital project, this one involving digital museums, producing such digital databanks as "Ch'ing Palace Imperially Rescripted Memorials", "Book Category Documents", and "Biographical Packets and Biographical Drafts for Ch'ing Dynasty Figures".

At the present, we have already completed the "Full Text and Image Databank of Ch'ing Dynasty Palace Archive Memorials and Council of State Archive Memorials" and opened the system for computer search by the public. When users conduct searches, they can enter search parameters in any column, such as the unspecified column or the ones for document number, memorial date, memorial person, official title, memorial reason, keyword, rescript date, or rescript, thereby making searches much more efficient and effective. For example, if you want to search the keyword "台灣 (Taiwan)" in the "unspecified column", that term will produce search results numbering more than 1,500 entries. You can also choose the "homonym" search in the "search assist" column and enter an alternate character or synonym characters used to refer to Taiwan or those from history, such as "臺灣", "台郡", or "臺郡". The results will yield even more information available to the researcher. You can even use such search methods as combinational operators and "and, or, not" operators to further refine the searches.

To complement the "Palace Archive Memorials and Council of State Archive Memorials", the Department has also established a "Memorial Person Name Authority Files", providing a biographical sketch of the officials who wrote memorials found in the "Council of State Copies of Memorials". The basic information of the main figures, such as birth and death dates, biographical overview, hometown, resume, clan relations, and alternate names are entered into the "Memorial Person Name Authority Database". Thus, readers who wish to learn more about the officials who wrote memorials to the Ch'ing throne can access this database for further information.

Since 2003, the Books and Documents Department has also begun the process of digitizing the National Palace Museum collection of rare books, dividing it into the three parts of "Metadatabase", "Image Files Database", and "Database Search System". The contents of the metadata on the books includes the naming (such as the frontispiece, cover label, block margin, and other naming of the materials), the author (including the writer of the text, those who wrote inscriptions or colophons, and others who contributed to the contents of the book), and other related publishing information (such as the dimensions, publisher's trademark, block format, number of lines per page, script type, impressions of collectors' seals, handwritten notes, comments and annotations, type of edition, name of the engraver, and format of the binding). The "Image Files Database" involves entering image files of the books into the database after they have been electronically scanned, thereupon being combined with the "Metadatabase" to allow users to access and view metadata and images related to the books via the "Databank Search System". For example, a user interested in searching the text entitled *Imperial Poetry of the Summer Palace* (御製避暑山莊詩) can find information on the text. By clicking on the first volume, all the entry names of that volume will appear. Then the user can access the desired chapters, such as "Windy Pines in a Myriad Valleys (萬壑松風)" or "Imperially Produced Poetry and Colophons (御製詩跋)", which will show the entire text and image contents of these two entries. Currently, the metadata files for more than five hundred rare books have been digitized along with complete text and image files for more than three hundred books, including a total of more than four thousand volumes.

Furthermore, the Books and Documents Department also includes many maps and illustrated documents, such as the "Map of Taiwan", "Geographical Map of Yangtze River", "River Construction Map of the Area North of the City of Hsü-chou", "The Pacification of Sinkiang", "Illustration of the Present Encampment of Rebels in the Attack on the City of Lanchow", "Portraits of Meritorious Officials in the Pacification of Kwangtung Bandits", and "Illustration of the Halls of the Ta-ming Palace". The contents of these illustrations include river construction projects, battles, figures, and architecture. In order to allow users to more conveniently access these materials and preserve them for the future, they are also in the process of being digitized. This first involves photographing them into 3x4- or 8x10-inch transparencies, which are then scanned and saved as either 350dpi or 600dpi TIFF image files. They can then be compressed into 72dpi JPEG files for electronic storage and provided for computer Internet browsing. In addition, the files are printed in color on oversize (60 x 84 cm) or A3-size (30 x 42 cm) paper, which can be borrowed by users without the necessity of exposing the originals to damage.

All of the above items in the archived catalogue databank can be accessed freely through the Internet, while the portion of the image file databank completed so far can be browsed in the library at the National Palace Museum or accessed via the Internet on a fee basis. Digital archives are the trend of the future, and it is turning out to be a blessing for both the Books and Documents Department in preserving these precious materials as well as for users who wish to access them conveniently. (Li T'ien-ming)

◄ Oversize color printout of a map in the collection of the Books and Documents Department.
Screenshot of the search page for the "Databank of Ch'ing Dynasty Palace Archive Memorials and Council of State Archive Memorials".

▲ Screenshot for the search page for the "Rare Books Image Databank".

Contributing to the Public: Services of the Library

In 1970, the National Palace Museum, as part of an effort to encourage its staff to conduct further academic research and in response to the needs of domestic and foreign scholars in the arts and history interested in paging and studying rare books and Ch'ing archives in the Museum collection, expanded and added to a small library room originally part of the Books and Documents Department to create the Museum's official research library. In 1984, with the completion of the new administrative building at the Museum, the library was the first to move into the new home. Stacks and shelves were readjusted and new facilities added to create the atmosphere of a modernized collection of books and periodicals. By 1996, the National Palace Museum library, with additions of new purchases, exchanges, and donations further adding to the collection, found the space for readers becoming increasingly cramped, especially with the use of new information

◀ **Exhibition on the history of Chinese books at the entrance to the Library.**

▲ **Reading area for new acquisitions.**

▼ **Research on rare books and archives paged from the collection.**

technology and audio-visual equipment. Therefore, in that year, the library moved to the newly constructed building housing it, hence becoming known as the Library Building.

The Library of Books and Documents at the National Palace Museum holds a rich collection of materials relating to Chinese art, the humanities, museum studies, art conservation, and Asian culture, making it an ideal place for scholars in these fields. The library collection is maintained in open stacks for people to browse and use, making this a library with academic and social education functions. The spacious interior of the library is neat and orderly, and it includes the latest in information technology facilities, such as a computerized cataloguing system, full search databank for the arts and humanities, computer network connection for browsing Internet sources, and microfiche reader and printer. At the entrance to the library is also a permanent exhibition in Chinese on the history of Chinese books. Through the fine cultural objects and chronological timeline, one can gain an introductory understanding of the development of Chinese writings, from those on silk to paper and from the historical development of handwriting to printing. In addition, the display also provides an overview of the important contributions of the Chinese people in the heritage of learning and culture.

At present, the services provided by the Library of Books and Documents at the National Palace Museum include reading privileges for books and periodicals in the stacks, paging rare books and archives, online search of materials in the humanities databank, reference questions, interlibrary photocopying, and others. Both foreign and domestic individuals of high school age or older can apply for library privileges, and the library card must be used each time upon entering or leaving the library. The hours of the Library of Books and Documents are from 9:00am to 5:00pm Monday through Saturday (closed on Sundays and national holidays). In addition, the paging hours for rare books and archives are from 9:00am to 11:30am and from 2:00pm to 4:00pm, Monday through Friday. (Sung Chao-lin)

**Getting to
Know the NPM**

The Art of Protection: The Preservation and Repair of Artifacts in the Conservation Department

Of all the museums in Taiwan, the Conservation Department at the National Palace Museum is the only one specifically dealing with the scientific protection and conservation of museum artifacts. Established in 1970, the present efforts include the prevention and protection of the collection from damage in terms of environmental conditions in the displays and storage, the restoration and care of artworks, and the promotion of scientific analysis and research on artworks.

Regarding the Repair of Artworks

The repair of artworks is one of the three major tasks in the field of art conservation, its history being older than that of the other two (preventative conservation and scientific analysis). Restorers in the past often focused on fixing the appearance of the object's surface. From restoration to repair, in the new field of the science of art conservation, there are no established rules or secret recipes, only norms and standards in a case-by-case approach. In other words, the professional ethics in the field of art repair are "an acceptable level of restoration" and "the reversibility of art repair materials and techniques".

Systematic repair of a work of art entails the following five steps: overall examination, the history of the object and its transmission in the past, study of the techniques used to make it, evaluation of the state of deterioration or damage to the object, and the proposal and execution of the protection and repairs. In addition, records and evaluations are kept, being an important part of the process.

The material(s) of the object will determine in large part the course of action to be taken in its repair. For porcelains, for example, there are the steps of cleaning, gluing, holding, filling, and touching up. Metal objects also include steps of preventing corrosion and sealing. The degree of the aging of an artwork will also determine in part the extent and materials needed for repair. In addition, the different requirements placed upon an object, whether it be for storage, display, or research, all will influence the course of action in its repair.

2   3   4

Preventative Conservation

Preventative conservation refers to separating, removing, or controlling elements in the environment that are harmful to the long-term preservation of cultural objects, the goal being to prevent damage before it occurs. Items in the task of preventive action include:

(1) Monitoring and recording temperature and humidity conditions all day and every day in the storage and exhibition areas: Stable and appropriate levels of temperature and humidity for different types of artifacts maintain them in optimal conditions for the long run, preventing changes that may adversely affect them.

(2) Maintaining appropriate lighting controls: In order to prevent deterioration from light sources, the level of ultraviolet rays in the lighting must be monitored and adjusted before the works are actually installed.

(3) Identifying and solving problems with air pollution on the Museum premises: In addition to including effective filtering devices in the air conditioning system of the Museum to prevent the circulation of adverse gases and dust in the air, the quality of the air must also be regularly monitored, and assistance is provided in checking the levels of sulfur dioxide, formaldehyde, nitrous oxide, and carbon dioxide in the gallery areas, storage facilities, and surrounding areas of the Museum grounds as well as the acidity of moisture in the air.

(4) Controlling pests: Work is done on newly purchased and donated works that have yet to enter the storage facilities in order to prevent the introduction of pests, molds, and mildew that can cause damage. Gentle freezing and heating, nitrous, and fumigation are used to eradicate pests from the materials used in the installation of gallery displays and the packaging of the artworks as well as to prevent dangerous pests concealed in the works from entering the system.

1. Conservation team cleaning the outdoor "bronze lions" at the entry to the Museum grounds.
2. Equipment used to record temperature and humidity in the lab facilities for art conservation.
3. Before the artifacts are placed in the gallery cases, extensive testing is conducted on the levels of temperature and humidity, dust, and volatile gases.
4. Museum facilities for using heat to eradicate pests.

Scientific Analysis

With the assistance of various types of scientific equipment, analysis can be conducted on the materials and structures of an object. This can provide further information on it and assist in the reconstruction of the techniques used in its production at the time as well as offer insights into the socio-economic conditions and cultural behavior of peoples in ancient times, thereby adding another dimension to the research available in the arts.

Image analysis of the objects can be done via scientific analysis in order to understand their structures. This form of physical analysis mainly involves the utilization of two major principles, enlarging the details of and seeing through the objects. In other words, a microscope can be used to enlarge details of the object's surface, and various types of energy sources can yield images of the inner structures of an artwork, respectively. The former refers to technology using, for example, a stereomicroscope, petrographic microscope, metallurgical polarizing microscope, and electron microscope. The latter involves techniques using infrared, ultraviolet, alternative light source, and X-ray photography.

Over the past few years, the Conservation Department has been able to use a specially manufactured handheld microscope for 150x enlargement in order to conduct studies on the surface bubbles, glaze flow, glaze contraction as well as stack points, glaze thickness, and broken surfaces of Sung dynasty Ju ware porcelains and imitation Ju wares of the Ming and Ch'ing dynasties in the National Palace Museum collection. This effort has added considerably to our knowledge of Ju wares. X-ray technology has also been used to gain insights into the interior structure of such antiquities as enamelwares, lacquerware, ceramics, and bronzes, providing crucial information of how to conduct repairs and also providing a basic understanding of the craft and technology that went into these art forms in the past.

Material analysis of the artworks is done in order to understand the specific materials that were used in their production and repairs. This form of chemical analysis employs non-invasive and non-destructive ionizing radiation energy to stimulate the elements in the matter of the artwork and give off characteristic X-rays, which are used to identify the materials used in the object. Some of the common precision equipment found at present include a X-ray fluorescence spectrometer (XRF), scanning electron microscope (SEM-EDX), electron microprobe, and a particle-induced X-ray spectrographic accelerator (PIXE).

In recent years, the Conservation Department has purchased a new portable X-ray fluorescence spectrometer to pursue research in the non-invasive study of materials in objects in museum collections. It is hoped that this instrument will be available for a wide range of applications in order to understand and identify the materials of artworks.

In general, the science of art conservation at the National Palace Museum can be said, on the one hand, to involve the preventative care and restorative repair of artworks. On the other hand, scientific analysis and research can be used to provide information for understanding the activities and living conditions of ancient peoples as evidenced by these preserved objects. With the museum as the medium, the beauty and knowledge provided by these objects can be presented to society.

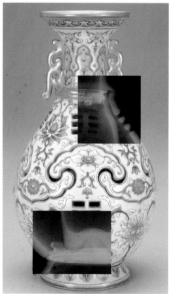

1

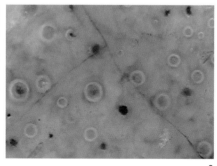

2

3

4   5

Digitization in Art Conservation

The science of art conservation actually is not all hard physical sciences or precision equipment. It also involves the computer science of digitization for the management of the artworks in storage, providing immediate information on the past history of repairs or those that need to be done. One of the more interesting aspects of this effort is the historical background of the artifacts in the collection. In order to create an efficiently integrated digital collection of resources and artifact information management, the Conservation Department has been included in the National Palace Museum's national digitalization project since 2005. It has taken part in the "Planning and Establishment of an Artifact Conservation Record System at the National Palace Museum". The databank of this system is part of the existing artifact storeroom management computer system at the Museum. As such, all basic information on artifacts, their past history of repairs, or related image files or X-ray image files have all been digitized to create links that can be accessed by Museum researchers. Providing instantaneous online search and information retrieval saves enormous amounts of time and greatly streamlines the coordination with the collection and research departments, thereby enhancing efficiency and effectiveness. It also ultimately provides for more ideal overall protection of the artifacts in the collection.

At the same, the results of these digitized efforts can be presented in terms of a systematic databank that can be extended into other digital projects of the Museum, such as the digital museum exhibitions of "Structured Space: The Art of Chinese Decorative Textiles", "Art and Science: Conservation at the NPM", and "The Workings of Nature: Digital Databank on Traditional Arts and Crafts", as well as the Museum's digital learning course entitled "E-learning on the Techniques and Conservation of Traditional Arts and Crafts: The Fate of Bronzes, Ceramics, and Artifacts and Their Conservation". The permanent exhibition in the Museum galleries entitled "The Mystery of Bronzes" also utilizes extensive information on art conservation and its promotion. (Wang Chu-p'ing)

1. X-ray imagery of the details of a revolving vase, revealing construction techniques otherwise unavailable to the naked eye.
2. Details of crackle and bubbles photographed on the surface of Ju porcelain using a handheld microscope at 150x enlargement.
3. X-ray fluorescent spectrograph showing past methods of staining in an old repair on paper. The spectrograph reveals the presence of iron (Fe), indicating that the coloring agent at that time included this element.
4. Screenshot from the digital museum website entitled "Art and Science: Conservation at the NPM" (http://tech2.npm.gov.tw/light).
5. The entrance to the gallery exhibit on the third floor of the Museum's main building entitled "The Mystery of Bronzes".

One Sows as Another Reaps:
The Education and Exhibition Department

"Open, Sesame!" As you enter the new lobby of the National Palace Museum, you face completely new interpretations of the exhibition contents, so it is not unnatural that you may be a little bewildered at first. In fact, you may ask, "How do I tour the museum? Are there any tour guides who can help explain the displays here? Are there any activities for kids?" Many of your concerns and questions are answered here.

As museums enter the modern world, their educational functions become all the more important. How do you make a great educational program of a museum even more universal so that it reaches all levels of society? How do you make the ancient objects of our cultural legacy an even closer part of the aesthetics and lives of people today? How do you make a museum even more approachable as a whole? Answering these questions and by making learning fun are all goals to which museums strive in their educational programs, and this is also a direction in which the Education and Exhibition Department at the National Palace Museum is actively heading.

As the name of the Education and Exhibition Department indicates, we are involved with the promotion of educating the public about the objects in the National Palace Museum as well as assisting in the presentation and explanation of the exhibits, playing an important role in the Museum. In terms of exhibitions, we coordinate with the curatorial departments in designing the displays of the objects, assisting with the production of the exhibitions, as well as the textual and image contents of the installation, providing visitors with a means of communication and interaction with the displays. In terms of promoting education, the Department creates and presents a variety of events and activities associated with the exhibitions. In addition to traditional services (such as regularly scheduled tours, student tours, special projects involving art and life, seed-teacher camps, and art camps) that continue to be provided to the public, changes in all facets of society mean that we have to work harder to meet these new challenges and demands. For example, we are promoting a series of digital learning courses on different types of Chinese artwork and presenting them online, combining art and technology. We also offer other new services, such as 3D animated film shorts, a children's museum, and creative workshops. The Education and Exhibition Department hopes that visitors and users will continue to provide us with continued suggestions and support, allowing us to continue to bathe in the glory of art and culture from the past in our daily lives today.

Promoting Art Education
Regularly Scheduled Tours

For many visitors who come to the National Palace Museum for the first time, cordial and knowledgeable tour guides can be of great assistance in presenting the many wonders of art and culture available at the Museum. In order to provide

1

2

visitors with friendly service, the Education and Exhibition Department provides regularly scheduled tours every day of the year. Mandarin Chinese tours are offered daily at 9:30am and 2:30pm and English tours at 10:00am and 3:00pm, given by tour guides of the Education and Exhibition Department and professional docents with many years of service. Following the course of historical developments in China over the ages, the tour guides at the National Palace Museum provide interesting and informative introductions for appreciating the beauty and legacy of these cultural artifacts, receiving the enthusiastic participation and joyful interaction of visitors to the Museum.

Student Tours

School trips to the National Palace Museum have long been one of the most joyous and unforgettable experiences of many a student in Taiwan. The tours provided to students by the Museum accommodate on average about 800,000 people every year. The objects at the Museum offer an excellent means for teaching outside of the classroom as dedicated and professional tour guides explain in a fun and interesting manner the importance of the display objects. The dialogue format of the tours leads students on a fascinating exploration of the mystery and allure of art and culture through the ages. They listen with rapture about the story of the "Mao-kung ting bronze", search with enthusiasm for the two insects hidden among the leaves of the "Jadeite cabbage", and marvel at the incredible detail and craftsmanship of the "Concentric ivory balls". Such innovative and supportive means of learning from the artworks themselves influence many young minds throughout their lives.

Seed-Teacher Camps

Appreciation of the treasures of art and culture at the National Palace Museum is not restricted to the exhibition halls, but it also should be a catalyst for stimulating education in various fields at schools in different levels of education. Utilizing the unique artistic and cultural features of the objects in the collection assist in the development of overall systematic courses. Maintaining this ideal, the Education and Exhibition Department holds "Seed-Teacher Camps" every summer vacation. The goal is to integrate museum resources and school courses, allowing teachers at schools in various fields to be able to effectively use what the National Palace Museum has to offer and to explore the thematic contents of exhibitions held at the Museum. Integrated into the courses that they design for their students, teachers design and create innovative curricula on "Thematic Overall Education Activities", encouraging students to use the educational resources at the National Palace Museum in their learning. After teachers participate in "Seed-Teacher Camp" activities, they become seed-teachers at schools for the National Palace Museum. As educational workers at schools who also participate and teach at the Museum, the curricula they have designed with Museum resources put their ideals and plans into actual practice. This special project arranges units on thematic courses, tour introductions, and brainteasers, providing teachers at schools with an interactive platform for the exchange of experiences and a way to "recharge their batteries".

Volunteer Services

Friendly and knowledgeable services at the Information Desk and energetic explanations in the galleries are the impressions with which many people come away at the National Palace Museum, and these are often offered by the more than three hundred enthusiastic volunteers and docents active at the Museum. At present, there are 307 volunteers in the Education and Exhibition Department, including youths and those of foreign nationality. In addition, the department also continues to actively recruit and train high school volunteers, annually recruiting fifty new "high

4

1. Personnel at the Information Desk answering a question.
2. A tour guide explaining a work of art to visitors.
3. Talk being given to student tour guides.
4. Seed-teachers appreciating a reproduction being opened by a member of the museum staff.

school seed-volunteers" of the National Palace Museum. As these new recruits grow up and become adults, often continuing to volunteer at the Museum, they become an invaluable source of experienced personnel who provide fresh and innovative outlooks for the new National Palace Museum.

Activities in the Aesthetics of Life

"Is all you can do at the National Palace Museum just look at the exhibitions or participate in their activities and events?" "Are there any half-day or full-day events that I can take part in?" These are just a couple of the questions that people ask at the Information Desk when they come to the Museum. In fact, since 2004, the Education and Exhibition Department has already begun planning for projects involving "Activities in the Aesthetics of Life" for half- and full-day tours. The contents include informative tours and courses on art arranged by the experienced tour guides of the Department as well as experiences in the creation of arts and crafts, offering a means to experience the aesthetics of life in the appreciation of Chinese arts. The art forms that one can learn and experience first-hand include Chinese knot-tying, innovative lacquerware, traditional bonsai arts and arrangement, and paper-cutting and fan production. The project for "Activities in the Aesthetics of Life" accepts advance group registration and can be held on weekends. Many of the more than one thousand people who participate in these activities end up signing up for it again and again. The art objects at the National Palace Museum are not just a feast for the eyes, but a visit can also allow you to experience the fascinating world of Chinese arts and crafts first-hand, providing stimulation and interaction within a group to increase interest in Chinese art and culture.

Art Camps

The Education and Exhibition Department also holds annual summer and winter art camps for a total of two weeks each, inviting researchers of the Museum, experienced tour guides, and outside professionals to provide a series of art lectures to the public on a variety of topics. These courses include subjects dealing with Chinese painting, Buddhist art, calligraphy, porcelains, collections of the imperial family, books and documents, costumes and accessories, architecture, and art conservation. Every year, there are about five thousand entries to these events and enthusiastically support them. The events provide an ideal opportunity for students and lovers of Chinese art to learn more about such topics in depth from professionals.

In addition to the regularly scheduled art camps, the National Palace Museum also holds non-regularly scheduled lectures on art and culture as well as small-scale academic conferences. With the completion of construction for the "Multimedia Screening Room" on the basement floor of the Museum's main building in January 2007, visitors to the National Palace Museum can enjoy a comfortable and artistic environment for activities to learn more about the Museum and its contents.

Bringing National Treasures into Life

The times are changing, and technology is making leaps and bounds as the 21st century presents us with numerous challenges while also offering and bringing new modes of living with it. As the Education and Exhibition Department ponders these new challenges that we all face in the modern world, we come to think about how to bring traditional art education into the new realm of museums in today's society, bringing cultural objects even closer into the daily experiences

1. Young and exuberant volunteers are the seeds for tomorrow's National Palace Museum.

2. Participants enthusiastically displaying their works of Chinese knot-tying.

3. Screenshot of the welcome page to the NPM e-learning website.

of people. One of these challenges, therefore, is how to take the treasures of art and culture in the National Palace Museum out into the world around us, universalizing and bringing them into life in ways not thought of only a few years ago. With these thoughts in mind, various programs and projects are being planned by the Education and Exhibition Department, including "Digital Learning", "Digital Tour Lobby", a "Children's Museum" inside the National Palace Museum, a 3D animated film short on "National Treasure Superstars", and "Creative Workshop".

3

It is hoped that, by integrating art and technology as well as the humanities and digitization, we can provide a new and complete round of activities and services to meet the needs of different groups of people in today's ever-changing society.

Digital Learning

In the past, the displays of objects in a museum were confined by the set limits of the spaces contained therein and the locations. For example, children in distant areas perhaps could only learn about the actual appearance of these treasures of art and culture through an annual trip to the National Palace Museum or a museum-on-wheels special project. However, now that many of us can enjoy the benefits of living in a digital age, the influence and universality of these objects can be enjoyed without constraints of time and space using a computer and the Internet. In fact, almost every corner of the world is available for instantaneous communication and learning. Together with the appreciation of the beauty of treasures in the museum and the promotion of the ideas of a "museum without walls" and lifelong learning in the arts, all levels of society can "visit" and "see" these objects at home and whenever they want.

Following the trends of digitization in society, the Education and Education Department at the National Palace Museum has a five-year plan for developing courses on "Digital Learning on Artifacts at the National Palace Museum". Integrating Internet resources and resources on cultural objects, online learning courses on series of themes are being produced. Interested people can visit the National Palace Museum's "NPM e-Learning" website at (http://elearning.npm. gov.tw) and take a variety of classes, including those Chinese bronzes, porcelains, and painting, learning about these art forms in classes that are interesting and informative.

Digital Tour Lobby

The newly opened galleries in the main building of the National Palace Museum offer visitors not only a completely new experience in terms of the redesigned spaces and manners of presentation, but also a reinterpretation of the eight thousand years of art and cultural objects in the Museum collection. As opposed to previous modes in which objects were presented in terms of format, the permanent exhibitions now take on a more cultural history perspective, presenting whenever possible the integrated course of development in Chinese culture from the Neolithic age down through the dynasties. In light of this reinterpretation of the permanent exhibitions, the Education and Exhibition Department has planned an integrated tour lobby and public space, introducing the contents of these exhibitions and providing visitors with a clear and concise index to the galleries and information on them. At the same time, digital technology is used to present digital learning films and classes, offering even more pluralistic and hands-on approaches to experience in the spaces used by visitors.

Children's Museum

During the promotion of art education, how can the beauty and importance of the art and culture at the National Palace Museum be spread in the most universal and efficient manner to all levels and age groups of society? This is one of the most pressing tasks of the National Palace Museum's Education and Exhibition Department. The children's museum currently in planning will be in a space isolated from the galleries in the Museum in the hopes of providing children with a new and separate area specially devoted to their learning and behavioral needs. Through the experience of learning about the exhibit themes while having fun at the same time, it is hoped that the interest and education of children will be stimulated, allowing them to come to think of a museum as a place where they can feel at home and learn something new at the same time.

Plans for the space currently call for a mobile theater, a hands-on crafts section, and various interesting displays on the exhibit themes in the Museum. It is hoped that children will not only be able to use their hands to learn about arts and crafts, but also be able to wholeheartedly experience and participate in the museum visit process, allowing then to be able to make things for themselves and also learn about the beauty and importance of art and cultural objects. The various themes of the exhibits in the children's museum will be presented in one of the manners they understand and appreciate the most--that of theater. By transforming the collection of art and cultural objects in the National Palace Museum into role-playing models, it will provide a creative space for action and appreciation, creating arts and crafts, and play.

What does the National Palace Museum look like from the viewpoint of children? The Museum hopes that with the opening of a children's museum on its premises that it can create even more stimulation for doing and learning about various art forms. Through this children's museum project, it is also hoped that the resources of the National Palace Museum can be spread among younger audiences and create a new mode of museum education for children in the arts.

"National Treasure Superstars" 3D Animated Short

In celebration of the completion the renovation project known as "The National Palace Museum's Makeover", the Museum prodrced an eight-minute 3D animated film for educational promotion purposes. This film breaks down the barriers of traditional filming methods and employs the latest computer animation technologies to reveal what the new National Palace Museum has to offer. By allowing visitors to understand the rich collection of Chinese cultural objects in the Museum, it is hoped that both domestic and international audiences will visit the museum through this lively and creative computer animated short. This is not only be the first 3D animated film short for a museum in the world, it also marks the significance of the new motto of the National Palace Museum: "Old is New".

This film uses the rich collection of cultural objects in the National Palace Museum as a stage for the story, integrating a world-class team of professionals in the field, including Gérard Pirès (the director of the 1998 world blockbuster French comedy *Taxi*), Desmond Crofton (who has more than twenty years experience in writing scripts), Teddy Yang (who is Computer Graphic Animation Supervisor in Hollywood), and the dazzling 3D animation team at Digimax. This short film introduces the "superstar national treasures" of the National Palace Museum in a light and easy manner, emphasizing the refinement and importance of these objects in the collection. It is hoped that each and every visitor to the National Palace Museum, both domestic and international, will come to more fully understand the treasures of the Museum as well as the unique background of its history, the humorous and amusing animated characters leaving people with knowledge about art and a smile on their faces.

Synopsis of the film:

After the sun goes down, the lights come on. Don't assume that everything is quiet and still inside the exhibition galleries at the National Palace Museum in Taipei. That's because every evening, after the last visitor has left the Museum,

1

2

1. Cartoon version of the Sung dynasty painting of "Children Playing on a Winter Day"
2. Still-frame of the 3D animated characters for a film short based on artworks in the Museum collection.
3. Kids proudly displaying the masks they made for a class.
4. Children personally taking part in the production of ceramics.

3   4

the works of painting and calligraphy and antiquities in the exhibition galleries come alive, throwing a party, chatting about everyday things, or just creating a general ruckus. The plot of this film involves three characters--a child pillow, a jade duck, and a pi-hsieh evil-averting animal. These three friends often romp around playing together. However, one night during their revelry, they lose one of the insects perched on the famous jadeite cabbage on exhibit, leading them on a chase of the insect around the premises. How does it end? Just wait and see...

Creative Workshop

The rich collection of cultural artifacts in the collection of the National Palace Museum represents the crystallization of the wisdom of arts and crafts among the ancients. In order to allow visitors to personally experience the beauty of ancient artworks and understand the techniques used in the production of these objects, the Education and Exhibition Department is specially preparing for a "Creative Workshop". The contents of the courses include the production of ceramics, lacquerware, and enamelware, and also divided into different levels for adults, student groups, and children summer and winter vacation camps. This series of courses will instill general audiences with basic knowledge about the production of traditional art forms found in museum collections, thereby making the National Palace Museum one of the cornerstones and motivators for a new cultural renaissance in Taiwan. The student groups will take the form of half-day trips. In addition to appreciating the beauty of the artworks in the displays, hands-on activities in the "Creative Workshops" will allow them to actually make works for themselves. The children summer and winter camps will be designed to complement the exhibitions that are on display at the time so that kids can have fun while they learn about art. Steeped in the culture of the past, it will stimulate children to use their hands and want to create works from the imagination based on the past, thereby stimulating a new generation to acquire a love of the arts and culture. (Lin Ming-mei and Liu Chün-ch'i)

Imaging the NPM:
Art and Technology at the Information Management Center

In response to ever-changing and sudden developments in technology around us today, the management of museums around the world is facing many new challenges. In light of these positive changes, "digitizing collections" has become one of the most widespread plans in solving the issues that major museums around the world are facing. The National Palace Museum is no exception. We have followed the ideas of "refined culture and universal appreciation" and "the NPM in a new age" to start the work of digitization, and the results are already becoming apparent after only a few years in the form of an overall strategy known as "A Mobile and Digital NPM".

Plans and Strategies for Digitization at the NPM

The National Palace Museum special project for digitization concretely describes the long-term goals of the task of digitization and sets annual plans for administering it each year. This long-term goal is as follows: "Based on the ideal of the fusion of art and technology, it is to establish museum digitization standards, to explore demonstration cases for the digital content industry, and to create a complete integrated economic model for the museum." In more concrete terms and to fully push forward the task of digitization, this involves developing the digitization of the NPM collection in upstream midstream, and downstream levels. They include the digital archives, digital museum, e-learning, a knowledge-based economy, and promoting art education, as seen in Diagram 1. It is hoped that by closely integrating the three levels, the digital results of each can be developed to their maximum advantage and efficiency.

The Course of Digitization at the NPM

The digitization of the collection of the National Palace Museum, starting with the promotion of the "Digital Forerunner Project" that began in 2001, has over the years completed the planning of the digital archives system for the NPM collection as well as the initial task of its establishment. The initial stage (2002, 2003, and 2004) involved the start of three major national digitization projects: "Digital Archives National Program: Developing and Producing a Digital Archives System of Artifacts at the National Palace Museum" of 2002 and "e-Culture Network: The National Palace Museum Digital Museum Special Project" and "e-Learning National Technology Program: National Palace Museum Cultural Artifacts E-Learning Project" of 2003. These three major projects laying the foundations of digitization at the National Palace Museum continue to be developed. The major foci of the initial period involved establishing the archives databank and the task of conducting digital photography, including the purchase of photographic equipment, the training of personnel, and the establishment of standards for the processes involved.

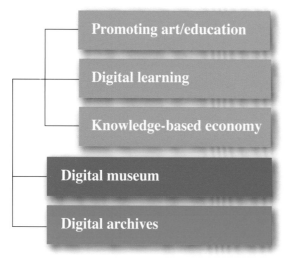

2   3   4

After the initial period, the Museum over the following two years (2005 and 2006) entered the growth phase of the project. In terms of the digital archives, the pace of photographing the cultural objects and establishing files was quickened, and the internal management system of managing collection objects and a public search system for the collection archives was completed. As for a digital museum, focus was placed on the utilization of technology to break through the physical barriers of traditional brick-and-mortar museums, bringing the beauty and importance of objects in the National Palace Museum to the people, facilitating education, and stepping out onto the world stage. As for digital learning, three kinds of major innovative museum e-learning projects were established in the form of the "Digital Courses and Online Learning", "Digital Tours and Mobile Learning" and "Digital Displays and Interactive Learning".

Starting from 2007 and led by the three major national projects involving digital archives, digital museums, and digital learning, the National Palace Museum has entered the phase of expansion in the course of digitization. In other words, the entire task of digitization will give rise to a cumulative efficiency, broadening its scope with results that will make the National Palace Museum a model for a composite economic system that combines both culture and industry.

State of Development in the Digital Archives Project

From the beginning of the plans in 2001 for the National Palace Museum's first five-year digital archives project, the following year (2002) marked the formal establishment of the NPM as one of the major institutions in the "Digital Archives National Technology Project". This project mainly deals with information on the objects under the care of the three departments in the NPM--Antiquities, Painting and Calligraphy, and Books and Documents--and proceeds with the task of digitization. In addition, some information related to the objects in other departments, such as Registration, Publications, and Conservation, including records, negatives, x-rays, and conservation records, are also being digitized. The Information Management Center is therefore responsible for providing technical support and management. This project has already digitized the most important parts of the Museum collection, providing users around the world an ability to search them using the Internet. In the end, it is hoped to be able to help achieve the goals of dissemination and exchange, educational promotion, and commercial added value to the world of knowledge associated with the objects in Museum collections.

In addition, with the development of new photographic methods and applications in the future, this project has also proceeded with bold new experiments, establishing a "3D virtual object display system" for such popular National Palace Museum pieces as "Jadeite cabbage and insects", "Set of concentric ivory balls in openwork", "Revolving vase", "Carved olive pit boat", and the "Mao-kung *ting* tripod". The contents of that project not only allow people to discover the culture and epitome of craftsmanship among the ancients, but through the eye and innovation of modern people and technology, allow even more people to achieve a form of resonance with ancient art in their lives today.

1. Charting the strategy for the development of digitization at the National Palace Museum.
2. Screenshot of the computerized search system for data on the collection of painting and calligraphy at the NPM.
3. Screenshot of the computerized databank for rare books at the NPM.
4. Screenshot of the computerized databank on Ch'ing palace archives and Grand Council archived memorials.

Developments of the Digital Museum Project

The digital museum project hopes to break through the barriers of traditional brick-and-mortar museums through the use of technology, bringing the beauty of cultural objects and educational resources at the National Palace Museum closer to the people and presenting them to the world. The production of the National Palace Museum website in several different languages, including Chinese, English, Japanese, German, French, Spanish, Korean, and Russian, along with the creation of various thematic digital museum websites, is done in the hopes that providing various forms of up-to-date museum information complemented by substantial contents on museum exhibitions can achieve the goal of raising the overall quality of museum services even further.

In addition, various multimedia videos and discs have been produced and presented. Those completed to date include such multimedia video presentations as "The Beauty of Famous Paintings", "Masterpieces of Chinese Painting and Calligraphy at the National Palace Museum", and "The Beauty of Calligraphy". Multilingual interactive compact discs produced so far also include "The Beauty of Enamelware", "Masterpieces of Chinese Painting and Calligraphy at the National Palace Museum", "The National Palace Museum for Kids", "Convergence of Radiance", "Age of the Great Khan", "A Great Garden of Chinese Painting and Calligraphy", "The Fashionable vs. the Archaic" (jades), "The Spirit of Jade", and "Emperor Hui-tsung and Northern Sung Painting and Calligraphy". In order to apply high-tech multimedia techniques and satisfy audiences' desire for a multifaceted museum as well as technological and digital experiences, the National Palace Museum has also established a multimedia screening room and interactive facilities. Completed so far are the multimedia room for painting and calligraphy and the multimedia interactive area for artworks at the second terminal at Taiwan Taoyuan International Airport. In 2005, a multimedia display hall meeting international standards was finished, providing high-resolution audio-visual materials for appreciation and thereby expanding the educational function of the Museum facilities.

Furthermore, in an effort to allow visitors to approach and understand the National Palace Museum from different angles, this project has especially incorporated the planning of films. The first film, entitled "Beyond the Palace, Beyond the Horizon", was directed by Wang Shaudi, who invited artists from different fields both domestic and foreign to come and appreciate works at the NPM and then follow up by creating works of art based on what they saw, a process which

1

2

3

4

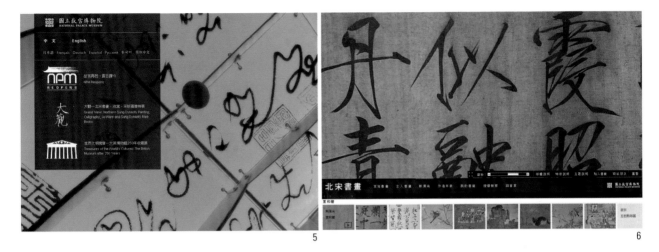

5   6

7   8   9

was documented by Wang. The entire film reminds us to reconsider, "Should objects in displays in museums just sit there statically in ancient history? Or, do they conceal a different form of life that awaits us to discover within them?" The second film is called "The Passage", and the Museum put up the capital for the filming. Directed by Cheng Wen-tang, it was the first dramatic film by the National Palace Museum that was shown in public movie theaters. Centered around a famous work of calligraphy by the great Sung dynasty scholar-artist Su Tung-p'o (Shih) known as "The Cold Food Observance", the lives of three different yet ultimately related people are woven together, interspersed with segments dramatizing the history of the NPM. The end result is a touching story that slowly unfolds before the audience's eyes. This film was nominated for several awards at the Tokyo International Film Festival and won Best Sound Effects at the 41st Golden Horse Awards in Taiwan. The third film is "In the Golden Age of Chinese Craftsmanship". A documentary by the famous Taiwanese director Hou Hsiao-hsien, the film reveals the extraordinary skill and beauty of various types of art from the Ming and Ch'ing dynasties in the collection of the National Palace Museum.

  The project also specially invited the director Wayne Peng to produce a 90-second image commercial for the National Palace Museum entitled "Old is New". The contents deal with the famous calligraphy of poetry by Huang T'ing-chien of the Sung dynasty entitled "Flowers' Fragrance Incenses One". In it, he invited the renowned Taiwanese computer music-artist Lim Giong to perform a completely new interpretation. The commercial involves the use of the Taiwanese dialect to chant this classical short verse along with inebriating computer music. Not only did it allow this nearly thousand-year-old piece of poetry and calligraphy to soar to new heights on monitors, it also fused age-old culture and tradition into

1. Screenshot of a virtual exhibition at the National Palace Museum.

2. Screenshot of an interactive display on an artwork.

3. Still frame from the title in a computer animation of the NPM.

4. Scene from a thematic computer film short on an NPM artwork.

5. Welcome page to the home website of the NPM on the Internet.

6. Screenshot from the "Grand View: Northern Sung Painting and Calligraphy" digital museum website.

7. Advertisement for the film "The Passage".

8. Still frame from the film "In the Golden Age of Chinese Craftsmanship".

9. Still frame from NPM image commercial entitled "Old is New".

modern life and aesthetics. This commercial won the Gold Award in the "Promotional and Marketing" category of the 2006 MUSE Awards presented by the American Association of Museums (AAM).

Finally, in terms of value-added applications, the digital assets produced in the various digital projects at the National Palace Museum can all be combined with or complement the research and marketing strategies in the private industry to further create various derivative value-added applications that benefit both parties. Such digital distributions of products published by the NPM include exhibition catalogues, compact discs, and reproductions. Using the Internet and online shopping methods for sale to consumers, the products related to the collection objects of the National Palace Museum can be made known throughout the world, even to the extent of creating a global market for value-added applications and products of the NPM collection. On the one hand, this promotes the domestic digital content industry and the development of cultural enterprises and industries. On the other hand, with the National Palace Museum as a public institution, the benefits of this enterprise also add to the national coffers.

1

2

3

4   5

Digital Learning Project

The goal of the "National Palace Museum Artworks Digital Learning" project is to use the rich cultural resources of the NPM to create multiple e-learning resources and to popularize the notion of digital learning. Creating a NPM digital learning demonstration center would also stimulate the trend of e-learning in museums and create a new paradigm for digital content education. In the five years of this project from 2003 to 2007, the source materials of digital learning based on the resources of the digital archives have been divided into stages to establish a museum digital learning demonstration center, to create a digital learning platform, to develop digital content materials, to provide synchronous and asynchronous as well as mixed online learning functions, and to establish a wireless tour learning environment in the galleries along with the development of its contents.

Numerous Domestic and International Awards

The websites and digital content products of the National Palace Museum have won numerous awards in domestic and international competitions, demonstrating their quality and bringing honor to the NPM for its efforts in the digital field. One of the most recent awards was for the "Old is New" image commercial, which won the Gold Award in the "Promotional and Marketing" category of the 2006 MUSE Awards presented by the American Association of Museums. The comments posted online by the judges are as follows: "This stunningly beautiful advertisement featured film-quality cinematography and a dynamic soundtrack featuring contemporary and traditional compositions. The dramatic imagery and music seamlessly presented the National Palace Museum's notion that the 'Old is New.' This dazzling piece of filmmaking drew us in quickly and kept our attention; by the end, we were excited to see more of what the National Palace Museum had to offer."

The National Palace Museum is actively digitization and globalization. Internet technology can allow those who cannot visit the NPM in person to enjoy the national treasures of Chinese culture and the Museum surroundings in a dazzling and trendy form of digital lifestyle. (Lin Quo-ping)

1. A selection of multimedia discs on art at the National Palace Museum.

2. The NPM multimedia interactive area at the second terminal of Taiwan Taoyuan International Airport.

3. Multimedia lecture being given at the NPM auditorium--Wen-hui (Literary Gathering) Hall.

4. Screenshot from the NPM online museum store (www.npmeshop.com).

5. Screenshot from the NPM e-learning course on Chinese bronzes.

Linking Old and New:
The Publications Department Creating Brand Aesthetics

We all know that the National Palace Museum represents one of the pinnacles in terms of collections of Chinese art and culture. Whether it be Buddhist scriptures, painting and calligraphy, bronzes, porcelains, or jades, each and every one of them reflects a refined expression crystallizing the wisdom of ancestors crafting materials from nature. These works also hold untold artistic value, representing treasures that are the essence of the artistic and cultural production. Beverly Barsook, Executive Director of the Museum Store Association in the US, has pointed out that the "selling point of a museum" lies as an extension of the museum's educational system and has the function of promoting aesthetics in life among people in society while also creating a new economic effect for the museum. Consequently, in consideration of such factors as expanding the range in popularizing cultural education and raising one's own funds to help meet operating expenses, the National Palace Museum is actively transforming for the future from a more passive to an active mode. The operating mode and framework of the Museum will be given reconsideration in the hopes of being able to attain a complementary relationship between the task of collection preservation and the business of the running a museum, both of which can work together without adversely affecting the other.

With this ideal in mind, several questions arise for the National Palace Museum. How will it cross East and West (traverse cultural differences while presenting the unique features of the East), combine old and new (from tradition to innovation, finding new ways to package old objects), and head into the future (creating beneficial conditions and developing cultural property value)? These are all important tasks that lie ahead for the Museum. In order to achieve these goals, the Publications Department at the National Palace Museum will work in the direction of changing into an authorized agent for operations and management with the ideal of maintaining a brand image for the Museum. The systematic planning of the contents of the NPM image and marketing strategies include the following items for management: issuing Museum publications, authorizing the use of Museum images, creating co-branding alliances, researching and developing derivative art-related products, and creating new domestic and international outlets for the marketing of its products. By closely integrating contemporary life and art, we can help create a composite economic platform for globalization while also being of economic benefit to the country as well.

Issuing Museum Publications

The National Palace Museum is home to a vast number of cultural properties, and the variety and contents of publications have already been divided according to marketing strategies in order to meet and cater to the different requirements and needs of various groups of readers. Methods of publication are also pursued along diversified lines. At present, an integrated approach in consultation with the actual experiences of domestic and international publishers is

taking place in order to raise the standards to meet international levels for design and print quality. In addition, considering the rising trend in digital publishing, the National Palace Museum also offers publications in digital file and POD (print-on-demand) formats. With the establishment of the NPM online bookshop, it is hoped that the Museum can occupy an important place in the global cultural market.

The National Palace Museum publications can be divided according to format and content into the following types:

■ Exhibition catalogues and guidebooks: To accompany important special exhibitions at the National Palace Museum, such annual events often involve the simultaneous issue of exhibition catalogues and guidebooks, while medium-sized exhibits are often accompanied by a tour guide. For example, the exhibitions for "Grand View: Painting, Calligraphy and Ju Ware from the Northern Sung Dynasty and Sung Dynasty Rare Books" that opened in late 2006 were each accompanied by an important exhibition catalogue and guidebook. In the same year, the exhibition "Early Dwellers of Taiwan: Illustrated Historical Documents in the Collections of the National Palace Museum" also featured a fine handbook to satisfy the needs of viewers during their visit and for further information afterwards.

■ Regular publications: These include the *National Palace Museum Research Quarterly*, *National Palace Museum Bulletin*, and the *National Palace Museum Monthly of Chinese Art*, which began publication in 1983 and has reached nearly three hundred issues, making it one of the most important periodicals on art in the domestic scene.

■ Research publications: These are publications mostly written by members of the Museum staff, including both text- and image-oriented series. They include *A Panorama of Painting in the Collection of the National Palace Museum*, *A Complete Collection of Calligraphy in the National Palace Museum*, *A Complete Collection of Calligraphy Through the Ages in the National Palace Museum*, *Collectanea of the National Palace Museum*, and Ch'ing dynasty archives and memorials in the Museum collection.

■ Digital audio-visual discs: Since digital publications have already become the trend of the future in the publishing world, the National Palace Museum has worked together with the digital information establishment to produce several award-winning multilingual discs, such as "A Great Garden of Chinese Painting and Calligraphy", "Convergence of Radiance: Tibeto-Chinese Buddhist Scripture Illustrations from the Collection of the National Palace Museum", "The Spirit of Jade", and "The Legend of Ju Ware".

Authorizing Image Use

Over the years, the National Palace Museum has actively established various types of digital images with the main purpose of creating a complete databank of image files of works in the collection. These completed image files not only provide the most detailed record of the collection objects, they are also offer the quickest, most reliable, and most convenient source of basic information for the development of value-added cultural products and the development of the Museum's cultural properties.

In order to increase the economic efficiency of these image files, the National Palace Museum has consulted such important international standards as those of the Art Resource in the US, Scala Archives of Florence in Italy, and the Réunion des Musées Nationaux (Photo RMN) in France. Linking up with international companies and using the Internet can offer services for image authorization. Based on a pay-per-use principle, a mechanism for establishing a set of fees that meet international market standards can be achieved, allowing an even wider range of domestic and international users to use the Internet and download conveniently, providing nearly instantaneous service.

Cross-platform Brand Alliances

As Director Lin Mun-lee has stated, the effort is to make the National Palace Museum "not just a museum brand, but also a lifestyle brand". This is why another important mission of the Publications Department is to raise the international brand market value of the Museum and use existing global outlets for brand names. To achieve this aim, the NPM has actively sought companies with great experience in international brands for cross-platform brand alliances, authorizing established companies to produce various reproductions of collection works and artistic souvenirs that meet high standards with the NPM registered trademark, and engaging in self-marketing both domestically and internationally. The principle of mutual benefit for the National Palace Museum and companies results in the most efficient and advantageous use of value-added applications licensed with the NPM brand.

From 2005 to July of 2006, five renowned domestic and international companies have already entered into brand cooperation with the National Palace Museum. They include cooperation with the famous porcelain maker Franz in converting the design in the painting of "Peach Blossoms", the second leaf in the album "Immortal Blossoms in an Everlasting Spring" by the Ch'ing dynasty court painter Giuseppe Castiglione (Lang Shih-ning) into two bas-relief porcelain sets entitled "Peach Blossoms and Two Swallows" and "Cherry Blossoms in Spring", with the flower vase, soup spoon, and tea pot featuring scrolling branches in bloom. There is also the "Free and Easy" series on the theme of goldfish in underglaze red that premiered in September at the 2005 Maison et Objet in Paris, the trade show for home decoration, giftware, and tableware. The white porcelain, embellished with several small goldfish, attracted the attention of many French companies. These three sets of porcelains from the Franz Collection were made available in over 5,000 outlets around the world, bringing the art and beauty of the National Palace Museum to audiences and places not seen before.

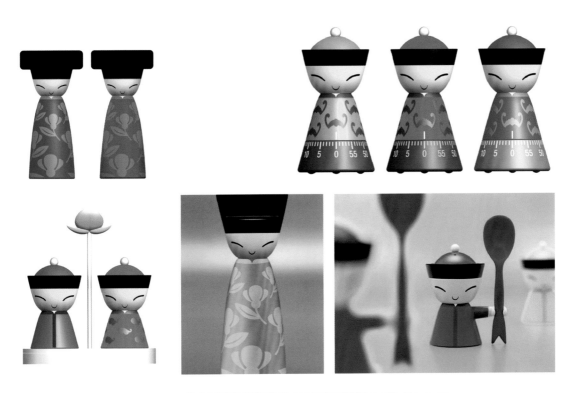

Innovating and Developing Art-derived Commercial Products

In the past, the National Palace Museum depended on traditional means of self-development or worked together with private companies in creating reproductions of objects in the collection or art-related souvenirs. Although nearly 4,000 have been made in this manner, the overall style, however, tends to be rather conservative and sometimes lacking in refinement.

The central point of "Old is New" involves shedding the stereotypical and old-fashioned views of the National Palace Museum and bringing in renowned domestic and international design teams to develop new and innovative products centering around the art at the NPM. At the same incorporating elements from the wealth of artworks in the NPM collection as a springboard for new products, trendy and innovative designs can remold and repackage the artworks of old, thereby adding even further cultural value to them. In the process, the art products of the National Palace Museum can become symbols of culture, technical innovation, style, quality, status, and a refined lifestyle. Starting from the innovative design exhibition of students in "New Design Ideas from the Y Generation" and the "Works of Cutting Edge Design Teams" held in August of 2005, the year 2006 witnessed even further developments along these lines. Five of the top domestic design teams took part in the production of trendy NPM products, and the "Modern T-shirt Design Competition" was held along with a workshop announcing concept products. In the two years since then, samples of products that have been designed so far have reached more than a hundred, including the plump icon of T'ang dynasty beauty "FéFé" based on Concubine Yang Kuei-fei designed by the Agua Design Team along with a series of modern stationery items. Then the design folks at ASUS computer used the traditional dragon-shaped jade pendant of the Warring States period to fashion it out of metal and make a dragon-claw bottle opener, combining both practical and aesthetic qualities into a single product. The Designburg team used the shape of a martini glass to create a transparent and totally innovative object, named a "shang" wine cup. The team at Bright Ideas gave new life to images of children playing from the Sung dynasty, transforming these cute kids from China's ancient past into modern and environmentally friendly three-dimensional dolls. Design Atelier02 chose a jade object from the Hung-shan Culture of China's Neolithic age to create a cute and delicious lollipop. In the T-shirt competition, more than 26 designs were selected, and most of them have already gone into commercial production and are now on the market.

Developing Domestic and International Product Outlets

In addition to the above-mentioned strategies for brand licensing, there are also plans to utilize the existing global outlets of current internationally renowned brands. The integration of outlets in the National Palace Museum's strategic methods of developing markets will become part of the permanent plan for its operational mode of design, produce, and market. This will involve regular evaluation of the market and the 4P's of strategy analysis, referring to "Product", "Price", "Place", and "Promotion". This will promote the quality and grade of commercial products derived from artworks in the Museum collection. As for cooperative mechanisms for production and marketing outlets, professional outside companies can be sought for cooperation to place these into effect. The National Palace Museum can also provide a variety of integrated plans to implement them itself, attracting even more companies to become involved in selling Museum products. In addition to these, research will also be conducted on the art products and their sale in both domestic and international museums along with evaluation of art products from the Museum in the market. Compiling relevant data can be used as a reference by design teams for consideration when they develop products. Furthermore, it will allow the National Palace Museum to control more effectively its products in terms of market demand, the use of materials, pricing strategies, and planning outlets.

Finally, the National Palace Museum has also established its own online store at <www.npmeshop.com> and is already operational. At present, there are many quality decorative and practical products available in such recommended gift categories as bronzes, porcelains, stationery objects, accessories, multimedia, apparel, and reproductions. From inexpensive practical objects of everyday life to expensive, high-class jewelry, something for everybody can be found there. Through cooperation on the part of the National Palace Museum and its managing agent, a wealth of information on products currently available related to objects in the Museum is offered for people to browse all over the world via the Internet. For those who love modern products based on traditional Chinese arts and crafts, this is an excellent opportunity of Internet cultural exchange that transcends the limits of time and space. Visitors can browse the quality products of the National Palace Museum at their convenience and make purchases securely online by fund transfer or credit card, making it that much easier to have the National Palace Museum become a part of life and home through the products it offers. (Hsü Hsiao-te)

Gardens of Elegance:
Mo-yeh Ching-she, Chih-shan-yüan, and Chih-te-yüan

Mo-yeh Ching-she: The Chang Dai-chien Memorial Residence

Located on the banks of the Wai-shuang-hsi Stream, the Mo-yeh ching-she ("Abode of Maya") is near the Chih-shan Junior High School not far from the National Palace Museum and was formerly the residence of the modern painting master Chang Dai-chien (1899-1983). After he passed away, his family respected Chang's wishes to have the residence donated to the government. In 1983, the "Chang Dai-chien Memorial Residence" was established under the management and care of the National Palace Museum.

The Mo-yeh ching-she occupies an area of about 578 *ping* (about 1,907 square meters) and its courtyard-style set of buildings composes both Chinese and Western features. There is a front, middle, and back courtyard, each of which is landscaped with an independent fish pond. The settings inside of the buildings are more-or-less the way they were when Chang Dai-chien was alive, the artworks on display being particular noteworthy for further appreciation. For example, there is a flywhisk with a handle made from chinaroot, a congongrass dragon brush, and a bamboo brush and exotic rock. Outside, there are many interesting garden scenes to appreciate, the back courtyard featuring four pavilions where one can rest and relax (named Fen-han, I-jan, Shuang-tzu, and K'ao). Inside of the pavilions are log tables and stools as well as a beauty back-chair designed in imitation of a girl in makeup from a minority people of Yünnan. The overall style of the buildings is simple and elegant, the spacious gardens dotted with trees and decorative rocks that reflect the taste and breadth of mind of Master Chang.

In addition, gibbons and cranes are still raised in the gardens, which also feature the bonsai trees that Chang Dai-chien loved so much. In the appropriate season, you can see such flowers as plum blossoms, tea blossoms, flowering crab apple, and lotuses. One can also find a variety of other plants belong to the pineapple, orchid, and fern families as well as various aquatic plants for appreciation that create for an exotic and varied assortment of flora on view. In fact, there are about six hundred different types of plants and trees in the gardens. Such an abundance of vegetation naturally attracts many animals. Among the birds that can be found at this site, there are Japanese white-eye, Chinese bulbul, and red-beaked black bulbul. The numerous kinds of lizards include the Chinese Formosan skink, Indian lizard, Formosan grass lizard, and Swinhoe's tree lizard. Such amphibians as the black-rimmed toad, Gunther's frog, Latocute's frog, and brown tree frog can be found as well. On top of all these, there are twenty-one kinds of butterflies as well as uncountable numbers of moths and beetles, making for a rich and diverse ecological niche.

The former residence of Chang Dai-chien is most notable for its Chinese garden features and its pure and elegant arrangement. Not only is it rich in poetic and painterly atmosphere, it also embodies the refined ideal of the literati of "plum trees planted in the front courtyard and cranes raised in the garden". Worth a trip in and of itself, the residence is open by appointment only through the Education and Exhibition Department.

1

1. Entrance to the Chang Dai-chien Memorial Residence--Mo-yeh ching-yeh. The term "mo-yeh" means "Maya" and comes from a Buddhist scripture indicating that the womb of the Buddha's mother is as grand as three boundless universes. The Dai-chien of Chang's name actually means "boundless".

2. Wax figure of Chang Dai-chien with a stuffed gibbon by his side. It is said that Chang Dai-chien was reincarnated from a black gibbon, which is why he often used the name Chang Yüan (homonym for "gibbon") when he signed paintings.

3. View of the dining room. On the wall behind the round table is a piece of his calligraphy entitled "Menu for a Feast", which he actually did for a banquet that he held.

2 3

4 5

6 7

4. Bonsai of Eurya japonica.

5. Grey cranes.

6. Treasure plum blossoms.

7. Garden stone inscribed with the characters for "Plum Hill", marking the place where Chang Dai-chien's ashes are interred.

Chih-shan Garden

The Chih-shan Garden is located to the east of the main approach in front of the National Palace Museum main building. Constructed in 1983, it occupies an area of 5,687 *ping* (about 18,767 square meters) and is in the style of Sung and Ming dynasty gardens. Many beautiful scenes have been carefully designed in the garden for the viewing pleasure of visitors. Among them are famous spots that combine both natural and man-made forms, becoming the foci of attention. After entering the garden, one follows an up-and-down path, featuring from right to left the following eight sites of interest: the Blue-green Bridge West, Listening Oriole, and Brush-washing Ponds, the Calling Crane and Pines in Wind Pavilions, and the Caged Goose, Flowing Cups Winding Stream, and Orchid Pavilions. In addition, entering the garden on the left includes a covered walkway for visitors to rest and view scenery. There is also a Treasure Vase arched gate that symbolizes peace and prosperity for all people who visit the garden. In the pond next to the Blue-green Bridge West Water Pavilion are beautiful black and white swans, while a variety of birds are raised in enclosures behind the Pines in Wind Pavilion, including such exotic species as the white peacock and blue-crowned pigeon. Leave your worries behind in a trip to the Chih-shan Garden, where you can enjoy the art of traditional Chinese gardens in a scenic spot renowned in northern Taiwan for its beauty and convenience of location.

2

3

4

5

1. Overview of part of the Chih-shan Garden with the NPM main building behind.

2. Entrance to the Chih-shan Garden. Standing on either side of the entrance are stone lion sculptures, while the decorative woodwork of the gate itself is adorned with openwork carving of plum blossoms, orchids, bamboo, and chrysanthemums, the "Chih-shan" plaque suspended above.

3. Blue-green Bridge West Water Pavilion. Done in imitation of the Ming-Ch'ing style, it is built over the water of the pond and includes an arched bridge to connect it with the bank. In the water swim carp of every color. Combined with the sound of songbirds at dawn and dusk along with the swaying of willows in the breeze, it makes for an unforgettable experience.

4. Orchid Pavilion. Based on the elegant gathering of poet-scholars assembled by the Sage Calligrapher Wang Hsi-chih of the Chin dynasty in Kuei-chi, Shan-yin (southwest of modern Shao-hsing county in Chekiang Province), this event marked an ancient purification ritual, for which poems and a famous piece of calligraphy by Wang were done. Here, the pavilion is rendered as an octagonal structure with a table and benches for visitors to gather, rest, and vicariously experience that memorable event in the history of Chinese scholars.

5. Flowing Cups Winding Stream. The offering of wine originated in the ancient rituals and ceremonies of China's remote past and eventually evolved into a custom of "purification drinking" in elegant gatherings of scholars. For the event, a winding stream was chosen or created and special wine cups used to make "boats" to float upon. When the wine cup floated in front of a person by the stream bank, he would drink the wine and compose a poem on the spot.

Chih-te Garden

The Chih-te Garden is located on the western slope of the exit ramp from the Museum grounds. Built along the grade of the land, it occupies 2,643 ping (about 8,722 square meters) and has a lotus pond at its center. Around the banks of the pond are the Tranquil Bamboo Zither Sound Path and the Banyan Shade Curved Path as well as the Green Embankment Curved Bridge and the Joyous Climb and Viewing Clouds Pavilions. The gurgling sounds of the stream flowing through the garden induce reflection and relaxation, in addition to allowing visitors to appreciate the wonderful scenery. A beautiful example of Chinese-style garden landscaping, it is another great place to unwind among elegant surroundings.

In addition to the garden's man-made beauty, there are also a number of flowers one can enjoy in season, such as the Nelumbo lily, Nymphaea lily, and the largest lily species in the world, the Victoria amazonia, which, as the name suggests, comes from the Amazon region in South America. Besides the flora, the pond itself features countless numbers of dragonflies and damselflies, making it an ideal place to photograph or sketch both flora and fauna in a garden setting. During the summer, the garden overflows with greenery as the Victoria amazonia bloom and float on the pond surface, the lily leaves and blossoms bending gracefully in the breeze. In the chill of autumn, the lilies begin to wither and the stalks and pods stand out starkly for a gentle reminder of the passage of time.

The natural and man-made beauty of the Chih-te Garden is a wonderful fusion of garden scenery of pond water, pavilions, and plants, placing the visitor in a landscape not unlike what one sees in a Chinese painting. (Tu Lu-jung)

2

3

1. Entrance to the Chih-te Garden. The view through the full-moon archway adds to the viewing pleasure of the experience.
2. The Victoria amazonia lily is the largest fresh-water plant in the world, with its pads reaching as much as 2.45 meters in diameter and capable of supporting as much as 100 kilograms.
3. Scene of the zigzagging Green Embankment Curved Bridge.

Browse and Relax: Gift Shops and Food and Drink

Ling-lung Hall Gift Shop

Location: Basement left, eastern wing, of the main
building (B1)

Occupying 200 *ping* (about 660 square
meters), this is the flagship gift shop of the
National Palace Museum, including a vast array of
Museum and Chinese art-related items from books
to souvenirs, approximately 3,500 in number.
Whether browsing or making a purchase for
yourself or someone else, it is a great place to find
something to take home after visiting the Museum
galleries.

Hsien-chü-fu Coffee Shop

Location: On the first floor left, eastern wing, of
the main building

The oversized plate-glass full-length windows
provide a stage that allows a panoramic view of
the beauty of the Museum surroundings. Here, you
can sip a cup of coffee and allow the beauty of the
art in the collection sink in.

Fu-ch'un-chü Café and Curio Box Gift Shop

Location: On the first floor of the Library Building
(Exhibition Area II)

An isolated corner of the building offers a
utopia to rest and relax as well as a chance to grab
a snack or drink. Before going there, you can also
peruse and perhaps pick up an item or two in the
nearby Curio Box gift shop to enjoy there.

San-hsi-t'ang Tea Room

Location: On the fourth floor of the main building

San-hsi-t'ang is a name derived from the imperial studio of the Ch'ien-lung Emperor of the Ch'ing dynasty. The interior design of this tea room is based on the theme of the *Complete Library of the Four Treasuries* of the Wen-yüan Pavilion, an encyclopedic compilation of books compiled under the Ch'ien-lung Emperor. The cases here therefore suggest a traditional scholarly atmosphere in a modern setting. The elevated site also providing a great view of the surroundings, the San-hsi-t'ang offers a variety of teas and Chinese-style snacks.

T'ing-yün (Lingering Clouds)

Coffee and snack area

Location: On the second floor of the main building

Why not stop and have a cup of coffee to relax during your visit through thousands of years of Chinese art and culture at the National Palace Museum?

NPM Grand Formosa Restaurant

(under construction, scheduled to open at the end of 2007)

Location: To the west of the main building

The building will have one basement level and three aboveground floors featuring glass curtained walls and offering a variety of meals and drinks, including renowned Taiwanese snacks and exquisite Chinese food.

(simulation)

Global Neighbors: International Exchange

International exchange in the arts and culture can take place via museums and cultural institutions through the loan exhibition of collection objects, reciprocal exhibitions, and visits. All of these represent some of the most direct and efficient means of improving mutual understanding between countries and fostering harmonious ties among peoples. Such exchanges also contribute to the spread of knowledge involving cultures of the world and to the development of peaceful and friendly relations in the international scene.

Following such major international exhibitions involving the National Palace Museum as "Splendors of Imperial China: Treasures from the National Palace Museum, Taipei" (1996-1997) that traveled to the United States, "Mémoire d'Empire: Trésors du Musée National du Palais, Taipei" (1998-1999) that went to France, and its reciprocal exhibition entitled "From Poussin to Cézanne: 300 Years of French Painting" that came to the NPM in 2001-2002, several other international exhibitions have been arranged involving the Museum. These include "Treasures of the Sons of Heaven: The Imperial Collection from the National Palace Museum, Taipei" (2003-2004) that traveled to Germany, "Genghis Khan and his Heirs: The Mongolian Empire" (2005-2006) featuring select works from the Museum collection exhibited in Germany, and "The Very Rich Hours of the Court of China (1662-1796): Masterpieces of Imperial Qing Painting" (2006) with selected Chinese paintings. The arrangement of loan exhibitions from overseas for display at the National Palace Museum has also included "Formosa: Taiwan, Holland and East Asia in the 17th Century" (2003) (featuring works from Holland, Germany, Denmark, and the US) and "A Century of German Genius: Masterpieces from Classicism to Early Modernism, Collections of the Berlin State Museums" (2004). Below is an introduction to a few of these important exhibitions:

Formosa: Taiwan, Holland and East Asia in the 17th Century (Jan.-May 2003)

This exhibition featured more than 270 objects borrowed from 17 domestic museums and private collections as well as 21 museums in Holland, the United States, Denmark, and Germany--representing the relations between Taiwan, Holland and East Asia in the 17th century. This was the dawn of a new age in the history of Taiwan, despite the fact that many people in Taiwan are still unfamiliar with this important period, having limited knowledge of the situation after the

1

2

3   4   5

Dutch assumed control in Taiwan. The holding of this exhibition provided an opportunity to explore Taiwan's early history, allowing people to come to a greater understanding of the land in which they live, something important and far-reaching for all folks wherever they are.

Treasures of the Sons of Heaven: The Imperial Collection from the National Palace Museum, Taipei (July 2003-Feb. 2004)

In response to an invitation from the Foundation of Prussian Cultural Heritage and the Bonn Art and Exhibition Hall of the Republic of Germany, the National Palace Museum helped arrange for an exhibition of four hundred objects from its collection at the Berlin Altes Museum and the Bonn Art and Exhibition Hall of the Republic of Germany. This exhibition was the fruit up to ten years of effort by both parties. Only after many negotiations and planning by the respective persons culminating with a revision of the "Law Protecting the Export of Cultural Properties" on the part of the German government, thereby ensuring within a legal framework the safe return of borrowed objects, was an agreement reached for the loan of objects from the National Palace Museum to the satisfaction of both parties. In terms of the selection of objects, the principle of the "imperial collection" was followed in the spirit of the exhibit title and important artifacts of antiquities, painting and calligraphy, silk works, and rare books were selected in cooperation with the German counterpart. This was the first time that the National Palace Museum objects were exhibited in Germany, and it had a major influence in Germany. It effectively stimulated mutual cultural exchange between Taiwan and Germany, and it also achieved the effect of international promotion, presenting the image of Taiwan not only in Europe but also around the world while opening up new realms for Taiwan in Europe.

A Century of German Genius: Masterpieces from Classicism to Early Modernism (May-Aug. 2004)

To reciprocate the National Palace Museum loan exhibition of "Treasures of the Sons of Heaven" held in Germany, the Foundation of Prussian Cultural Heritage in Germany agreed to lend 193 sets of objects from museums under its supervision for exhibition at the National Palace Museum in Taipei.

6

1. "Splendors of Imperial China" National Palace Museum exhibition in the US (1996-1997).
2. "From Poussin to Cézanne: 300 Years of French Painting" special exhibition at the NPM (2001-2002).
3. Opening of the "Formosa: Taiwan, Holland and East Asia in the 17th Century" exhibition at the NPM (2003).
4. Ceremony for signing the loan contract for the "Treasures of the Sons of Heaven" exhibition in Germany (2003).
5. Site of the "Treasures of the Sons of Heaven" exhibit in Berlin, Germany (2003).
6. Press conference for the special exhibit "A Century of German Genius: Masterpieces from Classicism to Early Modernism" at the NPM (2004).

The 19th century was a period of great historical significance for Germany since the Middle Ages, for it was during this hundred years' time that it was transformed from a country made up of dozens of independent, autonomous kingdoms, duchies, and principalities into a consolidated modern nation-state. It was also during the period when the Germans made great advances with far-reaching impact in philosophy, literature, music, historiography, and science. While the people of Taiwan are not unfamiliar with German achievements in these areas, German visual arts of the 19th century have gone largely unheralded here. With the rise of different aesthetic schools and the emergence of many art centers, Germany witnessed a period of intense creative activity between the 19th and early 20th centuries. In this golden age of German art, paintings, sculptures, handicrafts, and other media of artistic expression all reflected the Zeitgeist of Germany, projecting a general picture of the intellectual, moral, and cultural climate of the era. The presentation marks the first appearance in Asia of the collections of the Staatliche Museen zu Berlin, and of all the international art expositions that have been introduced to the audiences of Taiwan thus far it is also the very first one that is devoted exclusively to the art of Germany. The National Palace Museum took great pride in hosting this milestone cultural project with great significance in its own right.

The year 2006 marked the 800th anniversary of Genghis Khan establishing the Mongol state, and Mongolia held a series of events to celebrate. For the occasion, the National Palace Museum also presented Mongolia with a gift of a set of reproductions of Mongol emperors and empresses of the Yüan dynasty in China from its collection. This became part of the newly established Mongol national ceremonial hall collection, thereby stimulating cultural exchange between both parties. For that occasion, Director Lin Mun-lee of the National Palace Museum was invited to participate and lead the donation ceremony.

Every year, the National Palace Museum receives many figures in the academic, economic, political, art, and other fields. In 2006, for example, sumo wrestlers from Japan made a competition tour of Taiwan, being the first time since the end of World War II that sumo wrestlers from Japan have visited Taiwan. As part of their trip, they were invited to the

3

National Palace Museum. In order to receive these 42 "heavyweights" of the Japanese sports and cultural world, the NPM specially arranged a viewing of the "Jadeite cabbage with insects", "Meat-shaped stone", and porcelains. In addition, the portrait of Genghis Khan was approved to be specially retrieved from storage for viewing by the top-ranked yokozuna Asashoryu (born Dolgorsuren Dagvadorj in Mongolia), and a reproduction of the portrait was also presented to him to promote exchange.

The Southern Branch of the National Palace Museum, which will be devoted to the arts of Asia, is scheduled to open as early as 2010, and international exchange will become an even more important component of the operations of the National Palace Museum at that time. In June of 2006, Director Lin Mun-lee was a representative at the opening ceremony of the Musée du Quai Branly in France. This museum is devoted primarily to the arts of Africa, the Americas, Asia, and Oceania, one of its missions being a pluralistic dialogue among cultures of the world, which happens to coincide with the ideals of the NPM branch museum of Asian art and culture being currently planned for southern Taiwan. In addition to exchange in the international field of museums, the National Palace Museum is also researching and planning the development of cooperative alliances and relations with other Asian art institutions and museums in terms of artifact, history, and art research. For example, in 2005, the National Palace Museum co-organized "Southeast Asian Arts: An Assessment of Research" along with the École française d'Extrême-Orient, in which domestic and foreign scholars were invited to the NPM to present lectures on the state of the art in their respective fields. In addition, the NPM has also reached an agreement on a strategic alliance with the Guimet Museum in France on uniting each other's collections, joining hands to mutually curate the major opening exhibitions planned for the NPM Southern Branch.

In addition to exchange visits and establishing alliance relationships, the National Palace Museum has also increased considerably its cooperation with other museums around the world in terms of the mutual exchange of loan objects and exhibitions. For example, in April of 2006, the Guimet Museum in France held "The Very Rich Hours of the Court of China (1662-1796): Masterpieces of Imperial Qing Painting," which included two paintings ("Landscape" and "The Empress Supervising the Rites of Sericulture [Offering Cocoons]") from the National Palace Museum collection by the Italian Jesuit artist who worked for the Ch'ing court, Giuseppe Castiglione (Chinese name: Lang Shih-ning). In addition, at the end of 2006, the grand preview exhibitions celebrating the completion of the renovation project at the National Palace Museum ("Grand View: Painting, Calligraphy and Ju Ware from the Northern Sung Dynasty and Sung Dynasty Rare Books") featured major loan pieces from the collections of museums in the United States, Japan, and England. It thus goes without saying that the National Palace Museum has the ambition of becoming a strategic site for the research of Chinese as well as Asian artifacts. (Text: Ho Lai-hsiang; photos provided by Lisette Lou)

1. Director Lin Mun-lee presenting one of the reproductions of the Yüan dynasty Mongol portraits of emperors and empresses (Genghis Khan in this image) in the NPM collection to Mongolia (2006). (photograph provided by the Mongolian and Tibetan Affairs Commission)

2. Visit of sumo wrestlers from Japan in 2006.

3. Director Lin Mun-lee taking part in the ceremonies celebrating the opening of the Musée du Quai Branly in France (June 2006).

Paving the Way for the Future: History of the NPM

The Origins of the National Palace Museum

The wide range of treasures of Chinese art and culture at the National Palace Museum derive from the imperial collection of the Ch'ing dynasty, which was composed of many objects inherited from the previous Sung, Yüan, and Ming dynasties as well as works of the Ch'ing court. Not long after the Republic of China was established in the early twentieth century, these important and valuable objects remained hidden inside the Forbidden City. During the period of time when the deposed emperor still lived there, many of these objects were either presented as gifts by the last emperor P'u-i, borrowed by former officials, auctioned and pawned, or outright stolen and sold, leading to incalculable losses to the collection.

In 1914, the Republican government moved the objects from the former Ch'ing Summer Retreat in Jehol and the Ch'ing palace in Mukden (Sheng-yang) to the outer court of the Forbidden City and established display galleries open to public viewing. In 1924, P'u-i was finally forced to move out of the palace and the government established the "Committee for the Disposition of Ch'ing Imperial Possessions" to inventory and organize all the objects at court and in the collections. On 10 October 1925, the national day of the Republic of China, the Palace Museum was officially inaugurated and from this point on, treasures of the imperial collection and cultural objects of the court became the heritage and legacy belonging to all the people, who could freely enter the court and view these treasures of their past.

In the beginning, the Palace Museum was set up as an institution with a board of directors for making policies and supervision, and under them were council members. At that time, the makeup of the Palace Museum consisted of two divisions divided between antiquities and books as well as a general affairs office. Over the years, the political landscape changed continuously, and the Palace Museum came under the management of a conservator and custodial, preservation, and management committees.

In June of 1928, the Nationalist Revolutionary Army headed north and entered Peking, and the Nationalist government placed I P'ei-chi in charge of the Palace Museum. A law regulating the organization of the Palace Museum was promulgated, formally making the museum a government institution charged with management of the buildings, ancient objects, books, and archives in the Palace Museum and its subsidiary departments, as well as opening them to the public and disseminating information about them. At that time, the three departments of antiquities, books, and documents were established along with a secretarial and general affairs office. The regulations for the council of the Palace Museum were also promulgated, and in February of 1929, I P'ei-chi officially became the first director of the museum. During his term in office, the work of spot-check inventory and cataloguing continued as display galleries were increased, exhibit contents expanded, and the transmission and publication of information about the collection reinforced.

The Journey South

In July of 1932, the Japanese army invaded Jehol and set their eyes on China's north. The committee in charge of the Palace Museum, in order to safeguard the collection objects, began the task of selecting from the cream of the crop and packing them in crates to be moved at a moment's notice. In February of 1933, the situation in North China turned for the worse, and the first shipment of crated objects was moved south to Shanghai. By May of that year, five shipments were made to the south involving 19,557 crates, which included 6,066 crates of objects from such departments as the Office for the Exhibit of Ancient Artifacts, I-ho-yuan Summer Palace, and former Directorate of Education. In February of 1934, the Nationalist government promulgated the "Temporary Organic Statutes of the National Peking Palace Museum", and the Palace Museum was placed subordinate to the Executive Yuan with Ma Heng made as its director. During his term, an inventory of objects that had been moved to Shanghai and those remaining in Peking was begun, and a selection of more than a thousand masterpieces was chosen to participate in the "International Exhibition of Chinese Art" in London in 1935.

In December of 1936, the 19,557 crates were shipped from Shanghai inland to the Ch'ao-t'ien Temple in Nanking.

1

2

3

In January of the following year, the Nanking branch of the Palace Museum was formally established. In August, however, the Japanese army sparked an incident in Shanghai, and the situation in Nanking became increasingly unstable. As a result, Chiang Shang-yen and others sent the first shipment of eighty crates of objects inland west to Ch'ang-sha in Hunan, from which they were transferred even further inland to the final resting place at Kuei-yang (which, in the autumn of 1944 came under threat, so the crates were then transported to Pa-hsien in Szechwan). In November of 1937, the frontline at Shanghai was lost, and the government decided to retreat inland to Chungking. The second shipment of Nanking objects was evacuated by water and traveled to Lo-shan via the Yangtze River, Han-k'ou, I-ch'ang, and Chungking. The third shipment was transported on the Lung-hai Railroad to Pao-chi and then transferred by truck to Chengtu from Han-chung before finally reaching O-mei for safekeeping. At this time, the objects could take a slight respite, and in 1940-41 a hundred of the masterpieces were selected for the "Exhibition of Chinese Art" held in Moscow and Leningrad.

In this time of turbulence, the masterpieces of the Peking display halls were moved along with other objects of the Palace Museum south, and the "Planning Office for the Central Museum" was established in Nanking. And when the situation worsened in Nanking, these objects were moved by water routes westward to their resting place in Nan-hsi, Szechwan. Even during wartime, members of the Preparatory Office of the Central Museum still continued with their research, conducting studies of the Ch'uan-k'ang minority peoples, traditional handicrafts, geography and history of the northwest, and excavations of Han dynasty tombs at P'eng-shan. Following the move to Taiwan, the "Preparatory Office of the Central Museum" and the "Palace Museum" were combined to form the present National Palace Museum in Taiwan.

In 1945, with the defeat of the Japanese in World War II, the cultural institutions that had been set up by the Japanese were returned to their original institutions by the Republic of China government. At this time, the Palace Museum began the work of demobilizing, and the objects that had been in storage at Pa-hsien, O-mei, and Lo-shan were transported to Chungking, and in June of 1947, the Palace Museum began the task of shipping the crates by boat from Chungking to Nanking. By December, every single one of them had been returned safely, successfully concluding the task of demobilization.

The Move to Taiwan

In 1948, however, civil war between the Nationalist government and the Communists took a turn for the worse, and the committee in charge of the Palace Museum again chose the finest objects of the collection for transport, this time heading for Taiwan. A total of 2,972 crates were transported in three shipments, arriving in Taiwan in February of that year, and the treasures of the Institute of History and Philology at Academia Sinica, the Central Library, and the Central Museum

1. The archway of the Shen-wu Gate at the opening of the Palace Museum.
2. Scene of the western Szechwan-Shensi transport of the artifacts (photograph provided by Ch'en Hsia-sheng).
3. Map of the southern transport of the objects.
4. Display gallery at Pei-kou, Taichung, in 1957 (from *Liao-liao pu liao-liao chi*, last vol., p. 956).

were also included along among them. At the time, the Communists had already taken over the Palace Museum in Peking, so it was not possible to transport all of the objects. Although the 2,972 crates shipped to Taiwan represented only a quarter of the objects transported previously south by the government, many of them are the masterpieces of the collection.

In 1949, the "United Managerial Office of the National Central Museum" was established in Taiwan, incorporating the personnel and objects of the three institutions of the Palace Museum, Central Library, and Central Museum. These were placed under the administration of the Ministry of Education, and Minister Hang Li-wu also served as its committee director as they searched for a place in Pei-kou at Wu-feng Village in Taichung County to build storage facilities. In April of 1950, the Pei-kou storage facilities were completed and the objects of the collections moved inside. During the period of united management, the work of spot-check inventory and inspection of the objects was continued and a set of books entitled Comprehensive Overview of Chinese Culture was published.

In 1955, the united managerial office was changed to the "Central United Managerial Office of Artifacts Transported to Taiwan", under which was established the four divisions for the Palace Museum, Central Museum, electronic media education, and general affairs. Soon thereafter, the division for electronic media education was scrapped and reorganized as the "United Managerial Office for the National Palace and Central Museums". In 1957, the exhibition halls at Pei-kang were formally opened to the public. In May of 1961, masterpieces from the collection were sent on a traveling tour of the United States, spending a total of one year at venues in Washington, D.C., New York, Boston, Chicago, and San Francisco.

A New Home in Taipei

In 1965, the Executive Yuan promulgated the "Provisional Organic Regulations and Articles for the Managerial Committee of the National Palace Museum", and the committee director Wang Yün-wu appointed Chiang Fu-ts'ung as the director of the National Palace Museum. At that time, a site for the new museum building was chosen in Wai-shuang-hsi in Taipei and at its completion, the official name of the National Palace Museum was the "Chung-shan Museum", being opened on the hundredth anniversary of the birth of and named after Dr. Sun Yat-sen, the founding father of the Republic of China (Chung-shan being his posthumous name). Starting from 1966, the bulletin and research quarterly of the National Palace Museum began publication. In the following year, construction of the two wings of the main building was completed.

In 1968, to meet the needs of managing the collection, the original division between antiquities as well as painting and calligraphy at the National Palace Museum was reorganized into the departments of antiquities, painting and calligraphy, and books and documents, along with two divisions for exhibition and registration. A new inventory and organization of the objects was conducted and exchange with other academic institutions began, and later a conservation department was added. In 1971, professionals at the National Palace Museum were chosen to assist in the establishment of a graduate department of Chinese art history at National Taiwan University, forming the predecessor of the current Graduate School of Art History there. In the same year, the second phase of construction for the expansion of two wings for the new facilities was completed.

In 1983, Chin Hsiao-yi became the new director of the National Palace Museum, and in October of that year, the Mo-yeh ching-she ("Abode of Maya") studio-residence of the modern master Chang Dai-chien became a memorial museum under its care. In 1984, the third phase of expansion for the administration building was completed. Exhibition galleries in the main building were increased in size, and new measures for temperature and humidity controls as well the prevention of theft and damage from earthquakes, humidity, and fire were put into place. The "San-hsi-t'ang" (Hall of Three Rarities) tea room on the fourth floor of the main building was also completed in imitation of the Yang-hsin Hall, the residence of the Ch'ing emperor Ch'ien-lung. In 1985, the Chih-shan Garden was established in imitation of gardens of the Sung and Ming dynasties.

In 1987, the "Organic Statutes of the National Palace Museum" were promulgated by the Presidential Office, and the post of director of the National Palace Museum became an appointment of the Executive Yuan with jurisdiction over three departments, three divisions, and six offices. Director Chin at the time strived to improve the exhibition galleries, reinforce

1 2

3   4

academic research, and promote museum education. In two years starting from 1989, the complete inventory of the entire collection was completed. In 1991, the Executive Yuan replaced the "managerial committee" of the National Palace Museum with an "advisory panel", providing consul and advice for important matters related to the Museum. In 1995, the fourth phase of expansion was completed and the Library Building inaugurated. In the same year, the Chih-te Garden was also opened to the public. In 1996, at the invitation of the Metropolitan Museum of Art in New York, the "Splendors of Imperial China: Treasures from the National Palace Museum, Taipei" began as a traveling exhibition to four major cities in the United States.

A New Age of the NPM

In 2000, Tu Cheng-sheng was appointed as director of the National Palace Museum, and during his term in office he promoted the infrastructure project of "A New Age of the NPM", further strengthening academic research and holding conferences while initiating a multicultural perspective encompassing native, Chinese, and international viewpoints. Furthermore, to relieve traffic congestion in front of the museum and alleviate the lack of exhibition space, plans for a fifth phase of renovation involving the expansion of the main building commenced along with the beginning stages of plans for the establishment of a branch of the National Palace Museum in southern Taiwan.

In May of 2004, Deputy Director Shih Shou-chien became the new director and he actively encouraged cultural exchange with foreign museums, paving the way for globalization of the collection and loan exhibitions as he continued leading the effort in the renovation of the main building and preparations for the NPM Southern Branch, his goal to make the National Palace Museum into a treasure house of cultural properties for all the people while fully utilizing its collection, research, exhibition, and educational resources.

In January of 2006, Deputy Director Lin Mun-lee was promoted to Director, immediately bringing with her new ideas for the Museum, the reinforcement of planning and strategy, and new content for the exhibitions in the hopes of gradually shedding the traditional modes of museum thinking centered solely around the collection, preservation, and research while creating an approach that combines both the collection objects and "people" in a form of interaction taking place in a user-friendly environment and exhibition space. By the end of 2006, the main construction of the main building had been completed and the new exhibits installed for public view, presenting visitors with a National Palace Museum more in keeping with the times by having a stronger affinity with and closer to the people.

A modern museum must keep in touch with the pulse of the times and the society of which it is part, making flexible use of its research, collection, and exhibition resources while adopting the ideals of customer service as taking a leading role in its becoming a modern cultural institution. Since the new National Palace Museum in Wai-shuang-hsi, Taipei, opened its doors in 1965, it has undergone five expansion projects. In the future, how the National Palace Museum will adopt a new style of overall approach will depend of the course of social development, of which the NPM plans to play an integral part. This is always a goal that we will all strive with our greatest endeavors to fulfill and see come true. (Chang Ming-hsün)

1. The National Palace Museum as it appeared upon completion in 1965 in Wai-shuang-hsi, Taipei.
2. View of the renovated National Palace Museum main building in 2006.
3. New sky-lit lobby of the NPM main building in 2006.
4. New staircase from the first to second floor in the NPM main building in 2006.
5. New checkroom facilities at the NPM in 2006.

5

In Pursuit of Asia: Plans for the Southern Branch

What was originally a sugarcane field belonging to Taiwan Sugar Corporation in an area belonging to Taibao City in Chiayi County will by 2010 be transformed into the Southern Branch of the National Palace Museum. This project that began in 2003 includes not only the vision and hope of being able to bring the arts and cultures of other places in Asia to Taiwan, but also the ambition of using Taiwan as a starting point (more specifically, the seventy-hectare garden and museum facilities in Taibao) to understand and appreciate Taiwan's role in an overall Asia from many different points of view.

The main focus of the Southern Branch will be the "exchange and interaction of the arts and cultures of Asia", gradually forming a greater understanding of this vast topic based on the Museum collection and activities presented there. The six main permanent exhibitions that have been planned to date include "A Handbook to Life: Asian Texts and Writing", "Incarnation Represented: The Buddhist Arts of Asia", "The Ultimate Luxury: The Cultures of Asian Textiles", "Blue-and-white: An Aesthetic of Asian Ceramics", "Western Influences: Trends in Later Asian Arts", and "The Cultures of Tea in Asia". The three special exhibitions that will be presented include "Religious Folk Art in Taiwan", "Hindustan Jades", and "Asian Arms and Armor". The contents of these exhibitions take into consideration not only the spirit and material aspects of the arts and cultures of Asia, but they weave together a close-knit image of this region. At the same time, it is also hoped that several forms of multimedia and exhibition presentation methods will allow visitors to the NPM Southern Branch an opportunity to see, hear, touch and even taste the unique features that make up the arts and cultures of Asia.

A Handbook to Life: Asian Texts and Writing

Writings are treasures of wisdom produced by people. In Asia, five important types of writing appeared: Buddhist sutras, Hindu texts, Confucian classics, Taoist scriptures, and Islamic holy texts. These make up the core of the exhibition "A Handbook to Life: Asian Texts and Writing". The National Palace Museum already has many examples of such texts from various places and periods. Not only is it hoped to extract the core contents and spiritual concerns from these five different kinds of writings and present them here in one exhibit, the explanation of their spiritual and cultural significance will also recreate the regional characteristics in terms of the forms of writing and presentation of the texts themselves. By comparing these objects on display, one will be able to outline the spiritual passion and intellectual exchange and development that took place in the various places of Asia.

2

3

4

Incarnation Represented: The Buddhist Arts of Asia

Buddhism, which originated in India, is already in its 26th century of existence and has left behind innumerable artifacts and religious artworks in many areas in Asia, including India, Afghanistan, Pakistan, Bangladesh, Indonesia, and China, among others. "Incarnation Represented: The Buddhist Arts of Asia" will not only introduce the styles of Buddhist art in the three major regions of South and Southeast Asia, the Himalayas, and East Asia, it will also adopt the Buddhist notion of "incarnation" and use the Buddhist sculptures in the NPM collection to reveal the universal spirit of the Buddha by means of "personifications of the Buddha's likeness" found in the works of Buddhist art from various regions in Asia.

The Ultimate Luxury: The Cultures of Asian Textiles

Each of the major areas of Asia has its own rich tradition of textile production, and many of them paid particular attention to the use of refined materials and skilled craftsmanship to create beautiful works of art and daily life. Besides reflecting the highest standards of craftsmanship in textile production in the place they were made, these textiles also represent the unique cultural traditions and native stylistic features of their localities. Textiles were also always a means of exchange and interaction through which the effects of commercial trade, political expansion, movement of peoples, and religion spread. The textiles of various places traveled to other areas via land and sea routes, having a major influence on one another. For this reason, in the exhibition "The Ultimate Luxury: The Cultures of Asian Textiles", one finds not just an introduction to the beautiful and luxurious clothing and textiles found throughout Asia, but one can also compare the textile patterns, visual impressions, and techniques of craftsmanship from the objects to come away with a better understanding of the cultural exchange that took place in Asia.

Blue-and-white: An Aesthetic of Asian Ceramics

Blue-and-white (also known as underglaze blue) was one of the most influential and widespread forms in the history of ceramics, and Asia was the land where it blossomed on this stage. Originating in Western Asia and China, it spread to many areas around Asia, and the culture of blue-and-white even spread to other parts of the world. This is why the exhibition on blue-and-white ceramics will demonstrate the production, transmission, and use of this ware, explaining the mutual influence and competition witnessed with other wares. On the one hand, the exhibit will center on regions to

1. Computer visualization of the National Palace Museum Southern Branch building and park.
2. *Collected Sweet Dew Spring of Shri Hevajra*, gold handwritten text, 1439.
3. Detail of Indonesian batik skirt (Sumatra, Indonesia), late 19th-early 20th century.
4. Standing sculpture of the Maitreya Bodhisattva, Ghandara, 3rd century CE.

explain the different regional developments that took place, and on the other hand will also focus on the developments that took place in China to provide visitors a form of cross-cultural comparison.

1

Western Influences: Trends in Later Asian Arts

The exhibition on "Western Influences: Trends in Later Asian Arts" deals with the impact of the growing influence of Europe on Asia, dealing with the subject of interaction and exchange produced in the arts and culture. The display objects mostly date from the 17th to 19th centuries and are divided into the five intriguing facets of "Depicting the New World", "Rediscovering Nature", "The Lure of Science", "Sumptuous New Styles", and "The New Asia in Asia", revealing the last wave of major transformation that took place in the formation of the modern Asia of today.

The Cultures of Tea in Asia

"Tea" has already become a global drink, but the home of "tea culture" is undoubtedly in Asia and China in particular. For this reason, "The Cultures of Tea in Asia" exhibit takes China as its starting point to introduce two long and distant "tea routes". Furthermore, the history of tea in China forms a focus that provides a means of comparison with other regions in Asia that also developed unique tea cultures, such as Japan, Tibet, Southeast Asia, and India. By comparing the methods of drinking tea, the utensils and objects used, and the systems of thinking associated with the drinking of tea, one not only comes away with an awareness of the differences and interaction that took place, but also of the spread and great importance of tea in the cultures of Asia.

In addition to these permanent exhibitions, special exhibits are also scheduled to be presented annually. At present, the three main exhibits of "Religious Folk Art in Taiwan", "Hindustan Jades", and "Asian Arms and Armor" are now being planned and organized.

Orientation Hall, Traveling Exhibition Gallery, New Media Center, Children's Creative Center

In addition to the halls for permanent and special exhibitions, the National Palace Museum Southern Branch is also planning four exciting spaces for performances and activities. There is the "Orientation Hall" that integrates the various themes to present an overall picture of the flow of culture in Asia as seen in the Museum. There is also a "Traveling Exhibition Gallery" for special loan exhibits from other countries, which will spur exchange and cultural outlook among the people in Taiwan. The "New Media Center" will span the ages to interpret traditional art and culture with new technologies, and the "Children's Creative Center" will provide all people young at heart with an opportunity to lean more about the exhibits on Asia in a fun and educational way.

2

3

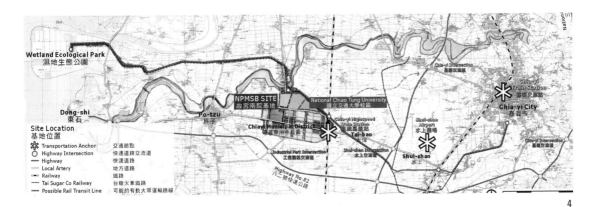

4

Rediscovering Asia with the NPM

For many years, the international outlook of Taiwan has been focused on Europe and North America, often overlooking many of its neighbors in Asia. The selection of Asian art and culture at the National Palace Museum Southern Branch is an attempt to rectify this situation. Using thematic exhibitions instead of traditional regional or chronological approaches, the process of interaction and exchange that took place in various places in Asia will be revealed, thereby reinforcing understanding of the historical and cultural pulse of this region in which Taiwan is located and placing part of the focus of attention on areas closer to home.

At present, the teams at the National Palace Museum involved with planning and organization of the Southern Branch have already begun work on arranging purchases, donations, long-term entrustments, loans, and exchanges with other museums to build up the collection and present the finest displays possible. The work teams have also begun research on the various exhibit themes and engaged in cooperation and contact with scholars in various important research institutions around Asia. As both part of the three-year academic cooperative exchange project with École Française d'Extrême-Orient of France and the sponsorship of the MAI (Ch'eng Yang) Foundation in Taiwan, various international scholars have been invited to Taiwan for the "NPM Southern Branch Exhibit Theme Lecture Series". These events are having the important effect of accumulating and promoting local achievements in research on Asian art.

The road to Asia turns out to be not as long as we had thought. Through the concrete formation of this process of building links with the rest of Asia by the National Palace Museum Southern Branch, we hope that more people will participate with the NPM in rediscovering the artistic and cultural wonders of Asia and help form a new outlook on Asia here in Taiwan. (Ch'iu Shih-hua)

6

1. Five-color blue-and-white large plate with mystical creatures, Vietnam, 15th-16th century.

2. Ivory-inlaid black sandalwood stationery box, India, ca. 1740.

3. I-hsing dark-red teapot with handle in the form of twisted bamboo, China, Ch'ing dynasty.

4. Local map showing the site of the NPM Southern Branch (NPMSB).

5. "The Arts and Cultures of Asia" preview exhibition of the NPM Southern Branch held in Chiayi in 2004.

6. Poster announcing a lecture sponsored by the MAI (Ch'eng-yang) Foundation on one of the NPM Southern Branch exhibit themes.

Visit Information

Effective 1 February 2007,the admission prices and hours for the National Palace Museum have been adjusted as follows:

National Palace Museum Open all year round, 9:00am-5:00pm
General admission: NT$160, discount admission: NT$80, group admission: NT$100 per person, and those 7 or under, aged 65 or above, or the physically/mentally challenged: free admission

Chih-shan Garden Open 7:00am-7:00pm
(except Mondays), NT$20 per person

Chih-te Garden Open year round, free admission

Chang Dai-chien Memorial Residence: Open by appointment only. Please contact the Education and Exhibition Department for further details.

Getting to the National Palace Museum

Bus **Neihu, Da-chih:** 213, 620, 645

Shih-lin: 255, 304, Red 30, Minibus 18, Minibus 19

Tour Information

Audio tours available Chinese, English, Japanese

Free tours Chinese -- 9:30am / 2:30pm
English -- 10:00am / 3:00pm

Museum Address and Contact Information

Add 221, Chih-shan Road, Section 2Shih-lin District, Taipei 11143Taiwan, Republic of China

Tel 886-2-2881-2021

Fax 886-2-2882-1440

Website www.npm.gov.tw

The "Old is New" NPM Guidebook

Splendors of the New National Palace Museum

Issuer	Lin Mun-lee
Chief Editor	Lin Mun-lee
Executive Editor	Chen Jie-jin
Assistant Editor	Tsai Ming-chien, Lisette Lou
Translator	Donald E. Brix
Photographers	Ts'ui Hsüeh-kuo, Lin Feng-sung, Lin Hung-ying
Address	221 Chih-shan Rd. (Sec. 2), Shih-lin District, 11143 Taipei, Taiwan, Republic of China
	Tel: +886-2-2881-2021(~4)
	Fax:+886-2-2882-1440
	Website: www.npm.gov.tw
Designer	FREEiMAGE Design Co., Ltd.
	Add: 3F, No.144, Pa Teh Rd., Sec 3, Taipei, 105 Taiwan
	Tel: +886-2-2577-0001
	Fax:+886-2-2577-0002
Printer	Chiu Yu Printing Co., Ltd.
	Add: 5F, 45, Tung-hsing Rd., Taipei, Taiwan
	Tel: +886-2-8768-2088
	Fax:+886-2-8768-1900
Price	NT$ 750
Distributor	National Palace Museum Staff Cooperative
	Add: 221 Chih-shan Rd. (Sec. 2), Shih-lin District, 11143 Taipei, Taiwan, Republic of China
	Tel: +886-2-2881-1230
	Taiwan postal remittance account #: 1961234-9

First printing July 2007
GPN:1009600812   ISBN:978-957-562-517-7